ESTABLISHING SHOTS

ESTABLISHING SHOTS

AN ORAL HISTORY OF
THE WINNIPEG FILM GROUP

KEVIN NIKKEL

UNIVERSITY OF MANITOBA PRESS

Establishing Shots: An Oral History of the Winnipeg Film Group

27 26 25 24 23 1 2 3 4 5

University of Manitoba Press
Winnipeg, Manitoba, Canada
Treaty 1 Territory
uofmpress.ca

Cataloguing data available from Library and Archives Canada
ISBN 978-1-77284-013-1 (PAPER)
ISBN 978-1-77284-014-8 (PDF)
ISBN 978-1-77284-015-5 (EPUB)
ISBN 978-1-77284-016-2 (BOUND)

Cover photo by Brad Caslor
Cover and interior design by Jess Koroscil

Printed in Canada

The University of Manitoba Press acknowledges the financial support for its publication program provided by the Government of Canada through the Canada Book Fund, the Canada Council for the Arts, the Manitoba Department of Sport, Culture, and Heritage, the Manitoba Arts Council, and the Manitoba Book Publishing Tax Credit.

Funded by the Government of Canada | Canada

For Caden

Catnip for Canadian Cinephiles

CONTENTS

PREFACE

In the summer of 2015, Cinematheque programmer Dave Barber and I began work on a feature documentary about the Winnipeg Film Group. With my interview background from past projects and encouragement from the Oral History Centre at the University of Winnipeg, I set out to capture extended interviews with the goal of eventually producing an oral history of the organization to accompany the documentary in production. We eventually interviewed fifty people associated with the artist-run centre, from across Canada and beyond. Each interview was transcribed and edited for clarity, with the transcript then reviewed by the interviewee. Not everyone approached was interested in participating in the documentary, or in the subsequent work of reviewing a transcript, which left some voices absent from the mosaic that follows. The challenge was ever before us, as Dave often reminded me: "In many ways, the Winnipeg Film Group is like the great Kurosawa movie *Rashomon*. Everyone sees their own version of the truth."[1] Our documentary would eventually be released in 2017 as *Tales from the Winnipeg Film Group*. Some of the interviews from the documentary are included here in edited form; one of these, with Winston Moxam, was conducted previously at the screening of his film *Barbara James*, at Catacomb Microcinema in 2007.

Establishing Shots is a story of creative individuals, a persistent community, and a particular place. The purpose is to head back in time, to reach the

---

Kevin Nikkel and Dave Barber, Winnipeg Cinematheque projection booth, 2017. Photo Leif Norman. Courtesy of Five Door Films.

NFG

headwaters, and establish a collection of stories from the early pioneers, as a means of contributing to the discourse on Winnipeg culture. My interest is to contribute to (and question) the growing mythology surrounding Winnipeg and the Winnipeg Film Group. I do situate myself as an enthusiast on this topic—not as an academic, but a filmmaker and a Winnipeg Film Group member and former executive board member.

Kevin Nikkel
Winnipeg, Manitoba
January 2023

Introduction

A SHORT HISTORY OF THE WINNIPEG FILM GROUP

I imagine a well-worn path in the snow leading to Leonard Klady's house. An assembly of the same people most Sunday nights, like some sort of religious cult. They gather in a darkened room to watch a print on a 16-mm projector (this being the early 1970s). Klady's uncle was a film distributor and he brought home 16-mm features every weekend for this dedicated crew of cinephiles. This group, existing in a marginalized city, was about to experience an infusion of new energy and purpose.

Several circumstances acted as catalysts upon this group of film enthusiasts. Film studies courses had begun to be offered at University of Manitoba, as across Canada. In the hinterland regions, individuals were searching to find a voice in what Andrew Burke describes as the "long" 1970s and the "afterglow" of Canada's centenary celebrations.[2] The protests of the era evoked a spirit of collective action and the need to organize. These factors would set the stage for Klady to organize a national film event in Winnipeg.

The Canadian Film Symposium was held in 1974, during the University of Manitoba's week-long Festival of Life and Learning. A chance for students to skip classes, watch films, and hear lectures, it even included a free concert by the then unknown band Kiss. Expectations were high. Insiders came from across the country to discuss Canadian filmmaking. *Cinema Canada* journalist Agi Ibranji-Kiss called the week-long event a "merry-go-round" of activities, "running from 10 in the morning to early the next."[3] Representatives from various funders, distributors, and filmmakers used the event to provoke serious discussion. Apart from the premieres, cathartic panel discussions allowed Canadian filmmakers to vent about the state of their craft in the face of federal inaction. From the "gloomy mood"[4] of the Film Symposium emerged a written declaration:

> *The Winnipeg Manifesto:*
> We the undersigned filmmakers and filmworkers wish to voice our belief that the present system of film production/distribution/exhibition works to the extreme disadvantage of the Canadian filmmaker and film audience. We wish to state unequivocally that film is an expression and affirmation of the cultural reality of this country first, and a business second. We believe the present crisis in the feature film industry presents us with an extraordinary opportunity.[5]

For the group that met to watch films at Leonard Klady's house, this was a chance to meet others, filling in their ranks. A local panel discussion was convened that included Klady, Robert Lower, Neil McInnes, Jerry Krepakevich, Ian Elkin, Leonard Yakir, Dave Dueck, Gunter Henning, and Leon Johnson.[6] This local panel would prove a catalyst. Penni Jacques, from the Canada Council for the Arts, spoke to the enthusiastic group of locals and encouraged them to form an organization that could be funded by the Council. Two weeks later, members of the new Winnipeg Film Group formalized a "Statement of Principles, Objectives and Structure."[7]

The Winnipeg Film Group joined a wider movement of artist-run centres happening across Canada, some founded as cooperatives and others as non-profit corporations. In all, there would be sixteen artist-run film centres.[8] The movement represented an effort to decentralize resources

Representatives from the Canada Council meeting Winnipeg Film Group members in the Bate Building, c. 1970s. Courtesy of Brad Caslor.

(*left to right*) Frederick Edell, Leon Johnson, David Cherniack, and Robert Lower at a Winnipeg Film Group Intensive Drama Workshop, 1975. Courtesy of Brad Caslor.

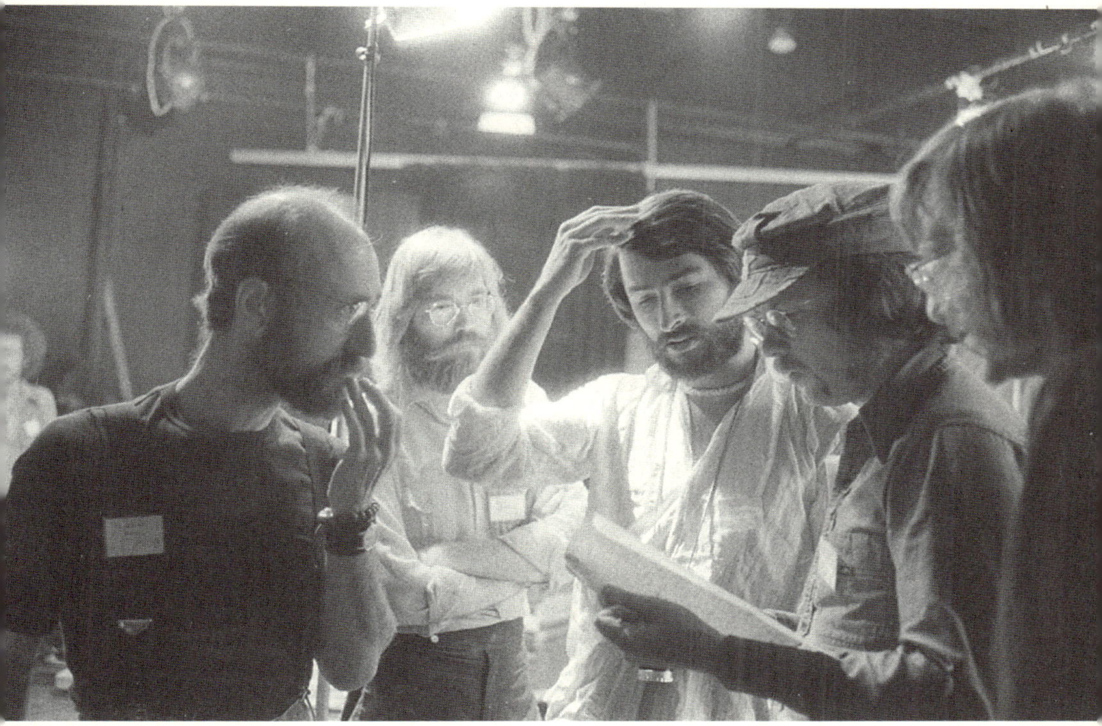

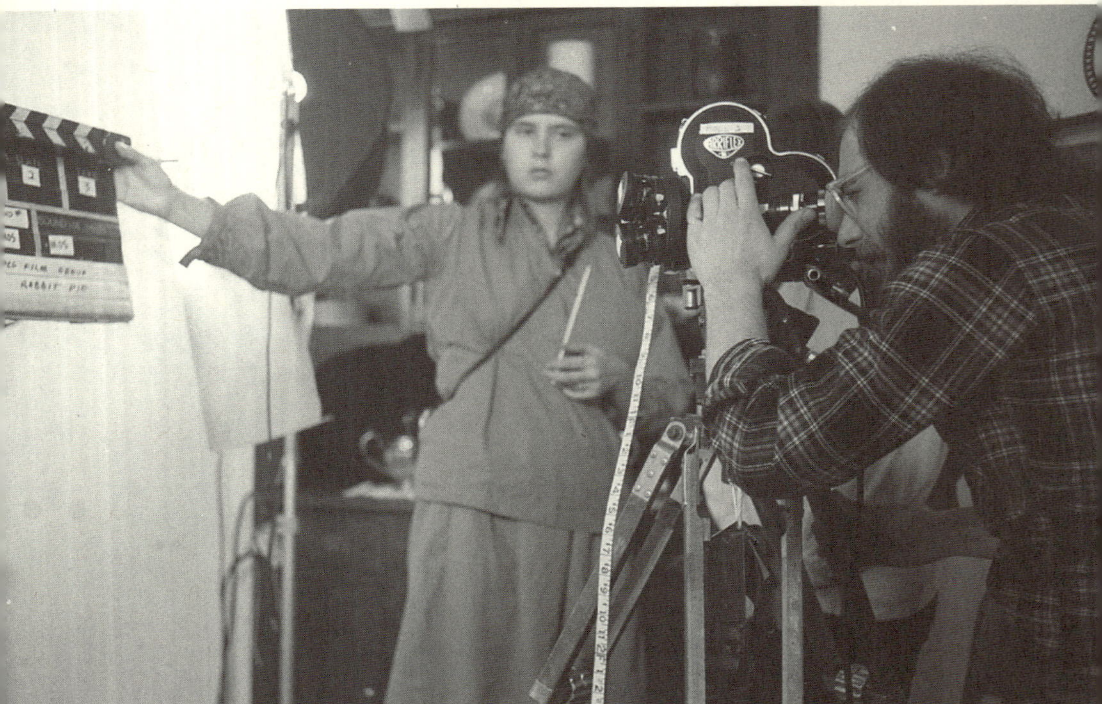
FILM GROUP

available to film-based artists through the funding for artist-run centres. Some organizations specialized in distribution, production, training, and/or exhibition spaces, and most also filled a gap as drop-in centres for artists. In a city of Winnipeg's size, the Winnipeg Film Group embodied multiple roles under one roof. The artist-run centres were networked together through various organizations such as the Independent Media Arts Alliance (IMAA). AA Bronson has suggested the phrase "connective tissue" to describe the dynamic networking of individuals within artist-run centres and between centres across the country—essential for developing the extensive art scene we observe today in Winnipeg and across Canada.[9]

Still, the local visual art scene was not completely harmonious. Individuals who emerged from institutions such as the School of Fine Arts at the University of Manitoba did not integrate easily with the crowd that gathered at the Winnipeg Film Group. In the early 1980s, one stream of creatives sheared off to form Plug In's Video Forum and Video Group, leading to the founding of Video Pool in 1983.[10] Video Pool maintained a distinct identity from the Film Group; cooperation was selective, with suspicion on both sides.

The Bate Building

The Winnipeg Film Group's first home was established in the Bate Building in Winnipeg's Exchange District, a dusty structure typical of the declining neighbourhood in the years before gentrification. The Group held regular meetings—gatherings which, due to the copious cigarette smoke, might have been mistaken for AA meetings. The Film Group occupied itself with existential questions and the office acted as a clearinghouse for members. Leonard Klady and Leon Johnston were in charge of writing grants for operating funds, equipment purchases, and to support film production.

There were two poles at the Film Group during these formative years: activists and artists. The former saw film as a hammer to change the world,

---

Elise Swerhone with slate, filming of *Rabbit Pie*, 1975. Courtesy of Brad Caslor.

Animator Richard Condie and Leonard Klady in the Winnipeg Film Group offices, c. 1970s. Courtesy of Brad Caslor.

the latter a brush for self-expression. This enthusiastic group of filmmakers demonstrated the essential qualities of emerging artists: energy, optimism, and innovation. Several collective projects offer case studies illustrating how the Group was learning to define itself and work together.

In the summer of 1975, a crew of Film Group members began shooting a documentary about the Winnipeg Folk Festival. The project was shelved for a lack of vision and insurmountable technical problems. A second collective effort was shot the same year: a silent-era-inspired comedy, *Rabbit Pie* (1976), in which a couple discovers that their restaurant meal of rabbit pie is multiplying all over their table.

In contrast to the failed attempt at a Folk Festival film, Elise Swerhone's documentary *Havakeen Lunch* (1979)—a film that observed the last days of a small-town lunch counter—was a much more confident success. Swerhone found funding for her project elsewhere but obtained equipment from the Film Group, a path that others replicated. David Cherniack's unfinished character-driven drama *The Crunch* began this way; partially funded by the Film Group, it stalled at rough-cut stage. *The Crunch* exposed a rift over which films should get funding—some felt the project was not worthy. Questions surfaced. What should be the Film Group's role in terms of production? Should the Film Group be a producer of its members' films? The debate simmered right up to the late 1980s, with Gene Walz's short comedy *The Washing Machine* (1988) in which a couple struggles over their faulty appliance—a metaphor for the Film Group itself during this era.

Inside the Film Group, the institution's maturity was

Cover of *The Moose*, Winnipeg Film Group newsletter. Courtesy of Winnipeg Film Group.

marked by the acquisition of a photocopier. Not everyone was as enthusiastic about spending precious grant funds—money that could go toward film production—on office appliances. Ed Ackerman and Greg Zbitnew's response was *5¢ a Copy* (1980), an animation made from photocopied faces and eclectic objects. This office conflict reflected the inevitable friction present in artist-run centres between bureaucracy and artistic practice. For the Winnipeg Film Group at that time, *5¢ a Copy* represented an alternative to a growing number of social realist documentary productions. A core of the Film Group was more interested in artistic expression and pushing the edges of experimental film than in changing the world.

Although its tides ebbed and flowed greatly, during this period the Film Group was marked by a high level of community engagement; but as the National Film Board (NFB) expanded its presence in Winnipeg with money for regional projects, many of the Group's founding members saw this as their chance to find paid work elsewhere. The Film Group would need to find ways to evolve.

Adelaide House

In 1982, the Winnipeg Film Group moved to a house on 88 Adelaide Street, on the edge of the Exchange District—a building more conducive to nurturing the Group's community. This turn-of-the-century house had that run-down, painted-over charm of a low-income rental. Wood trim and a curved banister welcomed newcomers to the offices down the hall. The living room was adapted for film screenings, much like the ones at Len Klady's house a few years earlier. Editing suites were upstairs.

Since the Film Group's founding, the most common type of production was the short film, and the Group's distribution department slowly expanded its catalogue from a stable of filmmakers.[11] A few stood out from the crowd. John Paizs began shooting animated films but switched to live-action drama. He was clear about what he wanted and it was not anything like what the Film Group had done before. Paizs observed, "It seems the film-makers of today are hung up on reality, showing things the way they are, including all the unsightly parts. I think they've thrown a lot away in terms of storytelling in sacrificing it to reality."[12] Paizs's string of successes shocked the Group's members into action. Not only was he breaking with the previous era's filmmakers, he took content from past film genres and began repurposing them for his own creative and comedic ends. Toronto film critic Geoff Pevere's article "Prairie Postmodern: An Introduction to the Mind and Films of John Paizs" applied a label that stuck. Pevere explains that by "subtly re-arranging the elements and iconographic road signs of American movies and TV shows Paizs establishes a distinct critical distance between the films and the object of their mimicry . . . it is precisely this funny and unfettered nature that ultimately facilitates the degree of intellectual resonance and political relevance the films unquestionably possess."[13]

The creative energy that Paizs brought to his films sparked others in their work, the most notable example being Guy Maddin with his first short film, *The Dead Father* (1985), a surreal story of a son dealing with a father's refusal to stay dead. As Paizs had reinvented genres, Maddin repurposed the tropes of silent-era German Expressionist cinema in an entirely different direction. The scene, in Maddin's film, of the son eating the father speaks to what was happening in the organization at the time, as filmmakers sought to establish unique identities for themselves, apart from those of their elders.

Filmmaker John Kozak observed that the artist-run centre attracted "filmmakers who brought with them an intense and personal vision, now far more interested in form than in content. It was this drive for personal expression, more than any other factor, that accounted for the Winnipeg Film Group's extraordinary growth, both in terms of membership and creative output, throughout the 1980s."[14] Gene Walz went further, detecting a Winnipeg Film Group "house-style" that played to the prairie postmodernist sensibility noted earlier.[15]

Artspace

In 1986, the Film Group moved into the Artspace building, also in the city's Exchange District, along with a consortium of other arts organizations. The Group became an anchor tenant which provided a permanent home for the Cinematheque, which would no longer need to borrow a screen at the NFB's Cinema Main, as it had since 1982. The Cinematheque, run by Dave Barber, was integral to the evolution of Winnipeg's film culture. It was a dedicated venue that championed films by local filmmakers. Emerging filmmakers had access to audiences—an invaluable opportunity to gauge response to their latest work. Films were more likely to be reviewed and the Film Group could thus build an identity in the broader community.

While the Adelaide space had been a home, the Artspace building—an aged but renovated warehouse building—was more like a factory. Members of the Group stepped up production. Although shorts were a consistent commodity, feature films—already evident in recent work at Adelaide—increasingly became a staple of local filmmakers' ambitions. Greg Hanec's *Downtime* (1985), consisting of scenes of bored Generation Xers failing to connect with each other, was the first feature film to be made under the auspices of the Winnipeg Film Group. Paizs released *Crime Wave* in 1985, in which he played a screenwriter who wrote great beginnings and endings but struggled with middles—a reprise of his "quiet man" role in his earlier short films. After a disappointing response to the film's premiere in Toronto, Paizs returned to Winnipeg to rewrite the third act.

Next came Guy Maddin's *Tales from the Gimli Hospital* (1988), with its fevered stories told by two patients in a sanatorium. It became a cult hit thanks to aggressive promotion by Film Group distributor Greg Klymkiw, overcoming its initial rejection by the Toronto International Film Festival (TIFF), then known as the Toronto Festival of Festivals. A brazen attitude in the face of rejection, together with Paizs's dogged reworking of his feature, exemplified a local resilience and provided a model for those who came later. More feature films followed soon after: one by John Kozak, another by Greg Hanec, and a first film by Gabriel and Jancarlo Markiw. The Group strove to keep the independent creative assembly line moving, while improvising and economizing outside the mainstream Hollywood factory models. Critic Geoff Pevere suggested that "the co-op had presided over one of the most fertile and idiosyncratic movements in the history of so-called regional filmmaking in Canada."[16] While the feature films that emerged from the Film Group did not fit neatly into a single genre or style,

the economic constraints reflected a common ancestry. Brenda Austin-Smith explains:

> While many Manitoba features did take stylistic detours from the straight realist road, they did so, at least at first, not because of their conscious adherence to a tenet of prairie postmodernism, but as a byproduct of the political economy of film production in Canada, which makes most features, particularly those in the regions by new directors, marginal to the commercial mainstream. Like filmmakers all over Canada, those in Manitoba can choose to compete directly for attention and audience share with American products, or can decide to make features that have no intention of locking horns with Hollywood releases. Many filmmakers in Manitoba made the limitations of small-budget, small-city filmmaking—poor lighting, cardboard sets, wooden actors, stiff direction—into what were regarded by later viewers and critics as intentional stylistic virtues.[17]

One of the high points for the Group, in terms of public attention, was a 1991 news documentary profile on the CBC program *The Journal* in which Pevere offered cautionary wisdom about a pattern he observed in Film Group films:

> Often the narrative becomes something that is practically irrelevant. I think particularly in the films of Guy Maddin, it's hard to fault those films for their lack of narrative because that's not what it's about. One becomes so captivated, and in some cases awestruck, simply by the ingenuity of the images and the sound and the references that are being made. You may forget the fact that the storyline itself is quite murky. For the time being, the weakness of storylines is something which can be compensated for by the incredible visual gifts that a lot of these filmmakers have, but I think that pretty well all of the feature films, whether

---

Tom Fijal shooting *Crime Wave*, 1985. Courtesy of John Paizs.

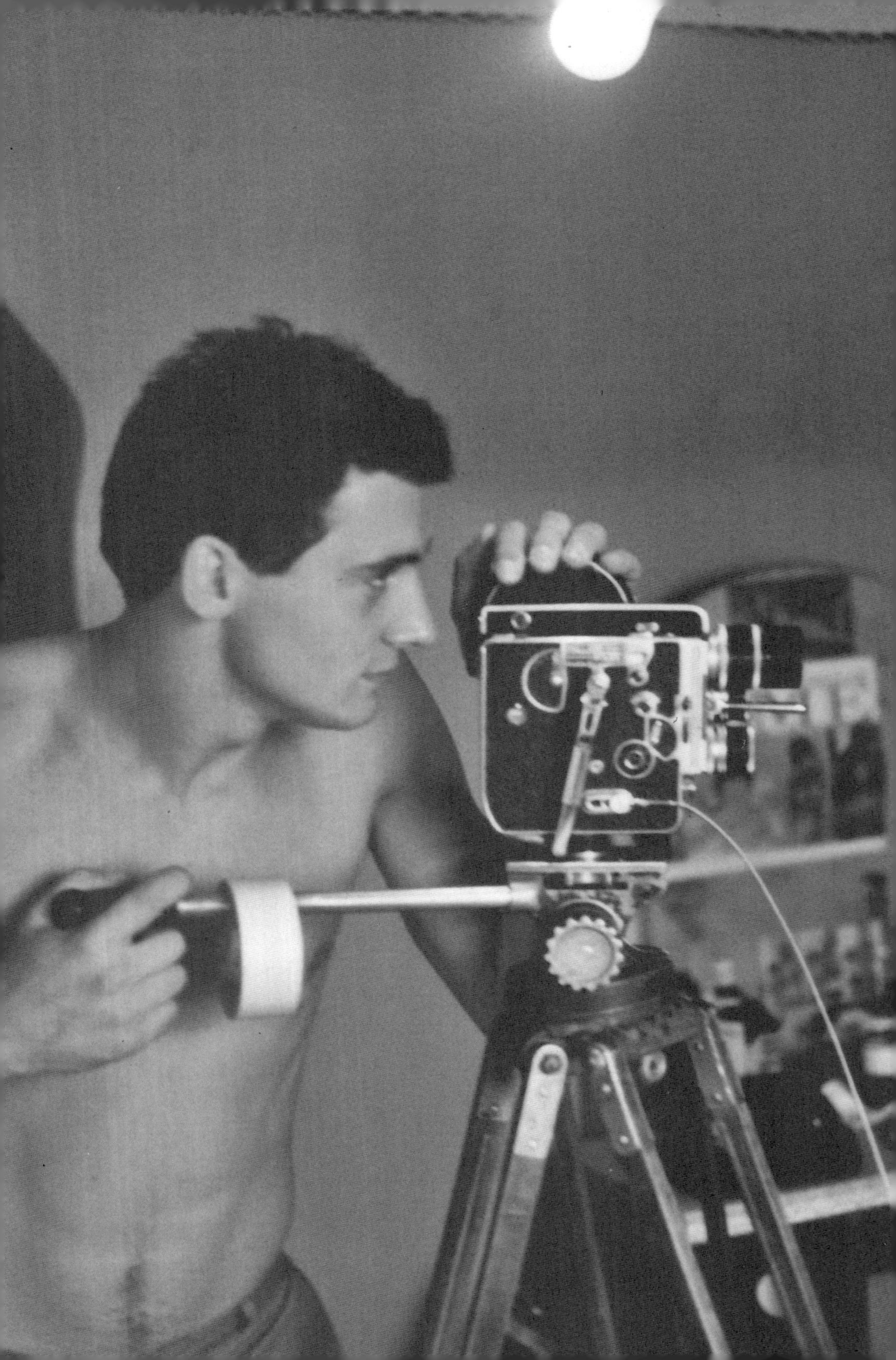

> it's *Smoked Lizard Lips, Crime Wave, Archangel, Tales from the Gimli Hospital*, occasionally you can see where that could possibly wear thin. I think that the thing that probably really needs to be improved, in order to ensure that this movement is not just a blip but is something which develops and which has a future, will probably mean stronger narrative lines from filmmakers.[18]

With *Crime Wave* and *Tales from the Gimli Hospital*, both released in the late 1980s, it seemed like the phenomenon of made-in-Winnipeg creative feature films would continue. Funders were ready to support local talent, sure that there would be a next hit. That project would be *Smoked Lizard Lips* (1991) by MB (Bruce) Duggan, except it would not prove as successful. While *Smoked Lizard Lips* was supported by Telefilm and had a distributor, response to the film was mediocre upon release. The film's failure meant that the honeymoon of attention from funders and distributors was over. Funders returned to their cautious posture toward most films, especially films from unknown regional filmmakers.

In the Winnipeg Film Group's anniversary publication *Dislocations*, Pevere claimed that the "movement of the 1980s is apparently spent" and that "there was no coherent purpose or manifesto for the practitioners of the Prairie Postmodern—it was made possible less by design than the almost climactic confluence of certain cultural factors—and since postmodernism itself is based in ironic detachment and ephemerality, the end was, to a degree, inevitable."[19]

Reflecting on the Group's anniversary and accompanying publication, Gene Walz concurred, adding a further critique: "Prairie Postmodern has degenerated into a series of empty mannerisms that lost the charm and the élan of the movement's first flowering. The result is a paralysis that will be difficult to cure without a complete change of direction or, better, a tremendous infusion of new talent."[20]

The Winnipeg Film Group has experienced something that literary critic Northrop Frye had observed: that Canadian culture "has felt the

---

John Paizs shooting *The Obsession of Billy Botski*, 1980. Courtesy of John Paizs.

CANADIAN

HOSPITAL

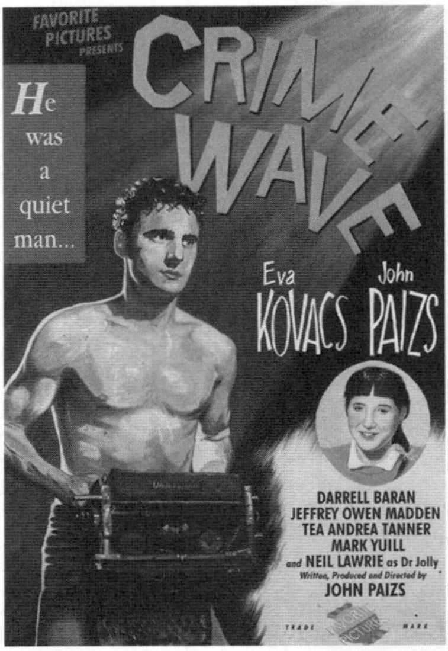

Members at the Winnipeg Film Group, Artspace location, 1988. Photo by Ken Gigliotti. Courtesy of *Winnipeg Free Press*.

Crime Wave movie poster, 1985. Courtesy of John Paizs.

Advertisement for film screening of hand-processed films, 2004. Courtesy of Winnipeg Film Group.

force of what may be called Emerson's law. Emerson remarks in his journals that in a provincial society it is extremely easy to reach the highest level of cultivation, extremely difficult to take one step beyond that."[21] In the film world, it is equally difficult to rise above a journeyman level of craft—a level that many Winnipeg filmmakers and technicians were able to achieve through their film school training or via dedicated Film Group workshop attendance. Trapped in a state of local pride, or perhaps a nostalgia for past film successes, the Film Group struggled to define itself in a larger creative field that was evolving quickly thanks to new technologies. Still, there were new seeds taking root in the Film Group garden.

Filmmaking Waves

Chronicling the history of an organization lends itself to a charting of creativity and community through the various locations that it inhabited: the Bate Building, the Adelaide Street house, and Artspace. But an examination of the surge of films produced over the years by individuals and groups is much more difficult; the Film Group's history seems less a story about waves and more like a river, widening ever more as it reaches toward the sea. In the early days, you could easily swim to the other shore, but with time, the output of films has given this river a vast width. There have been many hundreds of films, by emerging and mid-career filmmakers alike, produced at the Film Group over the years, but cataloguing and comparing each one is not the purpose of this volume. There are DVD compilations, streaming links, and online databases which chart the extent of the delta that resulted from the Winnipeg Film Group's downstream journey.

Although seldom unified in style and tone, certain periods of Film Group production, such as the darker, sensational films of the 1990s by filmmakers like Jeff Erbach, Gord Wilding, and Paul Suderman, exhibited similarities to earlier works. Filmmaker Deco Dawson's works were initially informed by the similar German Expressionist aesthetics of Guy Maddin. Dawson's multiple wins at TIFF demonstrate how the Winnipeg Film Group members were not merely riding on Guy Maddin's coattails but pursuing their own identity. The same could be said of many others interviewed in this volume—and many that should appear in the next.

What stands out about the Winnipeg Film Group generally is its acceptance of the short film as a valid genre of expression. In Winnipeg, filmmakers were, and are, willing to make their next short and thereby postpone, by a step, their road toward making feature films, which, in the dominant film culture, are the sole means of validation. Dawson explains: "I think Winnipeg has made short films a permissible and viable method of expression because really, unless you're making feature films, you aren't going to have any sort of recognition. . . . Winnipeg has said it's okay to make shorts."[22] This radical thinking fosters more experimentation and, subsequently, greater artistic maturity.

As the new millennium continued, the adoption of more digital technologies proliferated, prompting expectations of higher and higher pixel counts and CGI. But another trend was also at work in Winnipeg during these years: a resurgence of analog. Shooting on celluloid opened up new possibilities. This shift may be partially attributed to filmmaker Solomon Nagler's emphasis on processing film by hand. As Nagler explains, "Winnipeg filmmakers are always conscious of the act of filmmaking. That's why it's degraded—they're referencing the act of filming in Winnipeg. It started with John Paizs acting in his own films: we're always conscious of the filmmakers acting their roles. Guy [Maddin]'s texture has more to do with always making sure the act of filmmaking was referenced. By making the film look very degraded, sort of aged, fuzzy, and abstract, he moved this sort of ironic self-consciousness onto the material. That's the logical evolution of the current Winnipeg obsession with the material of film."[23]

Nagler's visit to Phil's Farm—a filmmaking boot camp run by acclaimed experimental filmmaker Phil Hoffman, in southern Ontario—brought back to Winnipeg an innovative set of tools for working with celluloid. Nagler and cinematographer John Kapitany began a hand-processing workshop at the Winnipeg Film Group, which led to notable works by Heidi Phillips, Cecilia Araneda, Victoria Prince, Carole O'Brien, Jennifer Bisch, Mike Maryniuk, and Matthew Rankin.

The history of the Winnipeg Film Group can be tracked with workshops, grants, commemorative events, and community engagement. For decades, the Film Group has operated a First Film Fund grant, a Production Fund and, more recently, a Mosaic project grant. Incubator events like the 48 Hour Film Contest attract members and foster the production of work. Another important event on the local calendar, and a staple for Film Group members, is the One Take Super 8 event run by the local WNDX Film Festival: participants shoot a cartridge of film but are permitted to watch the uncut film only at the public screening event. All of these contests and events play a crucial role in bringing members together and reinforcing the community.

In a number of situations, such collaboration with other filmmakers manifests itself in co-directed projects and film collectives associated, directly or indirectly, with the Winnipeg Film Group such as: Shawna Dempsey and

Matthew Rankin and Walter Forsberg, 2005. Courtesy of Walter Forsberg.

Lorri Millan, Red Czarina, the ITWÉ Collective, the Bent Light Collective, The Ephemerals, Astron 6, the Winnipeg Indigenous Filmmakers Collective and, perhaps most significant, l'Atelier national du Manitoba, made up of Matthew Rankin, Walter Forsberg, and Mike Maryniuk. From the Atelier's Horizontalist Manifesto, a mischievous yet sincere call for community:

> ***WE demand:***
> —away from the formal bouquet-throwing of the empty "contemporary Canadian" film; from the claws of imitative, careerist cinematic hucksters; from the sweet hugs of opportunistic critics and proclaimed authorities of movie.
> —away into the field of cultural introspection and civic self-loathing; toward the construction of film community worth its weight in Nips; closer to the Filmic Eucharist. [24]

L'Atelier's explosion of creativity, which continues to resonate years later, has been discussed by Andrew Burke and documented internally by Walter Forsberg.[25] This collective's season of productivity serves as a how-to guide for purposeful and playful collaboration. L'Atelier's work culminated in *Death by Popcorn* (2006), an experimental feature confronting the malaise of Winnipeg insecurity following the departure of the Winnipeg Jets hockey franchise.

Bureaucracy and Diversity

Growth, both in terms of members and of employees, is to be expected in an artist-run centre that survives this long. Although the organization's mission remains the same as when that group first gathered in Leonard Klady's living room to hash out its first principles, over time its policies and structure have made the Film Group less nimble. Board meetings have become more cautious and the annual general meeting more raucous. Arts organizations must satisfy the demands of funders, so the more effective an organization is at getting grants, the more accountability and paperwork it faces from those who provide them. There is a constant dichotomy between the organization's corporate posture and the demands of the members—a tension that marks the history of the Film Group.

Since its founding, there has been a recurring accusation that the Film Group was, and is, mostly a boys' club and that equal opportunities have not been available to women. There have consistently been strong female voices during each era in the Group's history. Things began to change as various executive directors implemented programs and encouraged individual women filmmakers. Carole O'Brien described what she has observed at the Film Group: "despite their low numbers, the women at our co-op have always managed to keep up with their male counterparts, artistically and technically. Until the late eighties, however, few of them made their own films, and those who did made documentaries. Public policy and the democratization of filmmaking technology is now changing the production landscape. For the past 15 years, a distinctly female voice can be heard. Out there, and at the Film Group, that voice is getting louder."[26]

The Winnipeg Film Group has made concerted efforts to be more inclusive, fighting the boys' club reputation and expanding the voices of its membership. The Mosaic Film Fund, for one example, was created in 2008 to support and mentor emerging women filmmakers and was designed specifically to support Indigenous and culturally diverse participants. Other initiatives have offered scholarships for training courses aimed at minority groups.

The Film Group's founding generation sought to use documentary to bring about social change. A few decades later, filmmakers such as Lorri Millan and Shawna Dempsey made the films *We're Talking Vulva* (1990) and *Good Citizen: Betty Baker* (1996) to address attitudes toward women in society. More recently, movements like Idle No More, #MeToo, and Black Lives Matter have galvanized Film Group members even further, resulting in important collaborations with groups like the Indigenous Filmmakers Collective and Black Space Winnipeg. Staff and board members who lack sensitivity to these issues have triggered confrontations, forcing the organization to examine its chemistry once again. The most recent conflict to boil over into the media was the dismissal of Executive Director Greg Klymkiw, formerly the Film Group's famed distributor, who had returned to the organization following some years in Toronto. *Winnipeg Free Press*

film critic Randall King wrote about the dismissal that, "it comes about two weeks after Ben Williams, the film group's former production centre director, published an open letter . . . highlighting what he referred to as a 'toxic' work environment under Klymkiw's direction."[27] More staff departures followed during this unsettled season. The Film Group's history is pockmarked with incidents of crisis and tension among staff, board, and members. Lorri Millan and Shawna Dempsey conclude that artist-run centres are "no more or less than their boards, their staffs, their volunteers, and their memberships. Anyone can get involved and help work to make an ARC what it is. ARCs are ever-evolving, and that evolution is by dint of the people who get involved. If you are unhappy with your local artist-run centres, get off your ass and work to make them better!"[28]

Regionalism

Like other regions, Winnipeg has struggled with its relationship to centres of cultural power—particularly Toronto. What is the significance of such a regional perspective to the story of the Winnipeg Film Group, and how have attitudes changed over the decades? Winnipeg's filmmakers have responded to the stigma of being from Winnipeg with what Brenda Austin-Smith identifies as a sense of "placelessness" in their work.[29] Gilles Hébert, writing in 1995, suggested that avoiding overt references to Winnipeg was a deliberate strategem, since "it is essential not to locate narratives in Winnipeg even though the stories are shot here or are about this place."[30]

While being from the prairies, and the term *regionalism*, are often considered pejoratives, as Lucy Lippard suggests, artists should think differently about their immediate locales because "regionalism is not a limitation but an advantage."[31] There are benefits to being from Winnipeg and there has been a shift in the representation of place in Winnipeg films. It may have been true, in the past, that filmmakers such as Paizs anonymized the

---

Actor on set, Winnipeg Film Group's Adelaide house, c. 1980s. Courtesy of Winnipeg Film Group.

KC
WFG
BULLS
1

location of their stories, and plenty of Hollywood movies have used the city as a setting for someplace else, but ultimately Winnipeg, as a motif, has come to be embraced by local filmmakers. Nowadays it matters less if people from elsewhere think Winnipeg is not cool.

Over the last few decades, thanks to the work of Winnipeg Film Group members and fostered by broadcasters like MTS TV, which for a decade funded hundreds of locally focused independent documentaries, a mythologization of the city has gradually gained steam. Perhaps not systematic, but certainly intentional, this mythologizing can be seen in the aggressive distribution tactics of Greg Klymkiw mentioned elsewhere; *My Winnipeg* (2007), Guy Maddin's celebrated filmic symphony to the city; the urban interventions of l'Atelier national du Manitoba; and the psychogeographic themes in the films of Matthew Rankin and Ryan McKenna, to name just a few.

More artists are choosing to live here and are making *here* a subject of their work. The Winnipeg Effect conference, held at the Winnipeg Art Gallery in 2016, examined the city's artistic influence and the dilemma of making work in Winnipeg. In their keynote address, Lorri Millan and Shawna Dempsey discussed the economic factors and attractions of locating their artistic practice in Winnipeg and questioned whether regionality matters, since "the geographic region now seems like an archaic designation."[32]

A local orientation can translate to resistance on an artistic level too, a connection aptly summarized by filmmaker Rhayne Vermette: "Because we are Winnipeg, and we're not Toronto or Vancouver or whatever, nobody really cares what we're doing, so we might as well do what we want. We can find freedom and liberation and that is what I'm trying to do. Just really think about my craft and really think about who's my audience? Where is this going to play? Be a little bit self-indulgent about it. Why not? I think Canadian cinema is a bit up for grabs, so let's just be innovative, let's be courageous."[33]

Group photo of the Winnipeg Indigenous Filmmakers Collective, 2017. Courtesy of Roger Boyer.

Production still from Guy Maddin's *My Winnipeg*, 2007. Courtesy of Guy Maddin/Buffalo Gals.

FAILU
FAILU
AILU

This attitude can be distilled to what Kenneth Frampton describes as an "arriere-garde" approach: if the avant-gardes in centres like Toronto will not accept us, who cares?[34] Similarly, in a letter addressed to the Canada Council many years earlier, artist Greg Curnoe wrote that people did not seem to understand that his hometown, the small, regional city of London, Ontario, is "not a cultural centre—it is a backwater . . . this is a good thing. . . . Because of this we can work without being bothered."[35] Today's maturation of local attitudes recalls the approach of the London Regionalists of the 1960s, '70s, and '80s, in the work of artists like Curnoe and Jack Chambers, among others, who centred their painting and filmmaking practices in London.[36] The collective spirit of their movement spawned galleries, exhibitions, and publications that championed regionalism and celebrated the work of local people who wished to practice their craft from where they lived.

Although initially appearing isolationist, this critical, or radical, regionalist posture is focused on universal targets that transcend place. Again, drawing a parallel to the London, Ontario art movement of the past decades is useful. London poet James Reaney (who lived in Winnipeg and taught at the University of Manitoba for six years) declared, "I don't believe that you can be world, or unprovincial or whatever, until you've sunk your claws into a very locally coloured tree trunk and scratched your way through to universality."[37] So, too, have Winnipeg filmmakers found local topics of universal appeal, whether in celebrating a local diner or a whistling lawyer. Filmmaker Guy Maddin's most lauded film, and his most accessible, is also his most local: *My Winnipeg*. Maddin's film became the centre of a major art exhibition, in 2011, of seventy-five Winnipeg artists at the Maison Rouge in Paris, one of France's top contemporary art venues. Since then, the gallery has launched a series of exhibitions giving other cities the same treatment—such as *My Joburg* (2013) and *My Buenos Aires* (2015)—but *My Winnipeg* launched the series.

Rhayne Vermette works on an animation, 2017. Courtesy of Five Door Films.

Winnipeg Aesthetic

Is there a Winnipeg aesthetic? Guy Maddin has honed his experimental low-budget approach through a repurposing of old film genres, and his influence on the community is significant. But not everyone fits that sensibility. Dave Barber asks if there is a way to answer this question without referring only to a few icons of the past:

> I honestly think the Winnipeg Aesthetic is a constantly shifting range of independent filmmaking styles ranging from irreverent works to experimental work, serious drama, animation, documentaries and a fantastic new generation of Indigenous artists. Every independent filmmaker is influenced by the friends around them and workshops and the spark of a great idea. The Winnipeg Film Group must always nurture that spark or it ceases to be of use. If there is a common bond it is that independent Winnipeg filmmakers forge their own path and won't let anyone tell them what to do. And we are all richer for it.[38]

While a Winnipeg attitude is easier to recognize than an overall aesthetic in the range of work made here, patterns surface when that attitude is put into practice. A fierce drive to create in a regional climate, with few resources, demands ingenuity and improvisation if funding is not available. Paizs showed how to make much from little money, and many have since done likewise. This necessity, and the "who cares" attitude which Rhayne Vermette describes above, are a reflection of a particular posture.

If this spirit drives a creator to be bold, to try something new, then that is where the Film Group has succeeded. A spirit of experimentation was something that George Godwin noted as "cause for optimism in the messier, less accomplished, but far more exploratory and inquisitive work of people like Sol Nagler and Victoria Prince. Ragged works to be sure, but actively building their creators' voices out of a wider range of sources."[39]

Some independent Winnipeg films also share a playfulness that has invited the label "fun formalism," a classification of the scene originally attributed to filmmaker John Kneller.[40] Filmmaker Clint Enns explains:

Still photo from Matthew Rankin's short film *I Dream of Driftwood*, 2006. Courtesy of Matthew Rankin/Winnipeg Film Group.

> There's definitely a regional aesthetic. There's definitely a school. It's more like a regional spirit that comes through. The best way to define it is through fun formalism. I also like the diversity of work that is still made. In that same sort of spirit that happens in Winnipeg, where zombie films are showing next to experimental films, they start to inform each other in some way. They may be engaging with a totally different aesthetic, but there's still this the same spirit. The spirit of play. There is a playfulness in the work that's here. I think a quintessential example of fun formalism would be Matthew Rankin's *I Dream of Driftwood* [2008], where it's about the zoom, but it's zooming into homes in Winnipeg. It's really humorous and it's really depressing. It really captures the spirit of Winnipeg, while using this simple technique, this simple form.[41]

The ant lines trudging from Artspace's third-floor elevator into the Winnipeg Film Group offices to sign up for the 48 Hour Film Contest or the WNDX festival's One Take Super 8 contest are great examples of this playful spirit in action. These contests are sold out at registration, and the subsequent screenings are too. Clint Enns relates this to "the posture of Winnipeg. Kids actually have fun making films out here. There's a lot of joy at the evening events. There's a joy to watch each other's works on the screen because of the sense of community in the city. It's a different attitude. Like Greg Hanec and *Downtime* [1985], which is a pretty humorous film, dealing with a very serious subject matter, and yet it has regional humour. You have Guy's work—these engage in a form of fun formalism. There's a lot more pretensions towards art in Toronto."

Resilience

In recent years, filmmakers with their own digital gear have been less dependent on the Winnipeg Film Group, but this has not meant the complete demise of the artist-run centre. It still offers unique gear, like an Oxberry stand or its arsenal of analog equipment, which includes a JK optical printer, positioning it to be a leader in celluloid-driven filmmaking. Workshops continue to be important to bring in new members.

AA Bronson suggests that "artist-run culture, like an iceberg, is 95% beneath the surface."[42] In Winnipeg, the local film scene extends beyond what is visible at the Film Group. Some cannot stand the Group's strong personalities and politics, contributing to a constant calving off of chunks from the berg, forming an archipelago of independents—but the climate of Winnipeg, with a seemingly endless demographic of emerging creatives adopting the local attitude, gives our iceberg a constant shape.

I approached this project to draw inspiration from individuals talking about the roots of their creative process and their relationship to an artist-run centre. I also take inspiration from long-time Winnipeg film studies

---

Film Group members participate in a film workshop, n.d. Courtesy of Dave Barber.

scholar Howard Curle, who remarked that "we need a history of film culture in this city and province, one that encompasses cinema as a commercial, social and artistic event. A lot of digging needs to be done, voices should be recorded before they fade, images deserve to be remembered."[43]

An exercise in oral history such as this one cannot possibly capture the whole story of the Winnipeg Film Group, as memories are limited by time. And some choose not to participate in articulating this past. The danger of anaesthetizing nostalgia is always a threat. Detailing (and mythologizing) the Winnipeg Film Group's story is a means to foster more creative work and build a stronger community—imperfect, but essential to working in a regional city like ours. Critical inspection of the Film Group's history will reveal its humanity and its flaws as our culture moves toward greater social equality. Still, the interview genre remains a highly productive means to document, inspire, and perpetuate the creative spirit and craft of independent film.

Following nearly four decades of growth since he wrote about the Manitoba film community back in 1983, perhaps Gene Walz's remark that "the film community here is still a very fragile eco-system" is no longer true.[44] The diversity and resilience of the Winnipeg Film Group community has helped filmmakers to withstand climatic shifts, which still come and go. Or maybe Gene is more right than we know.

Winnipeg Film Group meeting, c. 1970s. Courtesy of Brad Caslor.

Part One

THE BATE BUILDING 1974–1982

BOVRIL
Filmex76

LEONARD KLADY

Leonard Klady was born and raised in Winnipeg. He programmed films at venues around Winnipeg and attended the University of Manitoba, where he began writing film reviews. He was instrumental in creating the Canadian Film Symposium. Len was the first president of the Winnipeg Film Group. He went on to become a film critic for the Winnipeg Free Press *and, later, in Los Angeles for* Variety.

22 DECEMBER 2015, LOS ANGELES

Kevin Nikkel: Were there any hints that you would become the person you have become?

Leonard Klady: No. I grew up in the North End of Winnipeg. For those with some kind of historic perspective, I lived between the College and Deluxe theatres. I spent most of my Saturdays at one or the other. I liked movies. When you grew up in Winnipeg, you didn't think that you could be involved in the film industry. There were film houses in Winnipeg. There were mixing houses in Winnipeg. But these were primarily geared to advertising and commercial production. For some strange, unbeknownst reason, there were a lot of animators in Winnipeg. In fact, one of the early projects of the Film Group was an omnibus film using the animators in the city. It was a project that basically ended up not being done because I think there was a kind of suspicion amongst the animators of working together.

Leonard Klady at the Winnipeg Film Group offices in the Bate Building, 1970s. Courtesy of Brad Caslor.

KN: What was it called?

LK: It was called *Boarding House* [1975]. I think the idea had six segments. It certainly would be Richard Condie, Brad Caslor, Nancy Edell, Neil McInnes—and I can't remember the others. It would all take place in a boarding house and you would zoom into one of the apartments. Animator A would do a segment in that apartment and then you would zoom out. You'd zoom back into another apartment and see a segment from another animator.

KN: How far along did it proceed?

LK: It got far enough along that we had talked to all the animators and I think that we'd even decided who was going to do the framing story. They were asked to come up with a scenario for their section. Each section was to be three to five minutes long. It was like herding cats. People said they were interested and then, in most instances, didn't follow through.

KN: What were you doing in the city at that time?

LK: I was reviewing films and doing programming all over the city, which gave me the opportunity to see movies.

Canadian Film Symposium/*Winnipeg Manifesto*

KN: Let's talk about the idea behind the University of Manitoba Film Symposium.

LK: Perhaps the spark was the 1973 Canadian Film Awards, which were in Montreal. The Québécois filmmakers announced that they would not accept any awards, for some political reason. They'd essentially shot themselves in the foot. Whoever advised them to take that tack should be strung up because it was going to be nationally televised for the first time. If they really wanted to make a political statement, they would have let the awards go on. They would've gone up to the podium if they won an award, and made their statement on national television. So, by announcing this in advance of the awards, the CBC said, "well, if they are going to do that, we're not going to broadcast the awards." The awards weren't broadcast. I went to the event. There were some Quebec filmmakers there, but it seemed to me—wouldn't it be nice to do something with both the English Canadian filmmakers and the Québécois filmmakers on a neutral ground? The first year was kind of a trial balloon.

The next year it ballooned. I think we brought in forty or fifty people—filmmakers, government people, and a couple of performers. Showed films, had seminars. Created an environment where everyone could kind of interplay with one another. We had the world premiere of the jazz documentary that Budge Crawley did. That was also the year we had the English premiere of *Les Ordres* (1974).

At the same time, I thought we ought at least to have a program with local and regional filmmakers. We had a panel. I know Robert Lower was on the panel, I think David Cherniack, and maybe Leonard Yakir. Also on the panel was a woman named Penni Jacques, who was the head of the Canada Council's visual arts [section]. At some point during the panel, she said: "If you guys put together some kind of film collective, we would be open to a presentation for money." There was already the Atlantic Film Co-op and the Toronto Co-op. She almost said, "if you do A, B, and C, you will get a lump of cash."

After the event, those of us who were on the panel, and other people working in the industry who had an interest in doing things other than commercial films, all got together and basically said, okay, who's going to put together

Leonard Klady and Francoyse Picard, c. 1970s. Courtesy of Brad Caslor.

this prospectus? A couple of us wound up doing it and submitting it, and we got money.

KN: Tell me about the *Winnipeg Manifesto* that came out of the early discussions.

LK: It was basically a document to draw attention to the fact that there were filmmakers in the city who had aspirations to make films with a social and entertainment end. It was one page. We understood well enough that you had to make your points concisely if you wanted to get any attention.

KN: Was it really idealistic, like the French New Wave or Dogma 95? A lofty sort of thing?

LK: Yes, it was idealistic and it was lofty. But there weren't dictums that said we are going to make *this* kind of film. It wasn't Dogma.

KN: How would you summarize the *Manifesto*?

LK: The *Manifesto* was basically to get attention—to make people aware that there were credible filmmakers living in the city.

Winnipeg Film Group

KN: Where did these initial conversations take place?

LK: My house. My memory is that the meetings were very intense. You had a lot of strong-minded people, but somehow it didn't tilt over because we all wanted the same thing. As president, it was my task to ensure people worked together toward some kind of end. At some point, we said we should have some way to get these films out for exhibition or rental, and that's when Dave would've come into the picture, to have screenings. For years, the screenings were done at the National Film Board's theatre.

KN: It was a very young group with not much experience. Any memories of meetings?

LK: I'd been involved in different organizations. I knew *Robert's Rules of Order*. There was a meeting where we were electing officers and [doing] other business. There was a guy who was one of those guys who was opportunistic, who I could tell wanted to be on the board. I said, "Andrew, here's $20, go bring back beer." So, he left to pick up the beer and I said, "Okay, we're going to open elections now for secretary, treasurer, and VP." Someone nominated him for one of these positions and I said, "I'm really sorry, but we can't accept the nomination for this." He said, "Why?" I said, "Because he's not here and candidates have to be asked whether they're willing to stand." Whoever had made the nomination went: "Oh. Okay." He was someone who, a short time later, just wasn't involved with the group. So, I guess, in a way I was identifying who was serious. And by using parliamentary rules and deception, I could steer things in such a way that we wouldn't have distractions.

KN: Did you get flak?

LK: No. By and large, artists aren't really interested in the mechanical things that have to be done. I was aware that we had to file papers and I'd had enough experience in the past. I knew lawyers, I knew accountants, and basically decided what elements had to be in our bylaws. I could then go and make sure that the way it was set up was legally valid. It was a non-profit. Someone had to do that, and that was me. I was just the sucker who had to make sure that the i's were dotted and the t's were crossed.

KN: You began to hand out grants for people to make films?

LK: People would send in submissions and we would get updates on whatever project was under someone—either Bob, or Ian, or myself. The first time that Guy Maddin got a grant from us, in terms of rotation, it was Ian's turn. So, the first meeting subsequent to Guy getting money, I say: "Ian, what is the situation on Guy Maddin's project?" Ian, this quiet, unassuming guy, suddenly goes into a five-minute screed. He goes: "He's impossible! You can't communicate with him. I asked him something and he dodges the question. I don't know what he's doing!" Finally, he finishes and the rest of us are like, what just happened? There is this pause. I break it up and say, "Ian, how is the footage?" He says, "Oh, it's great. It's going to be a really good picture."

The Crunch

KN: I want to hear about *The Crunch.*

LK: Okay, so we have a chunk of money, and I think David [Cherniack] was the most motivated and was someone who could do a dramatic short, more so than anyone else. We open up auditions to get this money. David sends in a script. We read the script and we look at each other. We say: "It ain't there." We sit down and make notes, and send it back to David and say please address this and resubmit the script. David resubmitted the script, and we look at the script and it's worse. We said: "We can't recommend this to the group." David is arguing: "This is my vision. You do not see my vision. Can I take it to the group and argue my case?" We said fine.

The next general meeting, the committee talks about this project and how we have great admiration for David, but we don't feel that the script is there yet and so we're not recommending it. David gets up, is very eloquent, and says: "I'm a filmmaker. I have a vision. This is the Winnipeg Film Group! Are you going to back my vision or this administrative panel?" It went to a vote and the general membership voted in favour of David.

David did his first cut and showed it to the group, and it didn't go over well. I think David was a little bit in shock. He said, "I'm going back into the editing room to recut it." We would say over the subsequent months: "How is the cut coming along?" He said: "I haven't really been able to get to it." Eventually, David left town and took the film with him. So, other than that one screening, I don't know that it's ever been screened again.

KN: In hindsight, was *The Crunch* an important chapter in the evolution of the Film Group?

LK: My memory is that we just pushed on. From time to time, it would be a punchline to a joke. I don't think that the production committee was subsequently thought to be geniuses, as a result of having reservations about it. It didn't have a scarring effect on the group. Perhaps the fact that we were just starting out muted the potential.

KN: Did David get a fair chance to make that film?

LK: I think so, from my perspective. What is the quote about the democratic process—that it is the best of the worst kind of governance that we have?

Winnipeg Identity

KN: What were some of the most interesting works you saw over the years?

LK: There's something which is hard to define, that somehow gets at the environment of what Winnipeg is. I'd already moved down here when Guy had done the first feature, *Tales from the Gimli Hospital* [1988]. I was starting to hear this buzz about this weird, dreamlike, bizarre picture—they assumed that Gimli was a fictional place. They said, "It's called *Tales from the Gimli Hospital*." I said, "I know that hospital." Eventually, I saw that film and I went, that's not that strange. It's just the way we think in Winnipeg. It's a sensibility that seems endemic to where we grew up. That's what I think we all wanted to happen with the Group.

KN: Did all the Film Group members share a similar sensibility?

LK: It's part of your DNA. If it's part of your DNA, you don't have to go around and say "I'm a Winnipegger." You just *are* a Winnipegger. You will take it wherever you go. There were people within the Group who felt that whatever it was that they wanted to do, they were not going to be able to do it in Winnipeg. They would reach a certain point where it was time for them to go to Toronto or Los Angeles or Vancouver or London. And they did. Certainly, one of Winnipeg's biggest exports is talent.

Filmex76

LEON JOHNSON

Leon Johnson grew up in Minnesota, where he began working in advertising. He later settled in Winnipeg, where he helped found the Winnipeg Film Group and worked as its first coordinator. Besides making his own short films, he had a distinguished career as a sound recordist in the local film industry.

31 OCTOBER 2015, WINNIPEG

Kevin Nikkel: Any hint, from your upbringing, that you'd end up in the artistic life?

Leon Johnson: Artistic, yes—my father was a painter. And a farmer. We used to go to the Walker Art Center, in Minneapolis. I eventually took art in college, in Moorhead and Duluth. I started taking night courses in film.

I came to Canada in 1972. I was travelling and I eventually came here after a trip to Montreal and New York. I watched a lot of films from the NFB in Minneapolis because they had a big collection at the library. I got really interested in animation. I eventually did *Okeedoke* [1973], which is made out of a series of seven photographs. I was just travelling and I ended up in Churchill, and, from there, hitchhiking on airplanes around the Arctic. I saw a piece of sculpture in Churchill, in ivory, of a series of birds on little sticks: landing, coming down in the water, and

Leon Johnson in the Winnipeg Film Group offices in the Bate Building, 1970s. Courtesy of Brad Caslor.

coming up with a fish in its mouth. It was just like animation! I thought, I should go to Montreal and tell people. I was really moved.

I went to Montreal, not knowing a single soul there, and got to meet with Wolf Koenig and told him that they should send some people to the North to work with the Inuit, making films and animation. He said, "Interesting you're here today because somebody left this morning to do that very thing." He said: "Where do you want to live? What do you want to do?" I said, "I don't want to live in a big city anymore. I've had it. I grew up on the farm. I want to get into filmmaking." They said they're opening an office here in the next couple of years, and go back to Winnipeg and help make it happen. We need a body of people that can be there to start making films.

I came back, worked for Ken Perkins in animation, met Brad Caslor. From Brad Caslor, I met Len Klady and, every Sunday night, we watched movies. Elise Swerhone was there too because she was living in that house. We watched films and talked about it, and it really was the beginnings. Len brought together the Canadian Film Symposium, in '74. Major people making films in Canada were in town—it was a phenomenal amount of people. Out of that [came] a panel discussion of the filmmaking of Manitoba. The film officer from the Canada Council suggested that we form a film co-op. They were doing it in other places and, if we could put that together, they would be interested in funding it.

The Bate Building

Dave Barber: What did you talk about?

LJ: Who are we? How are we going to do this? How are we going to get an organization together? Where can we find money? It was a great, diverse group. It appeared that people from one part of the city didn't want to talk to people from another part of the city. I was neutral in all this stuff because I wasn't from here.

DB: Do you mean the North End and the South End?

LJ: I'm just saying that existed and I wasn't part of that. It even existed up until I rented a place for us in the Bate Building. People wanted it in their neighbourhood. I said, no—Portage and Main. The closest we can get. I just went and rented a place for $135 a month, and that was the place. It was central. It was not a very nice place, but it was big enough and perfect for the Film Group. It had a screening room out back. A place for an editing room.

At that time, there was one person who was already making independent films: Leonard Yakir, who had made the documentary [*Main Street Soldier* (1972), about Ray LeClair], and was working on putting together his film *The Morning Suit* (1975). I was really supportive and saying let's help with this. I was saying, if it's a success, it will benefit everybody. He eventually got the film together and, in the fall of '74, he shot it. I got to work on it, being the boom man and the second camera assistant. We actually shot in the Bate Building and the elevator.

KN: How soon, after the Group was formed, did you buy gear?

LJ: Very quickly. We were able to get an Arri camera and we bought a new Nagra, microphones, and an editing machine. We had matching provincial money with the Canada Council and then worked with the Manitoba Arts Council to try to get that started. Then, trying to get long-term funding in place. In the meantime, we did have little work projects. And the history of film—I don't know where that material went. There was a whole research project that went on for three months, on just the history of filmmaking in Manitoba.

DB: When I started at the Film Group, David Demchuk was working on that.

LJ: This was earlier. It was John Kozak and a woman—I can't remember her name. There was two of them that did that project, looking at the history.

KN: Let's go back to the conversations about how the Group is going to form.

LJ: We were meeting once a week. As the year went on, there was more and more people that found out about it and came around. We had to incorporate. We had to look for long-term funding and getting that in place. I guess it kind of fell to me to do a lot of that stuff. I was about ten

1

years older than everybody else, so I had some experience and I wasn't afraid of money.

We talked about what we wanted to do. Eventually, Robert Lower put it all down into the objectives, which—I don't know if anybody has a copy of those. There was a series of objectives of the Winnipeg Film Group. That was written down from all the discussions.

It took a long time for us to actually make our own first film, *Rabbit Pie* [1976], which was fun. It wasn't initiated by anybody from the Group. It was somebody from Prairie Theatre Exchange—David Huband. They had tried to do it. Couldn't do it. He came to us, and so, we just did it. We went around the room, with who was going to do what.

KN: In the early years, was there a sense that the embers were fragile and the fire might go out?

LJ: I spent a lot of time just talking to people—encouraging and giving direction to people that came in. When John Paizs came in and sat down and talked, I couldn't really give him any money but I could give him support. It was an organization to support those kinds of projects, and that was what I did. I listened and listened and listened and listened, and I typed an awful lot of grant applications.

At the time, there was grants through the Canada Council. There was support you could get from the Film Board, in terms of processing. We had a camera. Some lighting. We had [a] Nagra and microphones, and things like that. And an editing machine. So, there was that—there was a way of supporting that kind of thing. Other than that, just encouragement. And: there's this person that you might want to have, this person that knows how to do this. A lot of those projects, people did them for nothing.

On Greg Zbitnew's film *Muskeg Special* [shot in 1979; released in 2007], nobody was paid and yet we did that film and it was enjoyable. People were doing it, a lot of things, without payment, but they were learning

---

Leon Johnson operates the camera during a Winnipeg Film Group Intensive Drama Workshop, 1975. Courtesy of Brad Caslor.

their skills. I actually did this thing at [around] the same time, which was filming some scenes for *You Laugh Like a Duck* [1980]. There was money that the province of Manitoba and the province of Nova Scotia put up for the Year of the Child. That included a lot of people. I don't think anybody was paid to do anything on that, but we had money to do it and do a pretty good film. You learned a lot. I practically wore out a tape recorder just doing volunteer stuff, learning how to record.

DB: Was the National Film Board influencing the Film Group?

LJ: The Film Board kept people here. People had work. There was a practicality, for me, of actually working—I did really well in sound—and actually having a job once in a while. I hadn't had a full-time job since I quit advertising in '72. That's the last time I had to try to make a living.

KN: It's the siren song of making money that pulls people away, whether the NFB or the more recent film service industry.

LJ: Of course—the practicality of making a living. There's a few that can continue to do it and have access to the money that they need. It is not an easy task. Where is it going to be showing? How will you get your money back? It's difficult making a living, doing it. Independent film? It's hard.

KN: You made a choice of leaving advertising and went into independent film. Then you made a choice to become more involved in sound?

LJ: I became more involved in the sound industry. I got sucked in by Hans Comes from Montreal, with the Film Board. He came out here to get the industry going and do training. I did a lot of work with him. I would go there every Thursday. I had boomed on the show *The Morning Suit*—out of nowhere, just doing it—and then got a chance to work with him, and then he sucked me in. I was fairly good at it. I bought equipment and kept getting work.

KN: Let's talk more about your film career as well. You're in administration but you're also a filmmaker?

LJ: Well, wanting to be, yes. I had done one film, *Okeedoke*. I didn't have any real money to make films and so I went to the single-shot film.

Ten-minute films—that's *Christmas in Brandon* [1979] or *Park* [1983]. Or one that is not finished . . . with Richard Condie and his wife. I also did one with Peter Paul Van Camp. Then I did *You Laugh Like a Duck* and *Le Metif Enragé* [1984]. The film that didn't get finished, which I had $5,000 for, was *Yardmen*. It was done in the CP yards, with the old guys that switch trains. I've still got the footage—it's edited. It was never completed.

KN: Is it transferred?

LJ: No, it has sound in bits. It didn't have a sound edit done to it. It's got the sound from the shots, synced to the shots—but there are huge sections that don't have anything. But the dialogue and stuff is all there.

KN: Of the other films that you've made, which would it resemble?

LJ: None. Just straight documentary. Short documentary.

KN: I want to see this!

DB: Was it made around the time of *You Laugh Like a Duck*?

LJ: Oh no, way before. It would have been made about '76.

KN: Before *Muskeg Special*?

LJ: Oh yes.

DB: Sounds like a great idea. It reminds me of that NFB film by Roman Kroitor [*Paul Tomkowicz: Street-railway Switchman* (1953)].

LJ: I have an affinity to trains because I grew up next to a main line of the railway. When I was a little kid [living] outside of a small town, they switched every afternoon—the steam engines. They went back and forth, and I was on the front step and the engineers would know me. They would throw me chocolate bars. That was my life. So, I happened to see these guys and thought I should do this little film about them before they retired because it was changing.

KN: So, the film—you just have the film reels right now?

LJ: Yes, it's all in the basement somewhere.

KN: You have to finish it![45]

DAVID CHERNIACK

David Cherniack was born in Winnipeg. He studied sciences at the University of Manitoba and later attended the Prague Film Academy (FAMU) before returning to Winnipeg. He was a founding member of the Winnipeg Film Group, during its early years at the Bate Building. He later moved to Toronto, where he continued his film career in documentary, both at the CBC and with his own production company, All in One Films.

26 NOVEMBER 2016, TORONTO

Kevin Nikkel: Was there a hint in your upbringing that you'd become the creative person that you became?

David Cherniack: Probably not. I came to filmmaking a little bit later than most people. I was doing honours math and physics when I discovered, in my third year, I really didn't have any passion for quantum mechanics the way I thought I might. I spent my last year at university getting a degree in physics because I accumulated enough math and physics courses to do that, but I was interested in literature, philosophy, and photography. I studied directing for four years in Prague. It was a hell of a good film education. Really traditional—film as art. It had produced the Czech New Wave of the 1960s.

David Cherniack on set. Courtesy of David Cherniack.

So, coming out of that school, I really had no interest in going back to Winnipeg. But I had married. Vesna, my wife, was expecting and she wanted to be near my parents during the first couple of years. There weren't that many filmmakers around Winnipeg. Vesna and I quickly became acquainted with everybody in Winnipeg who was interested in making film. That's how we all ended up at the University of Manitoba one day, with the lady from the Canada Council, who said, "you should form a Film Group and we'll give you some money."

KN: Who was around? How did things come together?

Canadian Film Symposium

DC: Vesna and I had met Richard and Linda Condie, and Len Klady, and Bobby Lower. We would get together and Klady would get prints somehow, from some connection he had through somebody in the business. He would screen Hollywood and art house films in his living room. Everybody would just crash on the floor and we would watch these films. That's what the scene was like there. There was nothing organized, in terms of people who were actually working and doing films. As far as working in the industry, it was me and Bobby, and that was pretty well it because nothing else really had started yet. Richard was interested in doing animation and was in the initial throes of doing stuff.

KN: What was the Winnipeg Film Symposium like?

DC: I remember nothing except a meeting with the lady from the Canada Council because that was the critical thing. It was more than just that meeting—it was a whole symposium. It seemed to me there were about fifteen to twenty of us in the lecture hall at the university. We were just sitting around and she just got up and started saying, "Please, you're here, you're interested, form a film group. We'll give you some seed money to get started. Let's get it going. We want to get this stuff going all over the country." We didn't require much in the way of encouragement, let's put it that way.

Vladimír Valenta, Vonnie von Helmolt, and David Cherniack following a Winnipeg Film Group drama workshop, 1975. Courtesy of Brad Caslor.

David Cherniack and Leon Johnson at a Winnipeg Film Group Intensive Drama Workshop, 1975. Courtesy of Brad Caslor.

Czech actor Vladimír Valenta delivers a drama workshop to Winnipeg Film Group members, 1975. Courtesy of Brad Caslor.

KN: Do you remember what the conversations were like after you'd come together?

DC: We quickly got rental space on the second floor of an old building—I think it was on McDermot. The Bate Building. It was a nice building. Once people heard there was going to be a film group, it didn't take long for the numbers at those meetings to swell to thirty to forty people. We'd all sit around in a circle and talk about various things that could be done. The meetings were good and everybody was on the same page. There were no factions at all. There were various conglomerates of interest and philosophies. Some people were more political than others, but everyone was more or less on the same page. It was pioneering times and we appreciated that, and we were all quite keen to help each other out as much as we could.

The Crunch

KN: During those years, there were some important productions at the Film Group, *Rabbit Pie* [1976] being one. Another was *The Crunch*. You're a part of that story.

DC: *The Crunch* came about with Howard Gurevich and I sitting around. Howard said: "You know, we could probably get a Local Initiatives Project [LIP] grant to do a film. We can pay everybody. Why don't we do it?" So, I sat down and wrote a script. I was very influenced at that time by the work of Éric Rohmer. I wrote a very minimalist script for a man and a woman coming together, with an interesting personality clash. I wrote it for Jay Brazeau, who was acting in the local theatre at that time, and for Dianne Heatherington. Dianne was a singer on the Winnipeg scene, very much in the mode of Janis Joplin. So, we wrote it. We applied. Vesna, Howard, and I got the money. We went to see Dianne; she was performing at the beer room of the Viscount Gort [hotel]. We sat down with her afterward. I spent enough time with her to really know she was the kind of personality I wanted playing opposite Jay. She said, "Oh, I'd love to do this, but I'm moving to Toronto on Tuesday." We didn't have enough money in the budget to fly her back and we needed to shoot within a couple of weeks.

So, Dianne was out and we had to find somebody to play a female lead. There was nobody around in the acting community I felt could do it. We started doing casting calls. There was a girl who was visiting from Toronto. She was the girlfriend of one of the actors at MTC [Manitoba Theatre Centre]. I thought, well, maybe she could do it. We read her and she was fairly natural. But we had to shoot, so we went off and we shot. We shot it—I think it was less than a week. We got the equipment from the Film Board. It was winter and the locations were mostly in and around Selkirk and Salter [a corner in Winnipeg's North End].

One of the main locations was Obee's Steam Baths, and the two principals had to be naked together in the steam bath. It wasn't a sex scene or anything. It was more just the conversation and the awkwardness about getting naked. Jay was a bulky guy and was a bit self-conscious. And she [the woman from Toronto] had never been before a camera in her life.

She was a fairly attractive girl and she was self-conscious. There was a lot of skinny dipping going on at Birds Hill Park that summer, so I was not self-conscious about it at all. I said to the crew: "Hey listen, the only way we are going to do this is if we all get naked. That way, the two of them in front of the camera won't feel self-conscious." So, surprisingly—or not surprisingly—amongst the crew of guys and gals, we all shot the scene naked except for Henry Less, who was wearing the battery belt around his waist for the camera.

There was another scene in the front hall at Obee's and this led to the only disaster that befell the shoot. We were shooting in this very cramped area and prepping the shot, and suddenly I hear: "Oh no!" I look and the camera is doing a nose dive, right on the lens. There is a frozen moment of shock when that happens. The next thing everyone is thinking, how is this going to affect my career? Ian, the assistant cameraman who was responsible for the camera, was beside himself: "Oh no! I'll never work again!" It happens. You drop cameras. It happens more frequently than most people probably wish to admit who are camera people. The next day, the Film Board had a new camera.

The production itself didn't really work that well. We put a rough cut together. The chemistry between the two of them was not great, and it really required it to pull this off. I was young filmmaker, a year out of film school. Even though I had a really good education, there's a rule of thumb that it takes twenty-five years to make a filmmaker. There may be some truth to that. But in any case, I had put people into this film that really didn't have the chops to pull it off. It was a very internal performance that was required. I've long since learned that not every stage actor can be a film actor, not every film actor can be a stage actor, and very few are the actors who can shift between those two mediums. Jay was a stage actor and the girl was not an actor, and so it really didn't work too well.

We sat down and we figured, let's write some more scenes. I had written something that was very minimalist. I didn't feel that I had the ability to do the kind of dialogue that would be necessary to shoot additional scenes and make it less minimalist. Howard knew David King. David is principally a playwright, but he had written an NFB short drama that was shot in Winnipeg called *Fire Drill* [1975]. He was a good writer, so we brought him in and he wrote additional dialogue and additional scenes. We were pretty well out of money from the LIP grant. All the crew got paid—it wasn't much, but it was payment. We went to the Film Group for additional funding. I forget how much it was for—it wasn't for much, about $5,000. We showed the rough cut and people said, "Well, we're not sure what you got there." A lot of people did not really feel comfortable giving an additional five thousand bucks to something which really wasn't showing any promise that it would turn into anything. There was some opposition and the vote was taken, and it was decided not to give it money, which effectively shut everything down. It provided me with the first and only film that I never completed.

I got chosen for the dramatic directors training program at Studio C, in Montreal, at the Film Board. We had been planning to move anyway. Winnipeg had pretty well run its course, so we figured we'd go to Montreal for this three-month training program and then set up shop in Toronto, which we did. I brought the material with me, figuring I'll recut it. No—it died. That was the last of *The Crunch*.

KN: What was the attitude of the Film Group toward the production?

DC: They didn't have anything to do with the script in the development stage, and the script did not go through any kind of Film Group vetting and approval process. Probably it was given to Bob and Len for comments, but I don't recall [getting] anything back.

KN: When we talked to Bob, he was apologetic.

DC: Of what?

KN: He was feeling that he, Leon, and Len were not supportive of the project.

DC: I recall them being very negative. On the other hand, I don't begrudge them at all. In retrospect, it was a very ambitious project and may have been overly ambitious for what we had available. The only way it could work was if I had a Jeanne Moreau and I was an Éric Rohmer.

I was very influenced by Éric Rohmer's minimalism at that time, and was trying to pull something like that off. You really require very talented actors—not necessarily experienced—who can pull something like that off, where the internal kind of emotions and processes are visible on the face. If it doesn't translate, it's not there. It really wasn't there.

KN: It begs the question: what if that film had been finished? What would have happened if your vision had been realized as an early feature film? What would have been the influence on the Winnipeg film scene?

DC: That's an interesting question. Yeah, things would've been extremely different, but things are always extremely different no matter what happens. There are always these forks in the road. The choices you make either pan out and develop into something that sends you along and propels you, or they lead to a dead end. In terms of drama, I don't think I did another drama until the late seventies, in Toronto. I came here and started doing documentaries. I discovered I loved the freedom of documentaries. Within the Canadian film ecology of the 1970s, I could do expressionistic documentary filmmaking and not have to stick within a realistic worldview or artistic sensibility. That was conditioned a lot by the money that was available.

KN: Any regrets?

DC: I'm really a very serious Buddhist, so my philosophy is strongly conditioned by Buddhism in so many different ways, including its aesthetic. I don't look back. I'll look back and learn from the past, for sure—that's really stupid not to. Regret? No. Whatever events happen and trigger this or that, it's just the way things are. If I look back on *The Crunch*, for instance, with the wisdom and the experience of forty-plus years, would I have attempted a film like that given who the actors were? Probably not. But that's a lot of hard-gained experience. I can look back on it and learn from it.

KN: Do you still have the film reels for *The Crunch*?

DC: I have some old cans down in the basement that I haven't looked through in probably twenty-five years. But if they were down there, they would've rusted to dust by now. We're due to do some cleaning, maybe come the spring. . . .

ROBERT LOWER

Robert Lower grew up in Winnipeg and Rivers, Manitoba. He set out to become an engineer but found himself a few years later working as an apprentice film editor in Toronto. He moved back to Winnipeg in 1971 and was a founding member of the Winnipeg Film Group. He established himself as an editor, writer, and director with the National Film Board, and also edited for local independent productions.

21 NOVEMBER 2015, WINNIPEG

Kevin Nikkel: Can you introduce yourself?

Robert Lower: I'm Bob Lower. I grew up and went to school in rural Manitoba. Everything about that pointed me to a technical career, but that changed when I fell into a job as an assistant editor at CBC Toronto in 1966. I eventually became a freelance assistant working on drama films, the pinnacle of the profession in those days. It is a very stressful job, a lot of pressure. Everyone was terribly, terribly serious and yet what they were producing was utter, complete crap. Ignoring that, we would throw ourselves into it heart and soul, shortening our lives every day. I said: "I'm getting out of this." I decided to come back here and go into history and economics. I came back here in '71 and went back to school

---

Robert Lower demonstrating editing techniques at a Winnipeg Film Group Intensive Drama Workshop, 1975. Courtesy of Brad Caslor.

but, after being here a year, I was asked to edit something by the only film company in town, Western Films. I got back in the editing room and realized I was home. I was hooked.

KN: What was your training?

RL: My focus in high school was always physics and chemistry, and my intention was to go into engineering. I did half a year of aerospace engineering in Toronto and realized that I was in way over my head. I dropped out—was going to go back the next year but never did. Here I am today, recovering.

KN: What did the Winnipeg film landscape look like back then?

RL: Pretty bleak. Western Films had been here for a few years and then there was Film Factory. But both of them did nothing but corporate videos or productions for the [Manitoba] Department of Education. Mainly, they were sponsored films—*industrial films* was what we called them in those days.

It was the late sixties, early seventies. I was political and on the radical left. I thought film should be used for political and educational purposes. I can't even remember how we thought we would go about that in those days. We knew, when the idea of the film co-op came up, that was a great avenue. We couldn't do these things alone.

Canadian Film Symposium

KN: What happened at the Canadian Film Symposium in 1974?

RL: I was delighted it was happening. When you feel alone and completely ignored by people in Toronto, and not even on their radar, the symposium was a big deal. To have all those people here was great. I remember it being a very stimulating time. I came out of it feeling like I wanted to make films more than ever. I really wanted to make films with the National Film Board, but they were not doing anything here at that point.

KN: Tell me about how you hooked up with the crowd forming the Film Group.

RL: The meetings were at Len Klady's house. He had weekly screenings and movies in his living room, and I'd been to those. I think that was when I met Leon Johnson. I don't remember what the conversation was, but it's pretty easy to reconstruct. We needed a pool of equipment, we needed access to it, we needed other people to work on our films—if we ever found a way to finance films. We had a lot of interest. It was nice to talk to people who are interested in film. That was what was so good about the symposium.

Winnipeg Film Group

KN: Was there unity at the early meetings?

RL: There might have been an illusion of unity. What we knew was that we needed a grant to help run the thing—and we needed a central place where equipment can be stored, where equipment can be bought, where editing could be established—and so, in that sense, yes. Everybody agreed—but how that would be done? Not so much.

KN: How did things come together? When did the friction start to emerge?

RL: It is the Winnipeg Film Group as opposed to the Winnipeg Film Co-op, which is what it was supposed to be. Somebody read the provincial co-ops act and it said, if you call yourself a co-op, then anybody who has the money and agrees to the bylaws, you must take as a member. We wanted a choice. The Manitoba Club had choice and we wanted choice, too. So, we had to change it. No one could come up with anything less lame, so that was it.

We came together after it was incorporated. Len was the chair because he had a really obnoxious gavel and he would bring meetings to order. When I became chairman, I had to yell for order. You have thirty to thirty-five would-be directors in the same room. Enough said. Everything was a crisis. I remember some very stormy meetings. I remember way too many meetings, and I called them. They went on way too long, and I chaired

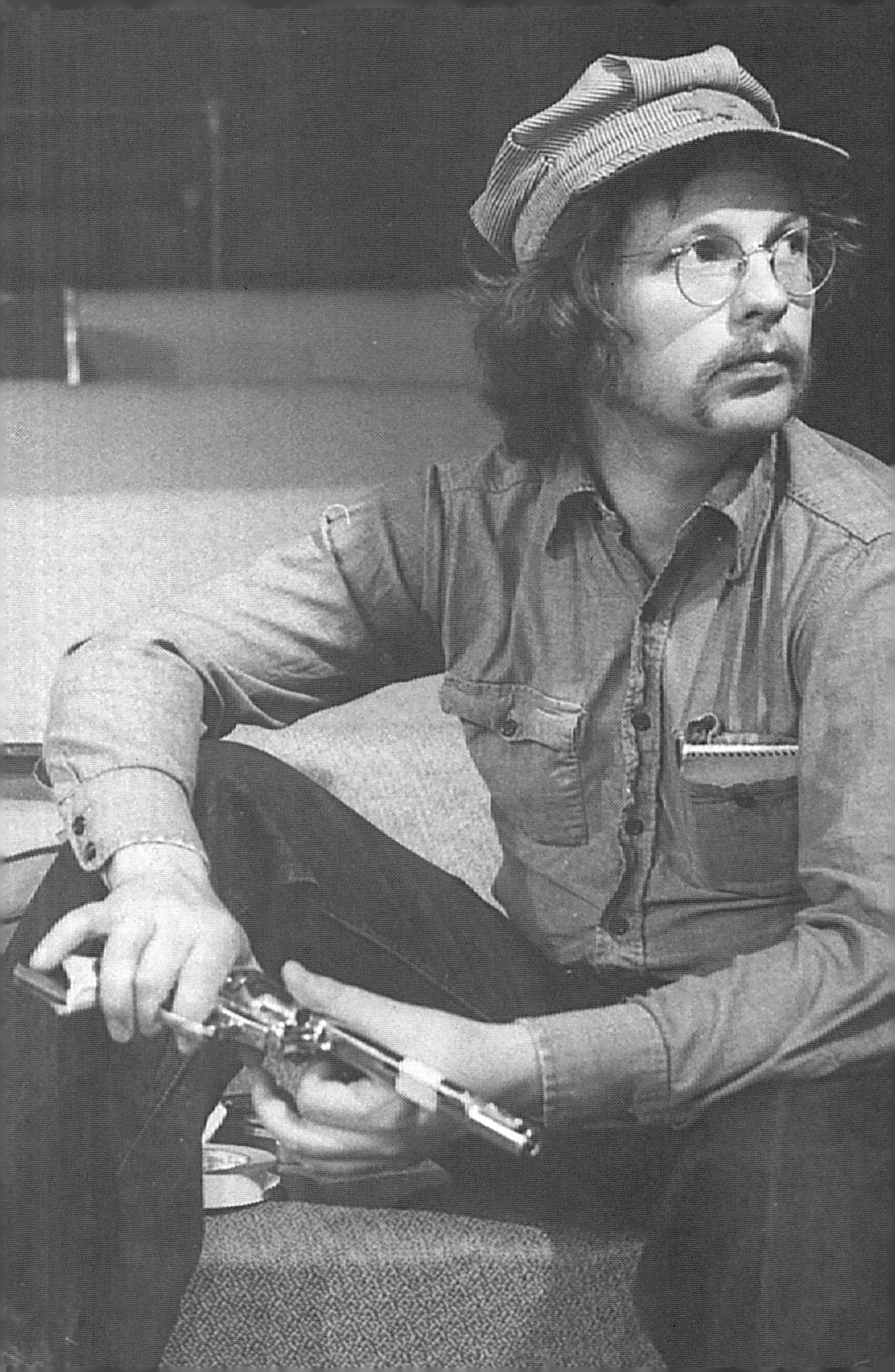

them. I would just like to apologize to everybody out there: I'm sorry about those meetings!

We had a number of meetings about how to acquire equipment, but we wanted to organize and get an office. We immediately got the offices in the Bate Building, and sweat and labour went into fixing the floors and fixing one room as an editing room. I contributed the rewinds and synchronizer, and bits and pieces like that. I don't remember where any production money came from; they must have come from grants of some kind. Everybody was perfectly willing to work for free on anything that anybody could raise money for.

In the beginning, we were pretty united. Everybody just wanted to make a film and we made *Rabbit Pie* [1976]. That was a good—you know those corporate games they play to make people into a team? That was pretty good that way. We had fun making that. Then came: what would the next film be?

The Crunch

A number of people were very much in the documentary stream. David Cherniack and a few others were very keen on drama. For one reason or another, the group voted for a drama: they voted for him to make *The Crunch*. I remember that the question had been decided way too soon. I thought the reason people chose this terrible script was because they just wanted to make a film. I thought, that's terrible. So, overnight, I wrote a competing script and, at our next meeting, tried to promote it. I am very happy that it was given short shrift and I'm not saddled with that. We went ahead and made *The Crunch*.

But Leon—the coordinator—Len, and I were quite strongly against *The Crunch* going ahead. My memory is, we put every possible obstacle in

---

Robert Lower at a Winnipeg Film Group Intensive Drama Workshop, 1975. Courtesy of Brad Caslor.

David's way, making that film. And I would also like to apologize about that. I am really sorry we did that because that's not what you do. Once the film is underway, the producer's job is to support, not to crush the spirit. I think that's pretty much what we did. I remember the three of us showing up on set one day and David said something like: "Here come the *no* brothers." I remember, even then, feeling a little guilty about that. But I thought it was a waste of our resources and I was going to make my opinion felt. Did that widen the cracks? You betcha. David, his producer Vonnie von Helmolt, the cameraman Henry Less, and several other people all left the Film Group, and not in good spirits.

KN: What came after it?

RL: In the summer of '75, we did a collective job, trying to record a second film on the Winnipeg Folk Festival. That worked out well, as far as shooting it. We shot on 8-mm synchronized sound. I think it was a disaster. It never got edited. I don't even remember it having a director. I think we just shot stuff. I remember it being fun, but that was the last collective thing I think the Film Group ever did. At that point, we said, probably collective films aren't a good idea. Probably, what we should be doing here—I'm probably making this way cleaner than it was at the time—but probably, what we should be doing here is treating this as a services resource and allow filmmakers to use it. Come together around it, if they want to, but not to act as a collective. We had, on one side, completely apolitical artists and, on the other side, very political polemicists. The twain were not about to meet.

Havakeen Lunch

I think the next thing was Elise Swerhone's *Havakeen Lunch* [1979]. She raised the money and did that on her own, but it was done through the auspices of the Film Group. I think it's produced by the Film Group and she used equipment from the Group. That was the pattern from then on.

When Elise made *Havakeen Lunch*, that was a perfect example of what we wanted to do. *Havakeen Lunch* was a film about a small lunch counter out in the Interlake, and the point was to feature these interesting people being themselves—the very foundation of the National Film Board–style documentary, which was to take ordinary people and bring them out as people worthy of films.[46] Elise's film was perfect for that. It really did a great job. It also brought Elise and I together—for thirty-eight years, so far. We basically did our honeymoon, editing that film in Starbuck, Manitoba.

KN: These early years feel a bit like a social experiment, or a reality TV show like *Survivor*. When did the crack started to appear in the wall?

RL: I can remember going to the Royal Albert for a drink after some meetings, and the contention would continue. There was a lot of anger and I don't remember why now. I know where I would've been coming from and that would be using the Film Group as an instrument for social change. I didn't like the fact that these poseur artists were trying to make—probably really excellent films, if they were allowed to make them—but didn't have any socially redeeming qualities. I remember my girlfriend of the time, now my wife, saying, "you gotta get off that board. This is crazy." But like most PTSD experiences, you shut it out.

I resigned from the board, but I felt like the Film Group definitely deserved support. I didn't deserve the stress it was giving to me. I stayed with it for a couple of years, but that was just at the time the National Film Board arrived—'76 or '77. I started making a film with them. That was the "big time." I did not feel the need of the Film Group. I slowly drifted away from Film Group.

Regionalism

KN: Despite the conflict, the Film Group still was important for the film culture in Winnipeg.

RL: We were united in a number of things. It did bring a group of people together interested in film in Manitoba. I think we all valued that. I valued the fact that there were compatriots. We really saw ourselves as Winnipeggers, as Manitobans, as prairie people who wanted to make films about that—and didn't want to make films for Toronto. There was a very strong sense that we wanted to show Toronto. Whenever anyone referred to any filmmaking on the prairies, they totally dismissed it. We wanted to make it very clear that there was a place for regional filmmaking, there were regional voices. There was something different that could come out of here than came out of there. Something that was valuable for the entire country. I never was a Toronto hater because I had been trained there. I've always liked Toronto and had friends in Toronto. But I really did not like that dismissive attitude, where they didn't even bother with contempt. They just dismissed us.

Because of our age—most of us in our twenties—we were very sure that we could overturn the status quo. I wouldn't be anywhere near sure now. But it was very important for us to make that statement and have not only Toronto, but the rest of Canada, hear it.

If somebody came from the CBC in Toronto, or someone came from the National Film Board, we always made that point. We're here! We're here to be recognized, and we're staying here. We're not here like somebody cutting their teeth at CBC Winnipeg so they can eventually get to CBC Toronto; we're here because we want to be here. We want to create a voice for Winnipeg, for the prairies, for Manitoba.

The great thing about making films in Winnipeg, especially in those days, is you did not have to specialize. I worked on commercials and documentaries, I worked on dramas and features and series. In Toronto, I would have to specialize and be a drama editor or a documentary editor. Not here. In Winnipeg, you were a filmmaker, and that's always been the case. It's always felt more like a community than it ever did in Toronto. Those are the upsides of spending a career in Winnipeg. The downside is income and security—and fame. I gotta say, if I were a young man now and wanted a career in filmmaking, I would head for Toronto.

KN: Were there seasons to the story of the Film Group?

John Paizs

RL: The Film Group has for years ebbed and flowed, and I think it ebbed quite badly in the late seventies and early eighties. When the Film Board came, a lot of the people who were at the centre of the Film Group began working with the National Film Board, and that took a core of the more experienced people away. I really expected the Film Group to die away because of that.

It was just a few years later that John Paizs emerged, and a bunch of others. Suddenly, it was this entirely different organization. Nobody in that first group of thirty or thirty-five would've wanted to make John Paizs's films, and suddenly they're making these films—films that I would roll my eyes at—and they were getting audiences. People were celebrating them. I remember sort of being disconcerted by this because this is not the reason the Film Group had been formed. Don't ask me why it'd been formed, but it wasn't for films like John Paizs's! Then I took the trouble to watch them, and they were good! Very Good! It was a whole different way of looking at the Film Group, that took me a little while to realize. That's exactly what this is: it's a process of maturation, dying, and then renewal. And that's been going on ever since. I've watched from a distance, but I never cease to be amazed at the way the Film Group rises out of the ashes, time and time again. I hear terrible things. The Film Group is in terrible shape, I'd think. I'm glad I'm not a part of it. And then—boom!—something terrific comes out of it.

ROLL 1
ARRIFLEX

ALLAN KROEKER

Born in Winnipeg, Allan Kroeker directed the Winnipeg Film Group's first collaborative film, Rabbit Pie. *He spent his early career in Winnipeg as a cameraman, editor, writer, and director. Kroeker established himself by making films for the National Film Board and dramas for Winnipeg's CKND TV before eventually settling in Hollywood, where he directed episodic television series.*

21 DECEMBER 2015, LOS ANGELES

Kevin Nikkel: Can you introduce yourself?

Allan Kroeker: My name is Allan Kroeker. I'm a filmmaker living in California and I come from Winnipeg—proudly from Winnipeg.

KN: Was there anything that hinted that you would end up a filmmaker?

AK: I grew up as a Mennonite, with social restrictions. We had to sneak off to movies. I grew up bereft of popular culture and specifically movie history. I had to catch up on that. I had to cram a lot. I'm still cramming.

I was studying literature and theology, when I got the compulsion to go into film. It was on a canoe trip that I met Bill Mason, a native of Winnipeg who made wilderness films for the NFB. *Paddle to the Sea* [1966] made a huge impression; it made me think differently about

---

Allan Kroeker on the set of *Rabbit Pie*, 1975. Courtesy of Brad Caslor.

what I saw on the screen. Directing was, I had thought, what guys did on a sound stage, with lights, actors, crew, movie moguls, and all that. But here were these pieces of celluloid Mason put together to create a cinematic illusion—the life of this little wooden canoe—shooting a piece here and a piece there. I was struck by the juxtaposition. Here's this little canoe rocking on the water and then you cut to a wider shot, and you see that he's in front of a huge freighter somewhere on the St. Lawrence. I thought: this is filmmaking! Maybe I can do this.

KN: Where did you go to college?

AK: I went to the University of Winnipeg and York University. Before that, I went to the Mennonite Brethren Bible College/College of Arts, where I discovered German and Russian literature.

KN: When did you take your first film courses?

AK: Between '72 and '74. I'd made a little film in northwestern Manitoba—Swan River and environs—a film about sawmills and lumberjacks. Rudolf Dyke was a relative, with a company that made wooden pallets and containers, like fish boxes and soft-drink cases. He was artistic, philosophical, and visionary; he introduced me to the art of Chaplin. He said: "You should come out here and catch this way of life that is disappearing."

I shot a Super 8 documentary called *The Summer of '72*. That was my first film. That, and a script based on a story by Stefan Zweig—*Episode am Genfer See*—got me into York University's film program. Though, after two years at York, I never recommended a film education to anybody. I figured, just get out there and do it. Spend time with the camera, learn how to make films. Learn from your mistakes. I was inspired by Jay Leyda, professor of Soviet film history, who had translated all of Eisenstein's works and imported these rare films to York, from which I learned about filmmaking. Not that I was into the Soviet mentality.

How Much Land Does a Man Need?

KN: You completed your studies at York?

AK: I finished York with a BFA honours degree, which remains somewhere, still rolled up in its cardboard tube. After getting this "education" in filmmaking, I went back to Manitoba and got a job with the Department of Agriculture for three years, in their communications branch. I shot farm news. I toured Manitoba, mostly the Interlake region. Because the Interlake was economically challenged, the NDP government did a lot there. I got to see and love the Interlake and discovered the works of W.D. Valgardson.[47] That clinched it for me. I'd never read Manitoba literature before. His stories were gripping and palpable, and had a strong sense of place.

KN: You transitioned from documentaries to dramatic films?

AK: I started to look at literature as movie material. I adapted a story by Tolstoy. I did some work for Mennonite Brethren Communications. They wanted me to do parables, little short films: two- or three-minute films illustrating life principles. They hired me and another filmmaker, David Dueck. We made little short parables for a TV show that they made for kids.[48] It was a lot of fun. I came up with these ideas and *How Much Land Does a Man Need?* [1976] became my magnum opus. It was ten minutes long. It was a simple fable about a man who is killed by his own greed. We shot the longest day of the year, June 21. Like the protagonist—in perfect irony—we almost did ourselves in, running around from sunrise to sunset to get this thing in the can. There I was with the Bolex chasing Jay, driving those red ribbons into the poplar trees.

Winnipeg Film Group

KN: Do you remember joining the Film Group?

AK: I had joined the Film Group when I returned from York, around the fall of '74. Leon Johnson recruited me from the Department of Agriculture straight from the yellow pages. That's how I met Leon

and the Film Group, and I worked with Leon many times later, over the years.

It was in the Exchange District. I'm sure by now it's been renovated, but back then it looked like a 1930s film noir set, with that old, dark wooden wainscoting and pebbled-glass dividers, the kind that would have names printed in gold leaf. That's how I remember the place. I was only in it a couple times. I'm loath to admit how few meetings I went to. I'm a lousy member of pretty well anything, but I was one of the charter members.

It was an exuberant bunch of idealistic fledglings, like myself, and a few pros. We all wanted to be moviemakers. It was intimidating but also heartening to see other people that wanted to do the same thing. Len Klady, who would tear us down in his reviews, and Gene Walz, who would build us back up again. Gene also had a running correspondence with Truffaut, which was pretty impressive.

Rabbit Pie

KN: What is the story behind *Rabbit Pie*?

AK: Leon Johnson coerced me to direct—if you can call what I did directing—*Rabbit Pie*. I've never seen the finished product. I got the job, I think, because I had some experience shooting sequences. It was a comedy of sorts, pretty hammy. The thing about comedy is, don't act funny. Watch Buster Keaton. Comedy is people being dead serious about what they're doing. I recall Harry Nelken asking: "Do you think I should play this guy like he's a professional wine taster?"

What I remember of *Rabbit Pie* is, we were shooting away, probably approaching eighteen hours. I dimly recall someone asking: "Are the pies hardened yet?" In the kitchen, they were filling aluminum pie plates

---

Filming in Gimli for Allan Kroeker's *God Is Not a Fish Inspector*: (*left to right*) Leon Johnson/Sound, W.D. Valgardson, Mary Anne Valgardson, Allan Kroeker/Director, Don Cambell/Director of Photography, (*kneeling*) Norma Bailey/Assistant Diector, 1978. Courtesy of Allan Kroeker.

with plaster of Paris. Those things were heavy. The gag was, the pies were multiplying like rabbits—they were breeding and reproducing, and crowding the people out of the café. They were humping right on the tablecloth. The patrons end up covered with them, drowning in rabbit pies. I don't think we knew about cheating the pies up with some kind of filler underneath. I think we just loaded the pies from the floor up. It was crazy.

The other Film Group project I remember shooting—I don't think anything became of it—was the Birds Hill Folk Festival. It was brand new at the time. We had Super 8 cameras, shooting cinéma vérité style. There were some big names and I got humiliated in front of the largest audience possible. There must've been twenty thousand people watching Ramblin' Jack Elliott. I had this big closeup of his hand on the fret board, filling the frame. I was pretty close, kind of up on the stage right, under his guitar. Eventually, I realized old Jack wasn't singing anymore, the audience were laughing, and he was just strumming. And he said: "Hey, you mind moving back?" I realized this guy is talking to me. "You got a zoom lens on that thing? Can't you move back and zoom in? Because you're freaking me out!!!" That wasn't the first, nor the last, time that I've been bawled out for getting too close with the camera. If they can find that old footage, there is some pretty cool stuff we shot, historically speaking. There must have been three or four cameras. We just shot like maniacs. There was no form to what we were doing, no vision—just shooting. A clever editor might do something with that footage. Someone should put it together, forty years later.

KN: How committed were you to the Film Group?

AK: In actual practice, I was a lousy member, perhaps because I was a loner and never fit in. My preferred way of working is alone and not necessarily directing. What I do now for a living—telling seventy-five crew people what to do—is at variance with that disposition. I'm still the kid that met Bill Mason and fancied shooting a little wooden canoe. Though I thrive on collaboration, I don't mind working alone on my own projects, maybe with a sound man or someone holding a light, but

I don't like asking people to help me when I can just do it myself. Early on, I would write, shoot, edit, and sound edit. I was a loner.

KN: The NFB was important for you as well.

NFB

AK: Mike Scott and Jerry Krepakevich moved back to Winnipeg from NFB Montreal, to set up a regional office. Guys like me were banging their doors down. I coveted working for NFB. I got more schooling from NFB than anywhere else. I think I'm still trying to emulate what the Film Board did in the mid-fifties to mid-seventies, when they were on the cutting edge of cinéma vérité.

A drama department was created, with Mike Scott, Roman Kroitor, Wolf Koenig, Colin Lowe, and a fine British director who was the head of the Manitoba Theatre Centre at the time, Eddie Gilbert. Eddie would have evening sessions with us film guys, essentially teaching Stanislavsky For Dummies. Eddie was a terrific teacher, and I wrote down everything he said and consulted that notebook on every project for at least twenty years. They sent us to Edmonton to learn from dramaturges like Vladimír Valenta.[49]

Eventually, NFB gave me a shot at my own ten-minute film, adapted from Rudy Wiebe's short story "Tudor King" [1979], a story of an old man who lives in a granary and believes he is the king of England. Later, they gave me a few more. I loved NFB. People from the Film Group ended up on NFB productions, as crew people or making their own films: animation, documentary, or dramas. I ended up quite happily in drama.

Strongest Man in the World

It was between the Film Group and the NFB that I met Halya Kuchmij, the Ukrainian-Canadian filmmaker. She had just been through AFI [the American Film Institute] in Los Angeles. With her, I shot memorable

Ukrainian films: *Strongest Man in the World* [1980] and *Laughter in My Soul* [1983]. That was one of the most creative collaborations I'd ever had.

KN: Why?

AK: *Strongest Man in the World* is a great story. We went to Olha, Manitoba, and spent three days shooting this guy who'd been a strongman with Ringling Brothers and met Houdini, and travelled the prairies during the Depression, doing feats of brute strength and hypnotizing crowds. That was my first full-fledged documentary. Halya was a very good leader. She would plant the story in your head and say, "Now do your thing." You can do that when someone inspires confidence, instead of questioning.

CKND

KN: You eventually left Winnipeg?

AK: I stayed in Winnipeg until 1985–86. Someone said, if you want to make God laugh, tell him your plans. In the film business, charting a trajectory is a joke. A film career is largely a matter of hard work and dumb luck. It isn't the door you're knocking on that opens. But you have to knock on some door. You have to do your homework. Like in the *Field of Dreams* [1989] movie, you build it and he will come—but "he" doesn't come from where you expect.

I'd done a couple of films with the NFB and *How Much Land Does a Man Need?* Then the Department of Education asked me to do a fictional film by a Manitoba author, and that became W.D. Valgardson's *God Is Not a Fish Inspector* [1980], about an old man trying to keep a step ahead of the authorities. Then NFB let me do two more Valgardson stories: *Capital* [1981], about a shifty used-car salesman trying to form his son in his image, and *The Pedlar* [1982], about an itinerant salesman/entertainer who brings light into people's lives and suffers.

While shooting *The Pedlar*, I got a phone call out of the blue from Stan Thomas, from what was then CKND (later Canwest Global). With his deep voice, he says, "I want to do a drama project." It became another

Allan Kroeker on camera for *Tramp at the Door*, 1985. Courtesy of Allan Kroeker.

carte blanche. I was invited to come to CKND and bring ideas for films. They liked what I'd done so far. They said: "With this model, can you do more? We want to make prairie films. Bring us a bunch of stories." So, I did. I was conversant with prairie literature by now and I brought them a big list of stories. They read them and they said, "this one, this one, and this one." I was really a lucky dog.[50]

The mandate from CKND had been to make prairie films to help along their CRTC [Canadian Radio-television and Telecommunications Commission] applications as they acquired TV stations across the prairies. So, it served them and served us very well. It gave us a lot of work. The films did extremely well. They won a lot of awards. I've never had a better partnership than with Stan Thomas. He'd put in a full day at the TV station, then have me over at his house, where we'd hash out story ideas long past midnight.

It was visionary of Stan Thomas to include a Cape Breton author among our prairie stories. "In the Fall" was by Alistair MacLeod. *In the Fall* [1985] worked as a prairie film because we embraced similarities between Cape Breton and Manitoba. Ches Yetman of NFB, a Newfoundlander, would say: "You drive across Canada and lose track of your roots, then you get to the prairies and hook up again!" And, of course, we had this great body of water that looks like an ocean.

KN: CKND was an era, maybe a golden era, for Winnipeg and prairie films. Why did it end?

AK: I think they realized their objectives. They acquired a few stations over that period and they used these dramas and the awards. They got a lot of recognition and they employed a lot of people.

KN: Are you are still in Winnipeg through this?

Toronto

AK: I left Winnipeg around '85. I found out the hard way that Winnipeg was not Toronto. Winnipeg had its own vibe. I don't know how it is now, but back then at the Film Group, there was an attitude somewhere between defiance and entitlement: we make the movies we want to make, the way we want to make them. Some of those qualities persist in me to this day, and I get into the occasional dust-up. But that was the Winnipeg way. Winnipeg was, screw you, we'll do it our way.

When I made *Fish Inspector*, *Capital*, *The Pedlar*, and *Tramp at the Door*, we made it up as we went along, kind of from scratch. I didn't know what a continuity person was; I'd keep it all in my head. I'd go to thrift stores hunting for props and buying costumes for people to wear in my films. The assistant director might also serve as art director. I would take the Bolex along to grab shots. We all put our heads together and did it that way, we didn't know any different. Good old days!

On my first Toronto job, they said: "You can't do that. We don't do it that way here. If you want to do that, go back to Winnipeg." We're talking about things like, you couldn't go into the woods a hundred yards away, because it's called a *crew move*. It made me crazy. I asked, "What's a crew move?" Winnipeg just did it their own way.

KN: You eventually ended up here in L.A. What happened?

Los Angeles

AK: In L.A. since '96. Hard work and dumb luck. I'd gone to Toronto around '85 for a six-hour miniseries in which there was one hour featuring Native Canadians, and the French director wasn't comfortable doing that. Pat Ferns, of Nielsen-Ferns, had seen *How Much Land Does a Man Need?* many years earlier, and remembered this and called me up. He said: "Can you do bigger stuff now? Want to come to Toronto?" So, I got to go to Toronto, to do this hour for this miniseries which wasn't very good. I don't think I was very good either, but he still gave me another job after that: *Heaven on Earth* [1987].

So, here is this 'Pegger working with a big crew. We were filming Mohawk people in the forest, most of them non-actors except for Graham Greene and Gary Farmer, and a few others. I figured a way to shoot non-actors was catch them unawares, just doing their thing, documentary style.

We were in the woods. I brought out the old Spectra meter and said: "Oh, 4.5. Okay. We've got enough light for this shot." So, I grabbed the operator and said, "Hey, see that guy walking through the woods?" The DP went bananas. "What do you mean? There's no slate! What are you doing?" I said: "We have to get that shot!" We had to get it *quick*. He said: "You do that again, I'm leaving the production." I didn't realize you couldn't do that either, but that's how I'd always done it. "No, no! We have to have proper procedures here!" So, that was my old Winnipeg way, butting heads with the Toronto way.

People in Toronto were harsh in those days. I don't know how it is now. If you were from Winnipeg, they'd give you a hard time. They thought Canada ended at Mississauga. What struck me about Toronto then: there wasn't really any indigenous filmmaking. They wanted to be Hollywood North.

Then, after that, I worked in "development" for a few years. It was a period when a lot of companies were developing scripts under tax shelters and made money by developing them and never shooting them. Then I realized, I've got to keep directing, so I ended up in episodic television. The first thing I ever did was a half-hour kids' show with Mr. T. That's how I got into episodic.

KN: You came down to L.A. for that?

AK: I'd never aimed to work in L.A., but it went into motion when I did a series in Toronto called *Beyond Reality* [1991–1992], a half-hour show with two investigators of the paranormal. It predated *The X-Files*. The showrunner of *Beyond Reality*, Hans Beimler, liked me and kept hiring me back. And then I got a call, in the summer of '96, inviting me to do an episode of *Deep Space Nine*. In those days, one thing could lead to another. Nowadays, agents assure me, it no longer works that way. I did over thirty-three hours of *Star Trek* [1996–2005] and I wasn't even a fan of sci-fi.

KN: Did you have a hard time reconciling this work with the passion you had, in the earlier years, for prairie literature?

AK: *Deep Space Nine* was closer to that than most of what I've done since. The *Star Trek* shows had similarities to westerns. The space station in *Deep Space Nine* was *Dodge City* [1939]. *Voyager* [1997–2001] was *Wagon Train* [1940]. So, I went into most episodes of *Star Trek*, not to mention countless other TV shows, imagining myself doing a western. To me, anything that's any good is analogous to a western. Go figure. It has to do with archetypes. I was able to get lost in those scripts quite easily. And I really did enjoy the time there. But still a long shot from prairie short stories, isn't it?

Making Mistakes

KN: Anything else you want to mention?

AK: I talked about the people you meet up with. It's very important to learn humility in this business. We filmmakers are mostly skating on very thin ice, in every way. Nothing is certain. Nothing is final. It is very precarious. Value these people. Be open to these people that come in and give you something. I've been really fortunate. If I look across my career, I see people that gave something to me that I probably hadn't earned.

You do it your way—make your own mistakes. Help comes from areas one is not expecting. Then you have to pay it back somehow. You have to pay it forward. To recycle an old saying that I recall from a lot of the Film Group people of the seventies: make the films you want to make, and like nobody else. Don't conform to anybody else's standard but your own, nobody else's taste but your own. Make it your own way. Make your own mistakes. That's vital to filmmaking. Don't make somebody else's mistakes, make your own. I certainly made enough of them.

ELISE SWERHONE

Elise Swerhone was born in Canora, Saskatchewan. She moved to Winnipeg to study at the University of Manitoba, and graduated with a fine arts degree. She eventually found her home in making films. Swerhone was a founding member of the Winnipeg Film Group and her first documentary, Havakeen Lunch *(1979), is an important early film. She enjoyed an accomplished career producing and directing films in Winnipeg.*

22 OCTOBER 2016, WINNIPEG

Kevin Nikkel: Was there any sign that you would become the creative person that you became?

Elise Swerhone: I don't know whether there were any signs in my early years that I'd become a filmmaker. I was always a tomboy, getting into mischief and trying new things. I grew up in a small town called Canora, Saskatchewan. My parents owned a bakery and I spent my early years living above the bakery. I left Canora to come to the city to study interior design at the University of Manitoba.

KN: Did you finish your studies in interior design?

Elise Swerhone and crew on set of *Rabbit Pie*, 1975. Courtesy of Brad Caslor.

ES: No. While I was studying interior design, I decided I didn't want to be an interior designer. At the time, I met a bunch of people who would become the Winnipeg Film Group: Len Klady, Brad Caslor, Leon Johnson, Bob Lower.

KN: What else was happening, around that time, with this group?

ES: I basically wanted to do something that was more socially helpful and I was finding that interior design wasn't doing enough for me. At the time, there weren't a lot of film courses at the University of Manitoba. I did take a couple of film courses from Frederick Edell and I met Len Klady. Len Klady was obsessed with film. Through a number of circumstances, we ended up living together in a house on McMillan Avenue. The house was one of those old houses that has a dining room and living room, with a long, thirty-foot throw. Len Klady had an uncle who had a film distribution company and he would allow Len to bring home films. Len would bring home one or two 16-mm feature films every Friday night that we would show on Sunday night in our house. People would come watch films that were really not available. That group of people that came to the house to watch films became the Winnipeg Film Group.

Canadian Film Symposium

KN: Did you attend the Canadian Film Symposium at University of Manitoba in 1974?

ES: Yes. Len was organizing the symposium, so he was very excited about it. They were bringing really interesting people into the city. That became an igniter of excitement around film.

KN: The meetings that went on at Len Klady's house and the symposium were important?

ES: There never were meetings at Len's. They were film screenings. We would get together and watch a Buñuel film, or we would get together and watch *Casablanca* [1942]. I remember watching *Casablanca* five times in one weekend just because Len brought it home and it was such a great film. He would take copious notes of what went on in the films and also the credits. I think he was responsible for getting all of us involved.

KN: Was there a common vision with those gathering?

The Crunch

ES: No, there was no common vision. We knew that if we worked together, we could bring the equipment in and we could actually get an organization that would help us make the films we wanted to. Some of us were very political, some of us were less political, some of us were very artsy. There was no common vision on the kinds of films that people wanted to make.

The lack of common vision came to a head when we tried to do *The Crunch*. We had done a couple of small films, like *Rabbit Pie* [1976], which is not a stellar example of great filmmaking—but it was amazing that we actually were able to come together to work on a film. But when it came time to do *The Crunch*, it was supposedly a feature film that we were going to do together to show that we, here in Winnipeg, could do feature films.

I think most of us were all still thinking of ourselves as filmmakers and *The Crunch* gave us an opportunity to decide what category we wanted to work in. Ian Elkin decided that the camera department was where he wanted to be. Henry Less, who was shooting *The Crunch*, was already working as a photographer but not as a cinematographer. I worked in the camera department on *The Crunch*—I was the clapper/loader. That defined things for me. At that point, for me, I wanted to stay in the camera department. I don't think I thought of myself as a director at all. I wanted to work as a camera person because, up to that point, my university training was all visual training. What *The Crunch* did was give me a credit which allowed me to work more as a clapper/loader and then as a focus puller—and then, eventually, I started shooting.

Dave Barber: Was it very contentious?

ES: It was divisive in some ways. Can you imagine: we were a whole bunch of creative people having to decide on one script. We were all directors or writers. Not many of us were producers, but we were all people that had our own vision of what we wanted to say and wanted to do. We had to decide on one script, and one director to do that script. So, there were a lot of egos involved, and it was contentious. I think that in some ways, what it did was it defined us individually. Some of us became dramatic filmmakers, some of us became documentary filmmakers. I think that *The Crunch* helped us mature in some ways as an organization, too. Because we were a co-op, it didn't mean that we had to do stuff together; it meant that we now had the infrastructure set up so that we could do our own individual stuff and use the Film Group as the facility that allowed us to do that.

KN: *The Crunch* was an important failure?

ES: Yeah, I think so. I think that is an interesting way to put it because it was a film that never really got finished. What we were trying to do is make films by committee and I think we all realized that this wasn't going to work. We couldn't do that. It really made us realize that we had to work on our own and, up to that point, we were trying to do everything. We had very limited resources and, as you know, it takes a lot of money to make a film. So, we were trying to do something bigger as a group and realized that it just didn't work.

KN: It seems like you are describing a textbook example of the stages of a social group.

ES: When I think about those times, 1973 to 1974, we were all young people, mostly in our twenties; and most of us were launching careers, though at the time none of us thought it. We were just wanting to make films. We were also setting up an organization that has lasted for decades. If you'd asked me, back then, if the Winnipeg Film Group would be around in 2016, I would say I don't think so. Would there be a Winnipeg Film Group in 1979? I don't think so. What we were doing was setting up an organization that was going to help us in the short term. We didn't think it would be something that would last forever.

We didn't know what we were doing. We would have to often refer to *Robert's Rules of Order* just to keep our meetings orderly. We thought, if it's a co-op, that means we have to do things cooperatively. That was a very difficult thing for us to do.

Havakeen Lunch

KN: Let's talk about your first documentary.

ES: In 1976 or '77, I started a film that I shot up at Eriksdale, Manitoba: *Havakeen Lunch*. A woman named Lois Brown and I did research on this little lunch counter called Havakeen Lunch. I did a photo essay for a course I was taking at university. The lunch counter was a bit of a throwback in time. There were a bunch of characters that would come and go from the restaurant. From that photo essay, I decided that it would make a nice short film. I was able to get a grant of $16,000 to help me make the film. We shot for ten days. It was an all-female crew. I did the shooting and a woman named Lorna Rasmussen did the sound. Joanne Jackson Johnson was my assistant and Michaelin McDermott was our production manager. It was the first independent production that the Winnipeg Film Group did—not financed by the Film Group, but some of the equipment came from the Film Group and a lot of emotional support came from the Film Group.

After that, I didn't make a film through the Film Group again because I didn't need to. The National Film Board had opened offices here and were very active. So, because there were no actual production grants, the Film Group became irrelevant in some ways, in terms of financing films.

KN: Do you remember at what point you said, I want to be a film director?

Women in Film

ES: What I love about being in the camera department is that it's purely visual. I've always been a very visual person and there's something about shooting that is very satisfying. There's something about having those

images come through your eyes, and into your brain, that is almost therapeutic. I never get tired of it. I still do that with my iPhone. I see an image and have to capture it in order to enjoy it. So, the camera came very natural to me, but it wasn't very satisfying in terms of self-expression. At that time, I knew maybe four or five women in Canada who were shooting film. Except for the two that were actually on staff at the National Film Board in Montreal, no one else was making much of a living. I realized that I probably wasn't going to make a living doing it. I used my camera-assisting money to support myself as a director because I wasn't making very much money as a director. Shooting without directing is not very satisfying in terms of personal expression and I seemed to need that, too. Directing became something that I wanted to do because there were things that I felt that I wanted to say and stories that I wanted to tell. The two complemented each other quite nicely, actually. For the first six films that I made, I shot them myself and directed, which was very enjoyable. Then I realized, as I had more experience, that directing became more interesting and more satisfying. I began to realize that the films that I was directing were more complex and I needed to have the help of a cinematographer. So, I moved away from cinematography.

KN: I want to hear more about your experiences as a female filmmaker. What was it like starting out in those early days, being in a room that was dominated by men?

ES: I don't really remember ever feeling excluded from conversations. The women that you had in the room were Vonnie von Helmolt, Val Klassen, me, Joanne Jackson Johnson. None of us are shrinking violets. We weren't stepping into leadership roles but we were definitely there. We didn't think much about being left out. We were really just doing what everyone else was doing.

Elise Swerhone, during the filming of *Rabbit Pie*, 1975. Courtesy of Brad Caslor.

I was on a panel, a few months ago, about women in film. There are a lot of statistics coming out about the lack of women in leadership roles in film. We've known that all along. It's always been difficult for women. The sexism was just one of the obstacles that you dealt with. I've always thought that Winnipeg was a very good place for female filmmakers, much more so than Toronto, or Vancouver for that matter. I think there are a lot of very strong women filmmakers that have come from Winnipeg, or that are still in Winnipeg making films.

DB: Why do you think that is?

ES: Well, I didn't feel that there was a lot of discrimination against women among the people who are making decisions about what films could be made. There are a lot of women who are making films in Winnipeg. I think there always has been. Whenever I went to Toronto, the women I knew in Toronto really struggled to get their voices heard. I didn't see that as much in Winnipeg, maybe because Winnipeg really is sort of a backwater when it comes to film in Canada—or the world, for that matter. We were all struggling. All Winnipeg filmmakers are struggling against the opinions of the centre, which is Toronto and the National Film Board in Montreal. We were just struggling, along with everyone else, to get our voices heard.

KN: Did it get easier with time?

ES: The whole thing gets easier with time because the more experience you have, the more credibility you have and the more knowledge you have. It's easier to navigate. I'm working with young filmmakers now and I see the struggles they face. If you have one or two credits under your belt, it's hard to go into the CBC and say I want $500,000 to make this film. They'll say, "I'm not sure that you can do that." But if you've got five or six, or even thirty credits under your belt and you walk in and say I want to make this film, they may say, "Okay, it's a good idea." It does get easier with time just because you've got more experience. Whether it got easier as a woman, I don't know.

In the last two or three years, broadcasters and producers are looking for women to direct because the statistics that have come out—the work that

Leon Johnson and Elise Swerhone on the set of *Rabbit Pie*, 1975. Courtesy of Brad Caslor.

Elise Swerhone with slate and Vonnie von Helmolt in the background, on set of *Rabbit Pie*, 1975. Courtesy of Brad Caslor.

Rina Fraticelli is doing with Women in View, collecting statistics on what the public funders are spending on women for television and the screen in Canada.[51] Those statistics are so embarrassing, especially for public funders. I think you are going to see a lot more women directing in the next five years. Things are very different.

National Film Board

KN: What did the arrival of the NFB do to the chemistry of the Film Group, to the pH balance in the ecosystem of the Film Group?

ES: The NFB setting up an office here in Winnipeg was a huge game changer. Suddenly, there was enough money to actually make a proper film. We actually got paid what was close to a living wage. And you also got the mentorship that came with Michael Scott, Jerry Krepakevich, and the whole institution in Montreal. You knew that you were creatively supported. You got the credibility that came with the National Film Board, which at that time had a huge name internationally for making fantastic documentaries. So, those of us who wanted to be filmmakers naturally wanted to work for the National Film Board.

Some of us spent less time in smoky meetings at the Film Group, but I think we all still felt loyalty and support for the Film Group. It was still an important part of the community and it became very important for the next generation of filmmakers that were coming into their own in Winnipeg—like Guy Maddin and that generation of filmmakers, who weren't really interested in doing National Film Board films at that point. They used the Winnipeg Film Group as their starting point. So, the Film Group continued to be very active and very important, even if a lot of those who wanted to actually make a living and buy a house went to work for the Film Board and other organizations.

Who Has Seen the Wind

KN: Can you talk about your career after that?

ES: I went to Saskatchewan to work on the film *Who Has Seen the Wind* [1977] that was being produced and directed by Allan King. I was from Saskatchewan and still a student, so, really, my permanent residence was still Saskatchewan, even though I was living in Winnipeg to go to university. The Saskatchewan government had put a considerable amount of financing into the production of *Who Has Seen the Wind*, on the condition that Allan King would train a group of filmmakers in Saskatchewan to work on the production. I begged my local member of Parliament to let me get on that production.

I was the only woman in all of the trainees (in the technical departments). I really wanted to be in the camera department. Richard Leiterman, who was the director of photography, was considered to be the best cameraman in Canada. I knew his work and wanted to work with him. I got to Arcola, Saskatchewan, and I met with the production manager, Gwen Iverson, and said, "I want to be in the camera department." She said: "No. Women just don't work in the camera department. Why don't you go to the sound department? Everybody wants to be in the camera department." I thought about it and said: "I've thought about it. I'm not interested in sound. I want to be in the camera department." She said, "Well, sorry. It's full." That evening, I went and talked to Richard. The next day, I was in the camera department.

That was my first opportunity to work with a professional crew and, as a result of that, I actually worked quite a lot as a camera assistant in Toronto. It was the beginning of careers for a number of people from Saskatchewan.

Toronto versus Winnipeg

KN: Did you ever think of staying in Toronto?

ES: Why did I stay in Winnipeg? It's a really good question—because we were always encouraged to move to Toronto. I tell people starting out today to move to Toronto. I met with a young woman yesterday who wants to be a screenwriter. I said: "It's possible—but really, you should be in Toronto." People are always saying that to me, and to Bob, too. I don't know why we didn't move. It was partly for family reasons, but also I just felt more comfortable in Winnipeg. I worked for about seven years as a camera assistant, from the time I made *Havakeen Lunch* in 1979. My main source of income was as a camera assistant or as a director of photography because you got paid a good union wage when you worked on big productions. I directed, too, but I didn't get paid as much as a director.

But why didn't I move to Toronto? I never felt comfortable in Toronto. I didn't feel like I belonged in Toronto. I felt that if I did move to Toronto, I wouldn't have a voice. There was a fair amount going on in Winnipeg. I felt I belonged in Winnipeg. I felt that there always was just enough opportunity here to keep me here. In 1990, Bob got a job in Toronto editing a series called *Millennium*, and I'd just had a baby, so I wasn't working. So, we moved to Toronto for ten months. At the end of that, we thought very seriously about staying in Toronto. Toronto is a very expensive city; you have to work all the time to be able to live. The people I saw who were small filmmakers and documentary filmmakers, having to work on stuff that they really didn't believe in all that much, just to keep the standard that they wanted to live at. We felt that we had more of a voice back in Winnipeg. Both of us made the decision to stay here. It's always fun to work with people from Toronto because you feel like Torontonians are somehow better in some way. You're working with the real filmmakers. But Winnipeg has always given me more opportunity to do the things I wanted to do.

MERIT JENSEN CARR

Merit Jensen Carr grew up in Vancouver, but studied at the University of Winnipeg. She worked as a summer student at the Winnipeg Film Group and eventually took on the role of distribution coordinator and later executive coordinator. She established herself as a producer, eventually founding Merit Motion Pictures, specializing in documentary for television.

10 FEBRUARY 2016, WINNIPEG

Kevin Nikkel: Any hints in your upbringing that you'd end up in the arts?

Merit Jensen Carr: Two things. I had a friend a couple of years older than I was, who would get all the kids together in the neighbourhood and put on a play, and invite all the parents to come and make them pay. That was my first experience as an entrepreneur. I thought, this is great—we can have all this fun and make a bit of money, too. I grew up in Vancouver and every day at six o'clock . . . I watched *The Big Show*; it was like a history of film. Classic films, from *Night of the Living Dead* [1968], to Fred and Ginger musicals, to *The Thin Man* [1934], to Fellini—it was all there. That's what I watched. I was transported. I loved it! But I never really thought of it as something that I would do as a career.

Merit Jensen Carr. Courtesy of Merit Motion Pictures.

I moved to Winnipeg, went to university and, for seven years, I just kept taking classes. I'd intensely study something and then get interested in something else and switch majors: philosophy, theatre, film, English literature, French literature, and political science. It depressed me when I thought I couldn't make up my mind about what I wanted to do but, really, I was interested in ideas and stories. Now I know that it's not a bad thing to have a restless mind.

My husband David used to volunteer at Liberation Book Store. They were throwing a party at the bookstore and, after seeing *Apocalypse Now* [1979], we decided to go. Elizabeth Klinck was at that party. David knew her but I'd never met her. Liz and I hit it off right away and we started talking about film. She was the coordinator, then executive director, of the one-person office of the Film Group. They had a grant to hire a student to start a distribution office and she asked me to come down and apply. I didn't know anything about distribution but I thought this was great. We put together the WFG's first tour of experimental films, created publicity materials, and had a fabulous time. I remember, at the time, I felt that this was where I was supposed to be. Finally, it all made sense.

Liz and I were a fantastic team, the two of us, because we were positive that we could do anything. We'd go to festivals like the Toronto International Film Festival and we'd talk about the independent cinema coming out of Winnipeg and how important it was. That was at a time when people were starting to think that regional film had a place in the country and there should be funding for it. We were that voice.

Independent Film

KN: What were some of the key events in those early days?

MJC: Independent cinema in North America was really starting to have a voice. There were a number of really strong personalities here, who had something to say. It was at a time when a lot of things were changing. We were coming out of the years where all the bad films were funded as tax shelters. Michel Brault's films were bringing in audiences and having a huge impact. Independent cinema in Quebec and the US was exploding. Don Shebib's *Going Down the Road* [1970] had just come out. English Canada wanted to foster its own culture and cinema.

The government had a real will to try to create a film industry where Canadian creators could express Canadian culture in a new way, and Liz and I were right there at the beginning. That was the beginning of Telefilm Canada, and they were looking for Canadian features with a unique Canadian voice. But, of course, most funding was being directed to Toronto and Montreal. We wanted to make sure that there were opportunities for people to tell stories from here.

At the same time, the Canada Council funded co-ops across the country. One of the wonderful things about being at the Film Group was that it gave us an opportunity to travel and represent filmmakers at national events. Not many people from Winnipeg had access to those events, so we had never had a voice at the table. Elizabeth and I were the ones who became the voice from Winnipeg. When there was a panel and everybody was talking about the problems that independent filmmakers were having, we were never shy about speaking up. *Cinema Canada* and all the publications would be like, oh, here is someone we haven't heard from before. Suddenly, the room would hear from these two women from Winnipeg who were talking about John Paizs's film *Billy Botski* [*The Obsession of Billy Botski*, 1980] and asking, why isn't anybody helping John Paizs? It was great.

KN: What was the Film Group like when you first arrived?

MJC: The Film Group was located in the Bate Building. Creaky old elevator. Lots of artists. Two rooms and a little closet in the middle. Bolexes, lights, not much equipment. The big dream was to get a Steenbeck. We didn't even have a photocopier; we had a Gestetner. It was very, very primitive. The office was full of rabbit pies—everywhere you looked were rabbit pies. It was ridiculous. *Rabbit Pie* [1976] was the big Film Group production the year before I started. And no one knew what to do with all the pies when it ended.

It was a different era. If someone simply wanted to talk about film, they could come in, hang out, and talk. Filmmakers were there all the time.

They'd come there and meet and have a cup of coffee, and they'd talk about independent cinema. That was great. It was community. I think we all knew there was a need for that. They were formative days. We were still discovering what this community looked like. How was it going to take shape? What kind of films do they want to make? People would come in there with a film idea and they'd talk, and then they'd find other people who would want to help them make it. In no time, that film would be made and they'd be on to the next one. It was a real collective. In the meantime, while everybody was talking and chatting, Elizabeth and I would be trying to get some work done.

KN: Were things changing quickly?

MJC: A big transition happened when the NFB opened in Winnipeg. A lot of the founding members of the Film Group moved over to the NFB because the NFB actually gave you production funding and paid you to make a film. Up until then, filmmakers worked as a co-op and volunteered. This provided an opportunity for a new group to move into the Film Group but it was also a kind of crisis. I think many of those people still feel like those were the glory days at the Film Group. They had an amazing sense of community and shared purpose.

After many of the founding members left, the struggle was to understand what the Film Group was without them. And how could we differentiate the Film Group from the NFB? It seemed like anybody making documentary, or even short drama, was making them at the NFB. Like it or not, people moved over to the NFB because production funds were so scarce.

Regionalism

KN: There was a need to redefine the Film Group?

MJC: I think a lot of the early people were trying to create more of an industry. Any experimenting they would have done got left behind. One of the strengths of the Film Group was that it was a place where people could really play. They could innovate, they could experiment, they could take risks. A place for people with unique visions—John being one of them—to make drama in a really interesting way. Some people would say he created a whole new prairie voice for cinema. Later that was followed by Guy. There may not have been that new wave, if that first wave hadn't left. It was a really exciting time. The Film Group was becoming a place where people with a unique style and voice could flourish and work.

Around this time, Elizabeth decided to go back to Ontario, where she was from. I took on her job and I became the executive director. And then, very soon after that, Joan Scott was the chair and she moved us into this beautiful historic house on Adelaide. I think some people would say their favourite memories of the Film Group were at that house. It was a real home. We had a really distinct presence. We had a little screening area where we could screen films, couches for people to sit on, three editing rooms, and a distribution office in the back. Much more space. It was an extraordinary place.

The Washing Machine

KN: Was there friction?

MJC: There were competing egos on Adelaide, absolutely. And there was a lot of testosterone—and a huge lack of female filmmakers. I had a daughter and I brought her to work with me for six months, and so I had my desk and the playpen. It had a big impact on all these young guys with all this ego and attitude. Many of them didn't know how to act around a baby. It was very humanizing.

I really wanted to encourage more women filmmakers because Elise had left and was finding more work at the NFB. That was when Shereen Jerrett walked in the door and she was a really fresh voice with a lot of great ideas. She was one of the first women members of that generation to really decide that she wanted to direct. There was a real tendency, at that point, for most of the men to want the women to produce, or production manage, and help them fulfil their vision.

Some members wanted the Film Group to be the producer, not just facilitate or provide equipment. Someone found the money to produce

Rabbit Pie, but that was before my time. We found some funding to make a short film and we held a competition. Gene Walz won the competition, with his proposal to do a short film based on a play that was called *The Washing Machine* [1988]. Mike Mirus was the producer. Everything that could happen *did happen* on that production. Long, long days. Lots of inexperience, and some big things like transformers blowing. Things that you don't want anyone to know about. Things that I can talk about now because it's thirty years later.

The Washing Machine created a real crisis. People were really upset that it wasn't managed better. After that, the decision was made that the Film Group would stop producing. That was a huge disappointment for some members, who had a real hope that the Film Group would play that role. There was a co-op in Quebec called ACPAV [Association coopérative de productions audio-visuelles] that did produce. It was a wonderful thing for the members of ACPAV because they could go there with their ideas and the co-op would designate a producer, find the money, and put together a kind of a financing model that made sense for that organization—one that included a kind of cooperative spirit of filmmaking that was really independent and didn't have to make a lot of compromises. That was the point where people decided maybe the Film Group was more about exhibition, distribution, professional development, and helping filmmakers to find their own production financing.

The Cinematheque

But what we didn't have was a cinema. What I kept realizing—and I think this was because I started in distribution—was that as long as our films were shown at the NFB's cinema, we couldn't really feel like we had a distinct presence in the community. They were all considered NFB films. It was a big problem because they had very limited exhibition slots

Merit Jensen Carr. Courtesy of Merit Motion Pictures.

and our films were so different. It was confusing. Because I travelled so much, I had a chance to see how fantastic the cinematheques were in other cities. BC had a cinematheque. Quebec had a huge cinematheque. Other cities, even if they didn't have a cinematheque, had independent cinemas that were showing independent films. And we didn't. So, we applied for a Canada Council grant and hired Dave Barber. A new era began for the Film Group.

Right after that, the Core Area Initiative was announced. It was an opportunity for three levels of government to fund very large arts projects in the core area of Winnipeg.[52] The visual arts groups all got together and decided that what we really needed—and this idea actually came from a conference we attended in Peterborough—was a visual arts centre. That was when we wrote the proposal for Artspace. The idea was that we could build this multidisciplinary, creative place where people could collaborate and exchange ideas. We always imagined that there would be a pub on the main floor, but that never happened, unfortunately. The big advantage, for all of us at the Film Group, was we'd have a cinematheque.

Exhibition, really, was the final piece. We started with production, and then I started the distribution office and then we found the money for exhibition. Dave Barber programmed the Cinematheque. . . . Those were the cornerstones. I felt like, at that point, the Film Group reached a point of maturation where we really started to create a presence that was known across Canada and around the world.

The Steenbeck

KN: Any other major turning points during these years?

MJC: There were a few seminal events that happened when I first started. We raised the money for the Steenbeck, and that took all of the films to a whole other level of professionalism. That encouraged a lot of people, who hadn't joined before, to join because it was one of the first Steenbecks in the city. It was a really big deal. Then, the second thing was the photocopier. We raised the money for the photocopier and Ed

Ackerman, in particular, used that photocopier continuously to make *5¢ a Copy* [1980]. We were in a situation that if somebody decided that they wanted to make 200,000 copies in order to make a film, that was okay. I think the thing that made that possible was the fact that we got charitable status. We got it because Elizabeth Klink lived in MP Lloyd Axworthy's riding.[53] We pestered Lloyd Axworthy for months until he finally gave it to us. In fact, the photocopier was partly a charitable donation.

KN: Do you recall any seminal crisis moments?

MJC: They were daily—with personalities blowing up. Egos. There were a number of times when we were just waiting for the next cheque. It was still a shoestring operation. We didn't have enough equipment, so lots of people would be battling over scheduling: who got the equipment when. And then I had this baby. One of the wonderful things about organizations that have working boards is everybody's really invested and passionate—but they aren't necessarily the people with the most experience working on a board or running an organization. I really like the model where everybody is really involved, but there are things that happen as a result of the inexperience and I attribute it to that. I think you'll find many crises have happened throughout the history of the Film Group that have to do with inexperience. Maybe that is the beauty of the organization? You can embrace that. Those crises are just part of the deal. If you're going to have an organization largely run by artists, it's going to have passionate moments and it's going to have more than a few crises. It could be what leads to greatness. It all comes as a package.

KN: What are your thoughts about how it has grown and where it is now?

MJC: It's huge. The Film Group is really huge. It's got a fantastic presence in the city. I think it's working really hard to reconnect with the filmmakers. But I think that it's really hard for an organization at a certain point, when it gets to a certain size, to be the kind of home that filmmakers might need. I think we need to ask, what is the vision for independent cinema today? Maybe that's a better question: what's the role? What kind of independent cinema do we want here? How are we going to foster that? How are we fostering collaborative, cooperative filmmaking? I think there is a huge yearning for that again. The industrial model in Canada hasn't produced very much good work. It's produced a lot of crap. I think there is a desire to really foster creative filmmaking that is really independent and telling stories that are really beautiful or remarkable or unique. That desire is still there and the struggle is probably stronger than it's ever been. So, that's the conversation I think needs to happen. The Film Group has to grapple with that. Canada is grappling with that—it's not just the Winnipeg Film Group. I'd like to see that conversation happen. I'd like to be part of that

Merit Jensen Carr and Bruce Duggan. Courtesy of Dave Barber.

conversation. I can't think of any other place that can create that conversation than at the Winnipeg Film Group.

Local Production Companies

Dave Barber: It seemed like there was a shift from an independent-minded scene to the industry model.

MJC: That's the story of film in Winnipeg, really. It's not Winnipeg's fault. It's not the industry's fault. It's one of the reasons why I work as much as I do in documentary. Much of the focus, for many years, has been on a service industry and on crews, and on creating jobs and employment. It hasn't been on developing the creators, developing the directors, the writers—even the actors, actually. The focus has never been on independent productions that are generated out of Winnipeg. That is not because people don't want to do that. It's because of the way the money flows and because so much of the money is triggered by broadcasters; it makes it difficult to make certain types of productions, here or anywhere. The national decision makers, for a long time, had a lack of confidence in our ability to produce a certain level of production here, particularly [in] drama. There was so much emphasis on crews and developing a full crew, or two crews, or three crews, and keeping them working for a service industry. I think there is a lot of glamour, bringing in the Hollywood stars and the big-budget productions at the expense of developing the talent that lives here.

DB: Is there more or less support than there was in the nineties?

MJC: Probably there was more support in the early years. In some cases, there has been real impatience in how slowly the industry was evolving and how quickly local companies were growing. Also, there were a couple of periods where production was really slow here and we lost a lot of our crew. We spent a lot of money training people and then, in one six-month slow period, many of those people moved to Vancouver and Toronto to get work and never came back. Then we'd have to start all over training crews again. That created this big emphasis on keeping crews instead of developing our own stories and talent.

The good news is that I think that's changing. I'm very hopeful, right now. I think that there is so much disruption everywhere we look in the industry that it is also creating opportunities—lots of opportunities. There's never been more opportunities for short films, for instance. People are doing amazing short films and making sales, establishing reputations, and getting lots of attention for them. I'm finding that there is more interest—maybe not more money, but more opportunity.

You can't talk about Winnipeg at that time without talking about Credo Group. Because Credo Group was one the biggest production companies and a major force: they were doing big-budget shows and hiring a lot of people. Joan Scott was the chair of the Winnipeg Film Group and she was also a partner in Credo Group. They encouraged some very good people to move here from Toronto.

KN: Can you tell me more about what happened with Credo?

MJC: Credo was left holding the bag for all the preproduction money on a big CBS drama that involved the Twin Towers and terrorism, right when 9/11 happened. CBS refused to pay. It was an economic hit that they couldn't sustain, even though they were a big company. Most people think that production companies have deep pockets and reserve funds, but there is no opportunity for a company to do that in this industry. We survive project to project. Most of the companies in this industry are barely making it. It was a really tragic thing for the industry when Credo went bankrupt. Today, I think we would've been smarter and somebody would have tried to step in and save them. When they went down, I think a lot of people lost faith in our ability to sustain an industry.

KN: How did you get to where you are today with Merit Motion Pictures?

MJC: I started out producing drama. I was the token woman from the West—Elise and I had a company together, and we developed several big dramas and drama series. Everyone gave us development money—and, in some cases, lots of it. It was a time when the idea of regional drama was very politically important, but no one in Toronto really believed it was possible to do a big series or movie out of Winnipeg. Elise and I spent ten years developing projects which everyone liked but no one green-lit. Then I went to the UK on a producers trade mission and met this woman producer who was very similar to me. I asked, "Why aren't you doing drama anymore?" I'd known she'd worked on a lot of dramatic productions. She said, "I decided I wanted to have a company, and I couldn't build a company on drama." It was like an epiphany. Then she said: "I can tell all the same stories I was developing in drama in documentary and, in a lot of cases, they're faster and even better." That really led to a change in my thinking. I moved to Montreal soon after that, and there were a few filmmakers, like Erna Buffie, that I knew and that I really wanted to work with, and they started asking me to produce documentaries for them. It made sense. It just worked out. I don't really want to work at home, in a little back office. I love having a group of people that I work with, coming to the office every day.

KN: You've made your own little Film Group!

12 min
8 min
cool down
4 min
7 min

GENE WALZ

Gene Walz grew up in Rochester, New York, and studied at St. John Fisher College. He began his university teaching career in the Faculty of English at Frostburg State College, in Frostburg, Maryland, and earned a PhD in film and literature from the University of Massachusetts. In 1974, he was recruited to teach film at the University of Manitoba. He was active in the Winnipeg Film Group from its early days, served on many committees, and made the short film The Washing Machine *with funding from the Film Group. He has had a full career teaching film studies and writing extensively about Manitoba cinema.*

10 JUNE 2016, WINNIPEG

Kevin Nikkel: Tell me about your background.

Gene Walz: I grew up in Rochester, New York. That's where the Kodak film company is, and the George Eastman House. George Eastman, the founder of Kodak, had a classic movie theatre in his mansion, and I got interested in movies because of the George Eastman House classic movie showings on Friday night. It got me so interested that I became one of the first people to work for educational television in Rochester [for the

---

Gene Walz, during production of *The Washing Machine*, 1987. Courtesy of *Winnipeg Free Press.*

Rochester Area Educational Television Association] as a production assistant. I started as a gofer and worked my way up to writer and director.

I taught English for the first seven or eight years of my teaching career. Then I was at the University of Massachusetts, when they were just introducing a film studies course. Because I had worked in television and had an interest in movies, they asked me if I would like to join the staff teaching that course. The course had no money and so we had to scramble to show films. The Canadian consulate in Boston had a cache of National Film Board films, so we taught a lot of the beginning film course at the University of Massachusetts in Amherst with National Film Board films.

The Canadian Film Symposium

When I took a job here [at the University of Manitoba] in 1974, I discovered that I had seen more Canadian films than anybody I met. I was an instant expert on Canadian film and was immediately slotted in to teach the course on Canadian film. I arrived at the perfect time. I couldn't have timed it better for my career: I got here when the National Film Board opened a production office in Winnipeg. I immediately made contact with them to use their movies. And I got here as the Winnipeg Film Group was getting started. The Festival of Life and Learning, at the University of Manitoba, brought in all sorts of filmmakers, and it was through the advertising for that that I met the initial members of the Winnipeg Film Group. I got involved with them as quickly as I could, in 1975.

KN: The Festival of Life and Learning—was that the same event as the Canadian Film Symposium?

GW: Yes. The Film Symposium was part of the Festival of Life and Learning.

KN: Talk about that.

GW: The importance of it, for me, was I met Claude Jutra. I met David Cronenberg. I met Jutra's cinematographer, Michel Brault, who made *Les Ordres*. There were eight or ten filmmakers there. They showed some of their films. It was a very exciting week. I had to run back and forth between teaching, talking to students, and hanging out with the people that I met for the first time, who were interested in making movies. Filmmakers from other parts of Canada.

I attended the panel discussion on getting funding for the Winnipeg Film Group. I don't remember much, except there was a woman from the Canada Council who was very important. She was very desirous of getting co-ops going throughout the country. She encouraged people to get their act together. Forms could be filled out to apply for money, so that a place could be rented and a program could be started. It was really that one woman, as much as the Winnipeg people, who was responsible for the Film Group getting started.

Winnipeg Film Group

KN: Was everyone on the same page?

GW: Arguments *are* the Winnipeg Film Group. There's always a dissenter. Some of it is spiteful. Some of it was healthy competition: it was your idea and not mine, but I got a better one. Some of it was a bit of resentment—but there's always been that kind of tension.

KN: What were your expectations for the group?

GW: It was an opportune time for me to come here—knowing more about Canadian film than even the people that I met there. Making it part of my focus in my teaching and then finding like-minded people. I met Allan Kroeker there. He and I were great François Truffaut film fans. Truffaut had a profound influence on both of us. We would talk François Truffaut films with the rest of the group. The Film Group got started because people met to watch movies. Especially, the core group were watching European and foreign films, and seeing that you could make money making films even if you didn't have an expensive, industrial infrastructure behind you.

KN: So, the Film Group is established—you walk in?

GW: My first meeting was at the Bate Building. A great building with a beautiful wrought-iron elevator. There were usually prostitutes in the doorway that we had to fight our way through to get up to the meetings. It wasn't a conducive place for meetings. The rooms were small and they were crowded and noisy. The Film Group was always argumentative and so there were always arguments. I had a feeling that the meetings weren't all that productive. I think a lot of people did, but they were necessary to get people together and see who was doing what.

It was just scattered. All sorts of people. There were people there who saw themselves as sort of hangers-on, not fully involved. There were others who saw themselves as the movers and shakers. I think the person that really wanted to make a go of it, besides Len Klady, was Leon Johnson. I think he was the core of the group. He was the leader. It was clearly his operation. I think he was the president of the Winnipeg Film Group, whatever title he had. I think he had some movies in mind and had some stuff started already, by the time I was there.

KN: Did you know, at that time, you wanted to make films?

GW: I knew I wanted to make films when I joined. But I was of two minds, really. I knew I wanted to make films, but I also knew that I wanted to document them. I just wanted to be part of that community. I had an enormous teaching load and I had a young family. I knew that I was not going to work on making my own films from the start. I had made some films before as a graduate student—just amateur stuff. But I was content to just be a part of the group. I think I was probably as much connected to the National Film Board as I was to the Winnipeg Film Group.

I split my time between them and was content to just wait my time and see how things went. To get my family going. To get my career going. To be honest, making movies didn't count for much in the academic realm at that time. It was only later that creative work was considered something that could be applied to tenure and promotion. I was busy working on writing about Canadian film, writing about Manitoba film, and writing a book on François Truffaut. It was only when I finally had my feet on the ground, and a little bit more time, that I was involved more closely in making my own film.

The Washing Machine

KN: The film I'm curious to hear more about is *The Washing Machine* [1988].

GW: Well, there was a competition to get the best screenplay and I decided to submit a screenplay to this competition—one based on a short story by my friend David Arnason because adapted Canadian short stories were a hit at the time. It came down to a script by Jake MacDonald and one by myself, and mine was chosen. I think that prize was $10,000 and I had to raise an additional $10,000. I did raise enough money, maybe not directly but in deferrals. I got assigned a producer, Mike Mirus, who had never been a producer before—and I had never made a scripted show before. We were both rookies and amateurs going about this. We had casting calls and we had the whole preproduction schlamozzle. I took a sabbatical to do the movie and, for some reason, the project collapsed in the spring. I went back to teaching in the fall. About mid-October, the Film Group got back to me and said, we've managed to get together a whole lot of money for you to make this movie. It was an enormous amount of money but they got it on the condition that everybody at the Film Group would be given an upgrade. It got money from the training budget, from the feds, to train people to make a movie. If we got a movie out of it, great. It was not just Mike Mirus and myself, rookies. It was everybody: all rookies doing a movie for more than a hundred thousand dollars.

I had to take time off from the university. I had to hire somebody to teach my classes for one week of preproduction and ten days of shooting—on the coldest days of the winter, in very odd places, with people that didn't know what they were doing. And a cinematographer who thought he knew better than the rest of us, but unfortunately hooked up all the electricity, down in the woods off of St. Anne's Road, to the electric wires going overhead and blew out the transformer. It went off like a skyrocket. The power to the whole neighbourhood went out. We had to pack up everything and get the hell out of there before Hydro came down and

caught us doing something illegal. We lost the whole day. We all thought, this movie is doomed. We needed every single minute that we had.

We had trouble with venues as well. We rented a laundromat across from the Park Theatre, on Osborne, and we completely redesigned it for the shoot. We told the guy that owned it not to come back while we were shooting. He came back in the middle of the shoot, in a long wolf-skin coat that was down to his ankles, wearing gold chains. He threatened to kill us all, threatened to burn our houses down.

Well, we somehow finished the movie. I went back to teaching at the end of that term. We thought we would be doing a fairly leisurely edit and, all of a sudden, it was announced to me that the CBC had bought it and we had to finish it in a couple of weeks. I had to take some time out, again, to get somebody to cover my classes. Ken Roddick and I, and a couple of other people, put a fast edit together. That was the movie! Considering all the difficulties that we had, it wasn't a bad effort. People laughed at it. We sold it to a couple places. The CBC played it several times. It was designed to be a sort of pilot for a sitcom, in that sort of crude American television style of the seventies. Not very subtle at all—sort of slapsticky and obvious. But in terms of what we were faced with and what we had in mind, I often likened it to having a baby with one arm and one foot missing. You can see that it was a lovable kind of movie, but it was insufficient.

KN: At that time, there was a fair amount of competition in the Group. Was there pressure?

GW: I didn't have time to think about that at all. If the film didn't get completed, it was going to come out of my hide. So, that brought me down a peg. I was more worried about the film not being done and about us getting a lot of footage that we couldn't put together into a film. Because we missed that whole day. Because it took so long. Because everybody was working at a level higher than they were prepared for.

Gene Walz and Dave Barber. Courtesy of Dave Barber.

John Paizs/Guy Maddin

KN: *Rabbit Pie* [1976] was a training film too, stimulating people.

GW: You can look at almost every film that the Film Group has done in those terms. People scrambling. People not having enough time and money, or experience—and yet somehow success is happening. Look at Guy Maddin's movies. Look at John Paizs's, even John Kozak's movies. There's a lot of scrambling because there's a lot of things that don't go right. There is a lot of improv that happens.

To me, the story of the Film Group is—it's a miracle. It's a miracle that this place has survived. It's a miracle that the films that they made have been successes. It's a miracle that it's got such a reputation around the world, the films continue to get an audience.

Dave Barber: Why is it a miracle?

GW: Because there's been so many things that have gone wrong. It could've collapsed so many times, when I was intimately involved in it, and so many times since. I think some outsider looking at the Film Group and studying what they've done, who's been there, and what's happened—they would say, wow! This place is still going?

KN: You've reflected on the eras of Winnipeg film in some of your writing. What contributed to the chemistry of these eras?

GW: John Paizs wanted to be a filmmaker from a very early age and made his own films before he enrolled in my classes at university—before he joined the Film Group. He just had his eye on the prize from a very young age, and he had his own peculiar way of looking at things. He had an artist's training in a fine arts program. He wasn't a very good student at all, but he knew what he wanted and he made some really interesting animated movies to start his career. Then he realized, this is just taking up too much of my time, I can spend my time better using real people.

I think this is the same thing with Guy and some other people—they knew that it's a process. You have to start small and master things, bit by bit by bit. Build your career. This is one of the great things that Allan Kroeker did before he joined the Film Group: he built his career very systematically. With this kind of film, a little bit bigger of a film for the Department of Agriculture, then *Rabbit Pie*, and then the stuff that he did for CKND.

There are a lot of people that joined the Film Group who really knew what they wanted to do. Only a small percentage of them succeeded. One of the things you have to remember is that the Film Group made some godawful films. The Film Group *didn't* make a lot of movies that *should* have been made, as well: good ideas that died, films shot and never finished.

DB: When did the Film Group start to get noticed?

GW: I think it was probably the mid-eighties. Merit Jensen was a very forward-thinking coordinator. During her tenure, we hired Bruce McManus, as a distribution manager, to flog our films nationally and internationally. We were helped by the fact that the [Manitoba] Department of Education gave us *God Is Not a Fish Inspector* [1980], a very popular short drama by Allan Kroeker based on a Manitoba story, to distribute. Then we moved into Artspace, opened the Cinematheque, and hired Dave Barber. That gave our movies local exposure.

Then television got interested in us. There are lots of things going on at the same time. There's the National Film Board, and a lot of people from the Film Group going to the National Film Board—and not just working for them but getting secret monies channelled into Film Group projects. I think that created a certain kind of buzz elsewhere. The co-op movement throughout Canada got strong in the early eighties.

We had meetings—between the Nova Scotia Film Group and the Toronto Film Group, and there were two or three others. Through the combination of us meeting with other people, exchanging ideas, and exchanging films, we made a film with Nova Scotia called *You Laugh Like a Duck* [1980], which Leon Johnson put together. I think that started to get us an audience. The National Film Board started taking films to show in Montreal. The television stations started getting interested in the movies the Film Group was making.

KN: You've written about various eras. Tell me about the next chapter, after Paizs and after Maddin. How would you describe what came next?

GW: Well, a couple of things led to a cratering of the Film Group, after the successes of John Paizs and Guy Maddin in the late eighties and early nineties. We got a bunch of imitators who weren't quite as good, and that sort of ran out the string. Then we got a couple of bad administrators and that almost sabotaged the Film Group. It seems to me that there's always been a top dog at the Film Group, and we didn't have as strong people as the top dogs after Guy Maddin and John Paizs worked their magic and encouraged people to make similar kinds of movies. The people that came in with the next generation weren't quite as different, weren't quite as magnetic, in terms of drawing people to them to get them to work on things.

The industry itself suffered. It wasn't just the Film Group—it was the National Film Board as well. It was CKND getting out of the business. There's always been a ladder, starting with people that made films in high school, or made films before the Film Group and then joined the Film Group, and then moving to do stuff at the Film Board, and then moving beyond that. It seemed to me that that ladder broke. The people that were at the Film Group, in the early years, were stuck on the ladder and prevented other people from moving up. We didn't have that nice progression. That seems, in my estimation, what happened.

KN: I like the ladder analogy. What is the next wave?

GW: The next wave, historically, is people that are willing to make films for the Film Group and make films for MTS TV, and not see feature films as the be-all and end-all. Content to make quirky, unique films and are willing to put them up on YouTube and put them up on MTS TV. Smaller, more manageable projects.

KN: Examples?

GW: You. Mike Maryniuk. I think, had he been of a previous era, he would have skyrocketed. The guys that made the *Death by Popcorn* [2006] movie—Rankin and that group. They decided that they would go elsewhere because I think they could see a ceiling. Who else is in that generation? Heidi Phillips. They're content to make these interesting movies and to try different things. They are more experimental. It's almost like they're going back to the early days of the Film Group.

KN: Are there other good stories you remember about the inside workings of the Film Group?

GW: The Film Group, like the Film Board, had a production screening committee that okayed projects. It was very contentious. It was when I was on the board—there were always battles. Filmmakers would come in and they would berate us for not okaying their projects—when the projects *shouldn't* have been okayed. I can remember rejecting a Noam Gonick film—it was going to be terrible. It wasn't planned out at all. It didn't deserve to be accepted, but we all felt bad rejecting it because we knew he had talent. We all encouraged him to do something else.

The Film Group, in its early days especially, what was considered a sort of a boys' club—Bob Lower, Derek Mazur, Leon Johnson, Brad Caslor, Richard Condie, and other guys. It was realized pretty quickly that it would be a better group if there were more women involved. We tried recruiting and we tried everything we could to get it to be something besides just the place where a bunch of guys hung out and made movies that interested them. There were some very strong women that were there, but not enough. It didn't have enough specific gravity, but there were enough of them to overpower the overwhelmingly male numbers. I think one of the reasons that Merit Jensen was hired, and one of the reasons that she did so well when she was in charge of the Film Group, was she was a very strong woman who had very good ideas, and has since made a very good career out of it. *Havakeen Lunch* [1979] came out of that same thing. We needed to encourage people with different points of view, from different genders, to make the movies that'll make a more well-rounded operation.

Regionalism

KN: It seems Winnipeg is often a test case for artists and co-ops. Maybe we can learn something here that can be applied elsewhere?

GW: I think, in my opinion, you've got to have a flexible group. You've got to have people that are willing to work with other people. It's not a one-person operation: it takes coordination, often not from the top. I think a good part of this is luck and persistence. Don't be discouraged, keep going, look forward. I think that Winnipeg is a tough town. I think Winnipeg is a place that encourages people—because of its climate, because of its isolation, because of its reputation. You have to have tough-minded people that aren't easily discouraged. If you can round up those people and get them working together, I think that's the secret.

KN: Do you think the Film Group has been able to ignore the latent insecurity of Winnipeg in general—the always being in the shadow of Toronto?

GW: I definitely think that Winnipeg has always felt that it doesn't deserve the demeaning reputation that it has elsewhere, that we're a backwoods, "flyover" place. But we're an art community with a kind of attitude that can be summed up in a couple words: "We'll show you." It takes D.W. Griffith's explanation about what he's trying to do—"The task I'm trying to achieve, above all, is to make you see"—and gives it a kind of chip-on-the-shoulder ethic. I don't think people here are discouraged easily. There have been some people that have made three or four terrible movies at the Film Group, and keep on going. There are people that have made some good movies, and then a bad movie and get discouraged, but come back. I think that's the strength of the community, across the board: singers and painters, sculptors and musicians of all types. I think our attitude is, well, I see you did that, eh? Well, we can do that. We probably can do it better. We can do it different. Or, at least, we should be able to control what gets on the movie screens as much as anybody.

I can remember talking to Allan Kroeker, being encouraged by the French New Wave and thinking, we can make movies like that. It's not all that terribly difficult. They studied movies, they had ideas. They were able to put together crews that weren't always professional. Because they were just that little bit different, they got noticed. That's what Winnipeggers thrive on: we're just different enough that our vision can captivate other people that are looking for things that are not quite down the centreline of the road.

KN: You are writing about Truffaut and the French New Wave at the same time as the Film Group's formation. Are there parallels?

GW: The parallels are quite apparent, if you think about it. Like the French New Wave: filmmakers got their interest in films from watching films obsessively, talking about them, and criticizing them. The same thing happened with the Winnipeg Film Group. That's how it got its start. It got its start because people were getting together, often in Len Klady's living room, and watching films that other people weren't watching and criticizing them and learning from them, and saying, look at how they did that. We can do that! That is one of the obvious parallels: working together, having a sort of community—a repertory group, almost, of people that work together, one project after another, and looked all over the place for inspiration. I think Leon Johnson got his inspiration as much from New York experimental filmmakers as he did from François Truffaut. But somehow, we could work on other movies and accept them and contribute to them. I think that was the same way with the Paris group, working for *Cahiers du cinéma*. Truffaut and Godard had famous battles; they fought and had a serious falling out. They were, in a lot of ways, completely different filmmakers, but at least they had the same belief in Paris as someplace that could equal Hollywood or London, or wherever else they were making movies: we can make movies better than our predecessors here in Paris, and be equal to what's going on in the rest of the world. I think we had the same attitude here.

The Dead Father

KN: Can you think of a scene from a film that is a quintessential Film Group scene?

GW: What comes to mind immediately is Guy Maddin's movie *The Dead Father* [1985]. There are many scenes in that movie that seemed to me to capture the quirky essence of the Winnipeg Film Group. Probably the one that stands out most is when the hero, the Guy Maddin substitute, takes out a spoon and digs it into his dead father's stomach, and consumes the father. That shocked a lot of people, when it was first shown. I can remember I showed it to people in a film studies conference one night, and they were blown away. They saw the symbolism. They saw the Freudian quality to it. They saw the quirkiness of it. They saw just what somebody working with a very limited budget, but a very strong idea, can do with almost nothing. I think that stands out for me as much as anything. When I showed that movie, people said, now I get it. Now I see what the Winnipeg Film Group is all about.

Winnipeg Film Group's home at 88 Adelaide, c. 1980s. Courtesy of Dave Barber.

Part Two

THE ADELAIDE HOUSE 1982–1986

GREG HANEC

Greg Hanec is a Winnipeg-based artist working in music, painting, and film. He discovered the Winnipeg Film Group at the Bate Building and eventually made the group's first feature film, Downtime *(1985).*

11 JUNE 2016, WINNIPEG

Kevin Nikkel: Was there any indication that you'd be the creative person you ended up being?

Greg Hanec: Thanks to PBS, and my brother and his girlfriend downstairs in the rec room, I was introduced to more complex films. When I was ten, I probably sat with them and watched European films like *Blowup* and *The Good the Bad and the Ugly* [both 1966]. That and Led Zeppelin because I inherited the record collection of my brother—it taught me about assemblage in art. With groups like that, and in films like *The Good the Bad and the Ugly*, you can see it's about constructing. Then you think, hey, I can construct things. I can put things together, too.

When my brother got a Super 8 camera, I started making these narratives. It was the era of Evel Knievel when I was a teenager, so we'd build ramps and we'd jump our bikes and stuff. I'd put on Jimi Hendrix's "The Star-Spangled Banner" and play it in slow motion on the projector.

Greg Hanec. Courtesy of Greg Hanec.

Winnipeg Film Group

I barely got out of high school and so university was out of the question. I thought, what am I going to do? I just wanted to be a filmmaker, when I was in my late teens. I looked into various things. Should I go to university? Somehow, I saw a notice for *Nose and Tina* [1980], by Norma Bailey. I went to that and then I talked to her about going to university. She said: "You know what, why not try this place first—the Winnipeg Film Group?" I went and took the incredible workshop that was there. It was for about $250. You got a twenty-two-week workshop where you made three films on 16-mm—my third ended up being my first film, *Work and Money* [1980]. Then it was just, oh wow! I'm in the right place.

KN: This is a formative moment for you. What was it like?

GH: It was the Bate Building. I walked in and, of course, I'm a little nervous. A really friendly person is there: Merit Jensen. She told me about the workshop, so I signed up for it. It was very friendly. I totally have only fond memories of Doug [Davidson] teaching that. He was a great guy—very patient. Very knowledgeable, too. Firm, but not ever overbearing.

There was always an air of "make shorter films." You have to pay your dues. Start with a short film. Okay, good—maybe get a grant, do a longer film. Maybe do a doc. But the idea of just being ambitious and making a feature or something—you wouldn't even think like that. You felt a slight limiting feeling there: we don't want to go too fast here. But what broke that spell was when I went to the first Film Group premieres and saw *The Obsession of Billy Botski* [1980], by John Paizs, and then I realized, oh wow, you can be ambitious! You can be ambitious and totally different. You don't have to make NFB docs.

KN: Did you have the DIY attitude early on?

GH: Very early on in my life, I had to figure out life for myself. My parents really weren't there to say, this is what you do, this is how you do that. I had to learn that myself. My dad was top of his class in his PhD, at the University of Wisconsin, of three hundred students, so there's definitely some IQ there, but also these problems too. I have the confidence that I could envision what I need to do, and then do it.

KN: You could see behind the curtain.

GH: It's practical. The very simple mixed with the complexity or the high-concept idea. Uniqueness was something that I really wanted to do. I really seem to be good at coming up with these fairly high-concept ideas, in terms of films. Most of my films are fairly high-concept. *Downtime* [1985] is a unique film; there's not really another film like it. Even with *Tunes a Plenty* [1987], it's [about] a band that never gets out of the basement—totally against the rags-to-riches scenario. I always like telling a different story, with a bit of a twist.

Dave Barber: What do you remember of the transition between the Bate Building and Adelaide?

GH: I loved Adelaide—that was the best. At that point, I was working on both *Downtime*, with Mitch Brown, and *Tunes a Plenty*. I had a key to it, and they had this beautiful Steenbeck upstairs. It was a beautiful, comfortable place. There was a nice window there, where you could do a few puffs of marijuana and blow it out the window. Once, someone came upstairs and said, "Hey, is that pot smoke?" So, that was really cool. And then, just come at ten o'clock at night, and have a beer or two and make films. No big-pressure thing, no security. It was like just going to a second apartment.

KN: What was the atmosphere like with other people?

GH: It seemed very calm and comfortable there. I don't think, at that time, Paizs was that well respected. I think there was still a core group of people that were thinking: what's he doing? Why is he doing these films? I followed the Paizs line of just doing my own thing and be ambitious. I still think that.

KN: What was the philosophy that drove you, during these years?

GH: It's more like, I'm going to make films. If they're good, they're good. If they're garbage, they're garbage. If you go in with that attitude, you generally get a few home runs, anyways. Trusting your intuition is an incredibly important thing. If you know your idea is good, not a lot of people can tell you it's not. What's there to stop you after that? You know your idea is good. You've got the means to do it: you've got a rental rate that's 10 percent of what the commercial rates are.

Downtime

KN: Were you talking about features at the Film Group, at the time?

GH: A little bit—but being discouraged to do it. Once I walked into Adelaide and someone said to me: "I hear you're doing a feature?" I'll never forget: like, what are you doing? I honestly said: "Yeah, I think it could be a masterpiece." Because I didn't want to be held back.

DB: What was the genesis of *Downtime*?

GH: I know exactly how it came about. Me and Mitch had made a short film called *Rigmarole* [1983] and I had made three short films. Then we just said, forget about short films. What are we going to do with them? It's time to just jump to a feature. What's the cheapest way we can do a feature? We need to use black-and-white. That's cheaper than colour and less problems.

Mitch wrote the script. It was about what me and Mitch were going through after we left school. When you leave high school, a lot of your friends go with it. Luckily, we had each other because we didn't have a lot of friends. He wrote it. *Canned Goods* was the first draft of the script. We tweaked it and started getting actors and actresses. Amazingly enough, we got a Manitoba Arts Council grant for $8,000 to shoot it, based on the script. It was really intense that we got the grant. We went to MAC to get finishing funds. I was told: "It's too boring. We can't support it, sorry." Then the Canada Council actually gave us the $8,000 to finish it. The Film Group too, of course, with a little grant.

DB: The visuals of *Downtime* are very distinct.

GH: For sure. We didn't want to do too much camerawork. We thought that would eat up film. Plus, the film is influenced by those really gritty

Maureen Gammelseter in Greg Hanec's feature film *Downtime*, 1985. Courtesy of Greg Hanec.

kinds of *Going Down the Road* [1970] Canadian films. But also, we were watching a lot of Bergman at the time, me and Mitch—because, at the Festival Theatre, you'd have a Bergman-athon. They'd show twenty Bergman films over a few weeks. And things like the French New Wave we were watching a lot of, too. The austerity of something like *Last Year at Marienbad* [1961] is also in there. That is one of my favourite films ever (although it's got tons of tracking shots).

DB: The casting for *Downtime* was great.

GH: Maureen was perfect, and that's the only film she's ever done. In fact, she wasn't going to audition for the film; she came with her friend because it was late at night, around the Exchange. That's when they had hookers around there, so she came with her friend because her friend was going to audition. Her friend was horrible in the audition, just terrible. Then we asked Maureen if she was going to audition. She said

no. She was kind of pissed off. We said, why not try one audition and just be mad like that? She said: "No, no. I'm not going to do it." They left. I went down the elevator and said: "Come on. Audition." She was the last person we auditioned, after about four people. Eleven o'clock at night. She came back up and she did it. We were ecstatic.

We did tons of video rehearsals to get stuff right. That's why Mitch Brown virtually co-directed the film, in many ways. I just said, we're not changing one word of your dialogue unless you approve of it. He ended up coming to all the rehearsals. We would have them count the pauses in their heads; they counted to fifteen or whatever. Then do the line.

There's a running joke in the film where the man, who is not named, keeps trying to ask her out. He even tries to rob her, as a way of asking her out somehow. He keeps saying, "Okay, forget it," when she refuses. But then, at the very end, when he comes and knocks on the door, and they have that talk through the door, and he leaves, he *doesn't* say "Okay, forget it." You know it's over. You know he's not going to try anymore; she's pushed him out of her life enough. They'll never be together, which is an anti-love story. I think her acting in that scene is absolutely perfect because she conveys a little bit of worry, but also understanding, even interest in him. You can see, in her performance, this kind of fear. But also sympathy.

DB: Were there a lot of rewrites?

GH: Tons of rewrites. In fact, rewriting due to rehearsals—this is not working, this is working, this isn't. Going away, coming back for rehearsals. That film is intensely rehearsed. It comes across as almost improvisation, but it's not. Every single word is rehearsed, as to how long the pauses are, just to create the tension of the waiting.

DB: The other thing is, the music is very sparingly used.

Still photo from Greg Hanec's feature film *Tunes a Plenty*, 1987. Courtesy of Greg Hanec.

GH: Yes, it's all incidental. The little sounds are so important. A little creak of the floor that speaks volumes to the thought of loneliness. The scuffing of feet.

KN: Or the sound of water in the bucket. It's a metaphor to me: the flow of water being life-giving—yet the film is about the absence of it.

GH: That's totally right. Even the much-commented-on fades, then a little arbitrary scene will come up for a few seconds and then fade—and then the next scene. We thought, why don't we have these arbitrary scenes that work almost like brackets, like quote marks?

DB: The Berlin programmer liked it.

GH: Yes—Alf Bold. That was pretty lucky that he was coming through Canada, visiting all the co-ops, and then saw *Downtime*. I remember getting a call at 9:30 in the morning. This was a time [when] I was staying up all hours and I was on welfare. He calls in the morning and says: "Your film is going to be in the Berlin Film Festival, so you're obviously coming." I said: "I'm on welfare." They got me an emergency grant from the Canada Council, to buy a ticket, and gave me an honorarium. So, that was good. I went with my $20 suit from the forties, that fit me perfectly off the rack. That's what I wore, whenever I was at one of the shindigs.

Think at Night

KN: Are you approaching *Think at Night* differently than *Downtime*? Is the process different?

GH: What happened with *Think at Night* is that, after *Tunes a Plenty*, I tried to write two scripts to get a lot more funding. I wanted to push it up to $50,000. I wrote a sci-fi movie script called *The Babies of the River*. It was about how people never drowned, that fell in rivers. It had really weird things in it. I couldn't get funding. Then I tried to do a Capra-esque movie called *Until It Happens Twice*. That was about a family that would welcome strangers into their home and give them half the money they had at the time; but when the person spent that money they had to leave. Those scripts were the hardest artistic projects I have ever done. I had two drafts of that script. One I gave to Greg Klymkiw. He lost it. Another I gave to my mother. She lost it. All that work—a year of writing, at a parkade on a midnight shift.

After that, I decided, I'm just going to shoot the opening scene of *Think at Night* and I'm gonna let that opening scene tell me what the next scene is. Then I'm going to let that scene tell me what the one after that is. I shot about half the film that way. The previous scene would make you see how to shoot the following scene. There'd be a few months, or even a year, of not doing any shooting. I was the lead. It takes place over one day—and I've been the lead for twenty-four years, so I have to shoot myself in weird ways, since I gained about forty pounds. I've had to keep my hair the same, all those years. Sometimes you just don't have the energy to do it anymore. So, at times, it would just be left for years.

Community

KN: The social nature of filmmaking is important to keep going, yes?

GH: That's what I liked about the Film Group and [it's] how I've wanted to live my life, whether it was filmmaking or making music. You do a project, you come together. Then another project. You'd meet up with people and would move on to the next project. Although, I must admit, I think now you can just edit at night, in your own apartment. . . . Without the Film Group, I don't think I would have done anything. You meet other filmmakers and they might say, hey, I really liked your film. Can you work on mine?

KN: What is the perfect metaphor for the Film Group?

GH: The Winnipeg Film Group is like a charming but rickety wooden boat going on a river, with a few holes in it. Way too many people on board. A few people are helping bail out the water and some people are lecturing them. Someone else is making up rules to ban this person or not allow this one in. Some people are pontificating about film theory. The ship, somehow, is going toward its destination—which it'll never reach, of course. Luckily for us, it will never reach its destination.

ED ACKERMAN

Ed Ackerman is a filmmaker and performance artist. He grew up in Winnipeg and attended Ryerson College (now Toronto Metropolitan University), in Toronto. Ed discovered the Film Group quite early on and was, at one point, its interim executive coordinator. He collaborated with Greg Zbitnew on the experimental photocopier animation 5¢ a Copy *(1980) using Winnipeg Film Group office equipment. Using an old typewriter, and an excerpt from the Kurt Schwitters poem "Ursonate," Colin Morton and Ed made the animations* Primiti Too Taa *(1986) and* Two Taa Too *(1992).*

9 APRIL 2016, WINNIPEG

Kevin Nikkel: Do you remember when you first walked into the Film Group?

Ed Ackerman: I think it was 1976. I was looking for other people that made film in Winnipeg. I think I found it in the phone book. The office was on McDermot. I would have been eighteen. It was after I made my first film on Super 8, called *Time Killer*, about a person who goes back in time to assassinate someone, and they killed the wrong person and it wrecks the future. I shot it for $118 on Super 8. After making that, I looked around for other people to make films.

Ed Ackerman. Courtesy of Kristen Andrews.

KN: Was *Time Killer* a student film?

EA: No. I had some money left over from something. I learned something important about filmmaking, that if you wear a jacket and look like you know what you're doing, people let you in places. The police were called because of an assassination scene. There was a parking lot on McDermot, across from where Plug In used to be. We had a soldering iron and part of a bicycle pump as a futuristic-looking gun. The police were called. When they saw what we were doing, they were like, hurry up and do what you're doing.

When I walked into the Film Group, I met Leon Johnson. We became friends right away. I hung out and kept going back there. He trained me in recording sound, in '77. I trained for two years in sound recording. In '78, I was nineteen. Leon did everything and then, for six months, I became an interim coordinator. I ran the place, all the equipment in one cupboard. I started the newsletter.

Animated Films

Dave Barber: When did you start working on *Sarah's Dream* [1980]?

EA: Summer '77. I worked at an old folks' home for a summer enrichment program and the idea was to have them doing things. I did film production and made an animated film called *Sarah's Dream*. I took all summer, working with people making the characters and the sets, based on their collective stories. I was accepted to film school at Ryerson; I turned it down to finish the movie. So, I did that at the Winnipeg Film Group, in the back. It was an official Winnipeg Film Group production, that eventually got done in 1980. I finally went to film school, in 1980. The first year at Ryerson, I learned nothing in filmmaking. It was all still photography. I was so pissed off about that, I came back here for the summer. I said, I'm making three films. I was a week and a half late going back to film school because I was finishing *Sarah's Dream*, *5¢ a Copy* [1980], and *Live Studio Sound*—the soundtrack of *Sarah's Dream*.

Ed Ackerman with his Alphabet Car. Courtesy of John Paskievich.

DB: Was the Film Group helpful?

EA: Yes and no. At the Film Group, there's times when it is the most fantastic place to be and also the worst place. It's cyclical, and I'm not sure where it is on the cycle right now. But at times, I'm a star. . . . It's a good place to be if you're from out of town. I think that's true with any cooperative. The problem with filmmakers at the Winnipeg Film Group is the filmmakers themselves. The films are great. If there weren't so many filmmakers around—that's the problem. I think there's a history of development of artistic bureaucracies. They become top-heavy. There's always antagonism that happens all over—in some places, a lot worse. Whatever bureaucracy that existed with the Winnipeg Film Group, it was able to limp along. Sometimes zoom along.

KN: When did you do *Primiti Too Taa*?

Dave Barber, Ed Ackerman, and Antero Lindblad. Courtesy of Winnipeg Film Group.

EA: It was originally done in 1986. The next, IMAX version was 1988. I reshot it all. First, I shot it on a camera I built myself. I borrowed a BD Coleman, a police mugshot camera that takes 70-mm film in a roll. I changed the lens. I made a Styrofoam lens mount. I was able to go close up on this animation. It was 70-mm, with no sprockets, so that if there is wandering sync where the frames were, it would still be okay. I shot a hundred feet—seventeen seconds on a home-built camera. I processed it and got some tests from that to make the IMAX movie. For the IMAX movie, I mortgaged the house for $10,000 and went down to Los Angeles, and I shot it. It was 3,809 sheets of paper.

Bureaucracy versus Art

KN: Lets come back to *5¢ a Copy*. Was it a response to your frustration with administration and the purchase of new photocopier?

EA: The way *5¢ a Copy* came about is, the Film Group was becoming more bureaucratic. Elizabeth Klinck was the coordinator and the Film Group was going to spend $3,000 on a photocopier machine. That was an extremely expensive thing. There was a Canon and a Minolta—we actually had two machines and the Film Group was trying them out side-by-side. We were going to buy one of them. Greg Zbitnew and I were so against the bureaucratization of the Film Group, funds going to office equipment. If we could make a film using it, we'd justify its existence. How could we make a movie using the photocopier? We were testing out the two machines. How can it be used as a filmmaking equipment?

The decision was made to buy the Minolta because the Canon machine quit working because of all the stuff we were doing to it. I'm not sure what killed it. But the Minolta was bought and Elizabeth Klinck said: "From now on, you have to pay for every copy—five cents a copy, in the box. You're having too much fun." It gave us the name of the movie.

We went to Minolta and said, we're making a movie—could you sponsor it? They gave us five thousand sheets of paper, and toner. I think it was $108 for the budget to make the film. We shot a hundred-foot movie, which is the smallest roll of film you can get. It's still a pretty wild movie, but it's an experimental movie we just did to show what you could do with the photocopier. The spirit of the Winnipeg Film Group is about that. There is a contest between bureaucracy and artistic use of things, and it's still a struggle. It's bureaucratic-heavy now.

KN: Did you pour beer onto the photocopier?

EA: It *looks like* we poured beer on the photocopier—but no, we put plastic overtop of it. A lot of that was fake-looking. It wasn't actually beer. It was Windex. The part where it looks like it's rolling waves—no, we did that with plastic. It was a special effect. That looked pretty neat and Greg Zbitnew, in his shooting of it, he repeated that so it looked like

rolling waves. The dart board was amazing, too. We did copies of copies. I did in-camera dissolves, but on a photocopier. One thing faded out, then another fades in. Then you do a copy of the two of them.

KN: Who were the people who you saw coming to the Film Group that were taking risks?

EA: Mike Maryniuk, *Death by Popcorn* [2006]. I thought that was really the spirit of the Film Group—to be *anti* the Film Group a certain amount. You can't just say, okay, I'm with the Film Group, I'm doing this. That's not the Film Group spirit. The spirit is to be antagonistic but also supportive. I mean being true to the art in the long run. John Paizs was one—he was never accepted by the Film Group, but he was doing stuff that lasts and carries on to this day and beyond. But he was really doing his own stuff and didn't really taint himself much with the Film Group. The Film Group doesn't really accept people. The Film Group accepts Guy Maddin, but he is out of town most of the time. I was accepted by the Film Group when I was out of town. *Primiti Too Taa*—oh yeah, he is one of ours. Another award for a Film Group production.

KN: Is this a universal problem, of the local artist not being recognized?

EA: The stuff you make is declared art by the critics and by history. The conflict between making stuff and the bureaucracy that somewhat allows it to happen—that conflict, every co-op has. Successful co-ops are the ones that end up having lasting work that's known years later, in spite of it. Looking at co-ops across the country, Winnipeg has done pretty well for doing stuff that's not bland. When bureaucracy wins, the art is boring. It's one against the other, but you can have no art by either one failing.

Ed Ackerman. Courtesy of Kristen Andrews.

MICHAEL GOTTLI
HEATHER NEALE

GUY MADDIN

Guy Maddin is currently the most acclaimed filmmaker to emerge from the Winnipeg Film Group. He was born in Winnipeg and attended the University of Manitoba. His first film, The Dead Father *(1985), premiered at the Festival of Festivals (today known as* TIFF*), in Toronto. Not long after, his first feature film,* Tales from the Gimli Hospital *(1988), established his auteur style with festivals and critics around the world. Guy's short films and features continue to inspire, his short film* Heart of the World *(2000) and feature documentary* My Winnipeg *(2007) being particularly successful.*

4 JUNE 2016, WINNIPEG

Kevin Nikkel: Thanks a lot for doing this, Guy.

Guy Maddin: Yeah, well, it seems like this is the for-the-record account of the Film Group, so I should be a part of it.

KN: What were the circumstances that attracted you to the world of filmmaking?

GM: Maybe around 1980, I kind of rotated my hemispheres. I'd been an economics major with a math minor and didn't really get goose flesh from either of those subjects. And I suddenly ran into a bunch of people that really influenced me a lot. My long-time best friend, George Toles,

---

Guy Maddin, 1988. Courtesy of Guy Maddin.

who became a screenwriting collaborator with me. Steve Snyder, a film professor at the University of Manitoba. Through them, I met John Paizs, a local filmmaker. Steve had shown me some films he had made in San Francisco. John Paizs showed a film in class—I think it was *The Obsession of Billy Botski* [1980]. I didn't even know that films could be made in Winnipeg. And I didn't know anything about underground film or anything. It was a real exciting eyeopener.

When I first saw a couple of little silent films that Snyder had made, I had a million questions for him. And then, when I saw *Billy Botski*—I can't imagine what my eyeballs would have looked like. They were really bulging out, and I was excited. I went straight up to Paizs afterward and asked him a million questions, and he was very generous with his answers. All of a sudden, it seemed that making a film was extremely possible. I didn't dare dream I could make one as good as him, but I had my own ideas. I'd been reading a lot and had been dreaming a lot about being a writer, but I was a good-enough reader to know I would never be a good-enough writer to enjoy reading my own stuff.

But I saw these films that seemed both primitive and sophisticated at the same time, and had conspicuously used non-professional actors and really stylized performances, and were basically collages of ideas done with panache and style. They were really affective. I just wasn't used to feeling those kinds of effects on film. It was just such an eyeopener to me, and I suddenly realized that maybe instead of writing, as I was so fruitlessly dreaming of doing, that maybe this was the way in—if I could just get some people who knew how to load a camera and point it at some things.

Steve Snyder had shown me Buñuel's film *L'Age d'Or* [1930], his second film with Dalí, and that one also has a certain primitive look to it, a spirit of just being pasted together. Mostly non-actors—except for the male lead, Gaston Modot, is so great. But the film created so much confidence in me that, if I just could take some of my favourite feelings from the page. . . . I'm not talking about making a literary adaptation the way Merchant and Ivory so famously did for so long—or any prestigious literary adaptation. I just wanted to take the effects that books could produce, when metaphors were *just so*. I was really reading a lot of Nabokov, Bruno Schulz, and Rilke in those days, and I wanted to make film versions of their stuff. Their stuff can't be done on film properly because filmmakers are always trying to adapt the wrong aspects of their work. I was just trying to recreate the feelings that those works produced in me rather than the literal storylines, or plot points, or characters, or settings, or anything like that. So, suddenly watching *Billy Botski*, I think, and then re-watching *L'Age d'Or* a million times, I started to dream that someday I'd make film.

I was also starting to hang out with my first male lead, John Harvey, a young law student at the time. I don't even think he was in law yet. He was very charismatic and he, too, had the filmmaking bug. He's one of those people who could, and still can, just spin a confected myth around him, wherever he goes. Whenever he talks, his language is dripping with mythic possibility and everything is alive. He just experiences life with all six senses. He was talking about taking over the sleepy town of Lockport and turning it into Hollywood circa 1912, and I just believed he would do it.[54] And so, we drove around a lot in the back alleys of Lockport and discovered little chapels that you could break into. He had me hypnotized into believing that this little, rural Manitoba town near Winnipeg was going to be the next Hollywood, and that maybe, just five or six years down the road, we would be churning out our version of *Intolerance* [1916]. We'd have different sound stages going all at once. It was based mostly on the fact that it was just sleepy, that it wouldn't know what had hit it, and that it had a lot of abandoned Quonset huts. It just seemed ripe for the rewriting of movie history.

So, all these things intersected in my life at once. I just decided, I need to make films. As I did so often in the beginning, I went to Paizs and asked him how he did things and what should I do? He just told me to join the Winnipeg Film Group. He did say that the chief advantage of doing so was the cheap equipment rates. You join and you pay an up-front fee, and then you get really cheap equipment after that. He didn't really say anything about the community of filmmakers or anything like that.

He seemed really focused on working by himself and the way he worked was *almost* by himself. He had Gerry Klym, his camera operator, and another good friend who helped run the set with him but, other than that, he just made the films by himself. Framed the shots and run around front. And he never moved the camera in the early days—he had it always on a tripod. I saw that as a real strength because I'd seen a lot of Canadian films and they didn't give me the same thrill. It was American-style filmmaking, but not up to snuff. What Paizs had done was really impressive: he had just turned his back on Canadian filmmaking circa 1980, and just made his own. He is an excellent animator and cartoonist. He had just turned his movies into story panels with a tripod locked down. He told me that your best chance of getting a well-framed shot was to carefully compose it beforehand.

So, I became a *tripodista* myself, right off the bat. I guess I was imitating him. I noted that he had very few spoken lines of dialogue in the movies—quite often, a voiceover. One good voice is the most you could hope for, and he was smart enough to get someone who was a professional voice person. It just made sense: hire someone who's got a good voice. I subconsciously filed that away as: that's how you make a movie, here in Canada. That's how you steer yourself clear of all the Burmese tiger traps, that huge crews of Canadian films had been just blithely driving themselves into. It was a sudden ignition of film possibility in my head that really got me going.

I guess now I realize: maybe he just evolved separately, the way platypuses evolved separately down in Australia? He evolved separately, maybe even without being aware of George Kuchar at all—but there's a bit of Kuchar in Paizs. But his big influences, I know from talking to him, were Walt Disney and then some schlock films. He really loved all that stuff. He just didn't want to be influenced by Prairie Realism or any of that stuff—and I decided I didn't either because I never enjoyed watching that stuff. I've since softened my stance on it considerably but, at the time, it was important to have a manifesto, and that manifesto was to ignore everyone else—except John—and just make my own thing.

I was already interested in dreaming bigger things. For some reason, I felt an inner confidence—I've no idea why. I think this is very common among young people picking up cameras: they really feel that the whole world is suddenly revolving around them and that everyone should do them a favour, and even thank them for making the film. There's no other thing—other than maybe a gun—that messes up your ego as much as a camera. But I was holding it and just feeling like the world really needed to watch what I could make with this thing.

Winnipeg Film Group

KN: Talk about what it was like when you first arrived at the Film Group.

GM: By the time I joined the Film Group, it was 1982. It was on Adelaide, in the old house. I went in. I expected it to be a bunch of Winnipeg versions of Stan Brakhage and [James] Broughton. Kenneth Anger, I heard, had been there. I'd just missed him. He'd been there to present some films and discuss things with members. It would've been just the living room of this house [where] Anger sat and visited with local filmmakers. I expected it to be an underground, samizdat kind of organization. A Bolshevik frenzy with people sitting around arguing, spitting saliva at each other in the vituperation of their passion over montage filmmaking versus *caméra-stylo*, or something like that.

I went in and it was pretty quiet. There were a couple of people reading four-year-old magazines. Someone at the desk, trying to figure out how to turn the coffeemaker on, or something like that. I got a membership and was reassured that the rates would be affordable with this membership, and was just sent off. Then I just decided to make a film. It was a matter of borrowing equipment. So, I wore quite a path up and down the stairs of that address on Adelaide—the old house.

I had so poorly planned my first film. I thought I could shoot it in one or two days. After the first night of shooting, I pronounced myself about a half—or a third—done, little realizing that there'd be another fifty days of shooting, or something like that. Not that the film was long. I just had no idea how much time went into making a film. I didn't know anything about the stages that happen after you shoot: editing or sound mixing or colour timing, whatever. I just didn't know about it. I just started shooting and figured I was about done. I didn't know what kind of film to get, or anything. But I just went ahead and did it.

KN: Was the Film Group important to help you navigate this first film?

GM: The Winnipeg Film Group was extremely useful in that they existed, but I didn't take any workshops from them. Even the word *workshop* sends a kind of tsunami of ennui through me somehow. They are obviously very valuable learning experiences—but I don't know. I just like on-the-job training, just being thrown into the fire. I learned a lot by going to the School of Guy Maddin, at which I was the only student. And a series of really ruthless, cruel mistakes were the instructors—especially since I was paying for my first film out of pocket and I didn't have much money. When you make a mistake and it's your own money, you learn.

KN: When you were reading about some of those pockets of film history and art history, were you wondering about the Winnipeg scene and what was available here?

GM: Yeah. The romantic history of the Paris surrealists and all those people—Miró, Dalí, and then Max Ernst—and all those people that worked together, fought against each other, slept with each other, cuckolded each other. Some succeeded, some offed themselves. Some of them were still alive in the early eighties—Buñuel didn't die until 1983. They were all living, or recently deceased, and it was incredibly romantic to me.

I was always tracing my steps through what I figured would be, someday, legendary territory. John Harvey and I formed Extra Large Productions on the very top of Garbage Hill one midnight, almost like it was a Black Mass or something like that.[55] We signed these documents with two total strangers that we found in a bar. We told them not to tell us their names, and they were [our] witnesses. And then we just dropped them off back at the bar again and never saw them again, and can't discern their names on the registration paper—that sort of thing.

KN: I wonder what you think about Winnipeg and the Winnipeg Film Group, and if what's been happening here over these decades is something unique?

GM: Right from the beginning, they were pretty intoxicating atmospheres because I hadn't even made a movie yet. And that's perfect: the movie hadn't even come out all wrong yet, and so I was just walking around in this possibility of perfection—this *certainty* of perfection, as a matter of fact. And everyone around me was becoming co-stars in our collective legend. It was very easy, at the Film Group, to start assigning roles in a mythic cosmos. Those mythic universes are formed of really strange relationships, of people who've had ill-advised relations or really volatile, adversarial relationships, with rivalries.

There was something I'd noticed in starting to watch the older films that John Harvey turned me onto. I realized film—almost more than any other art form—in its industrial haste, film has always discarded its vocabulary units before they were completely exhausted.

But there is something about the way the language of cinema just exploded out of its invention and was fuelled by popular taste. But the decision to go to talking pictures was made and then all the other studios had to do it at the same time. And so, this incredibly rich, yet-to-be-fully-matured silent film language was just abandoned, like a lost city. It was something that was not fully functioning, but still growing. And it really excited me to watch these films and to realize I could just go back and pick up all these—still in perfect working order—vocabulary units and tropes and devices. And really, I could pick and choose. I could leave out the horrible attitudes of any time period and take the ones that excited me, that still seemed modern. I could mix them with my own contemporary attitudes and recontextualize them and do things.

KN: Is there anything that is significant from the early days of the Film Group that has been forgotten?

GM: Yeah, the Film Group has changed a lot since I joined—you know, a third of a century ago. I'll always love the dilapidated old house that it was in first. There's always something lost when you move into more

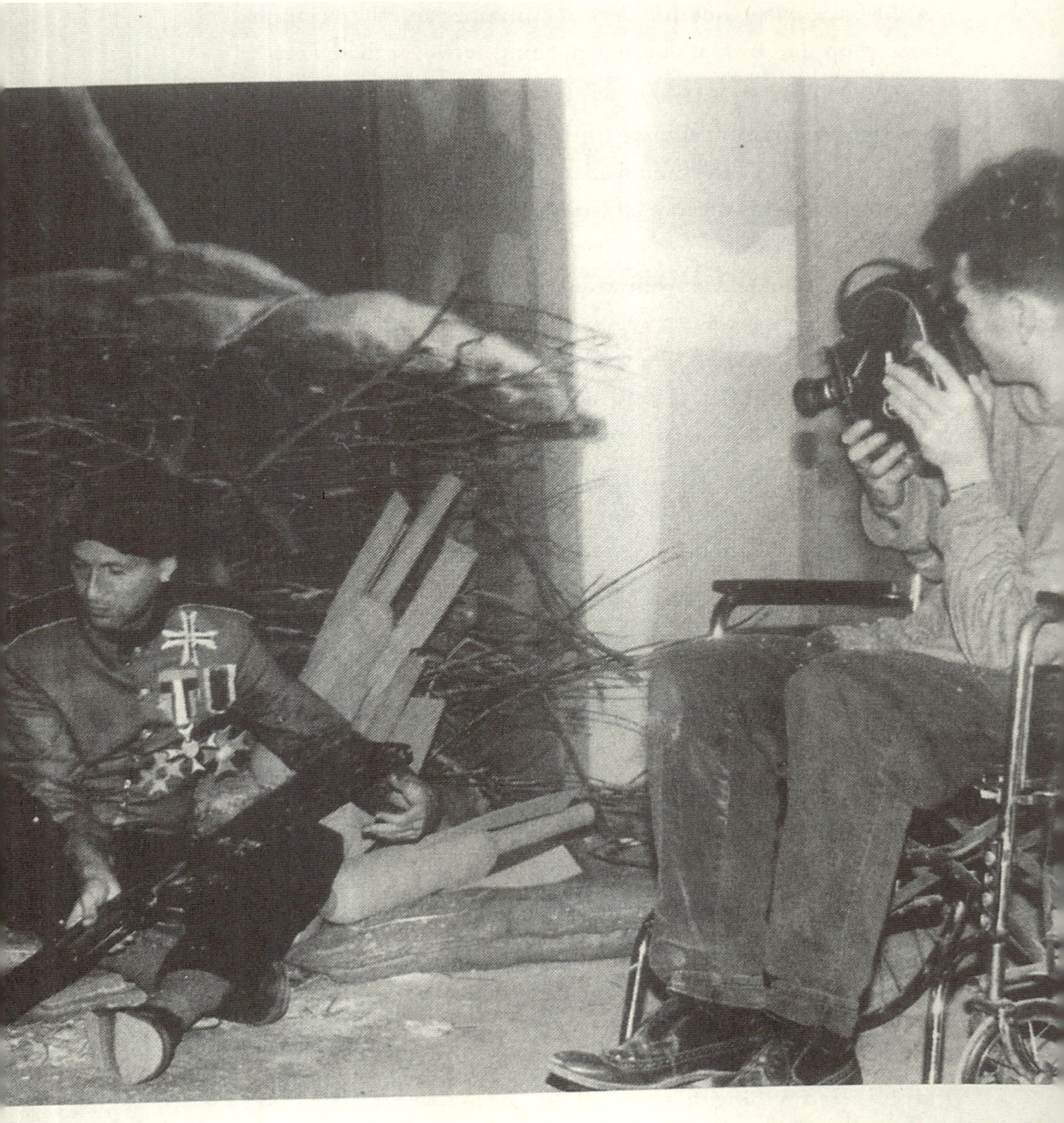

Guy Maddin shooting *Archangel*, 1989. Courtesy of Guy Maddin.

sensible and more modern environs. It certainly wasn't fatal to the Film Group to lose it, and I only made one film—my first film, *The Dead Father* [1985]—at the old joint. But there was something lost—but it's more or less the passage of time that saw some people just give up on filmmaking altogether or move on into other levels of filmmaking, get legitimate jobs in the film industry, or move to other provinces, or just evaporate like people tend to do. I miss a lot of the early people. Some of them, I guess, I've completely forgotten.

I say this about every five years: that we should always be making baseball card collections of Winnipeg Film Group members, so that you can just put them in a shoebox and then, every now and then, pull them out and look at a 1983 Pierre Naday, or a 1991 Patrick Lowe card, or a 1985 Greg Hanec card, or a 1994 Barry Gibson card, and then flip it over and look at the stats. With a little cartoon: "Barry works at a bookstore," or something like that. You'd see his stats, all his filmography, and the running time on them, his height and weight. Maybe it's bilingual. Of course, it smells like gum. We probably should have just been getting Canada Council grants since day one, to get Winnipeg Film Group cards made—and include the cavalcade of receptionists that we've had, and other staff members. It would be a novelist's delight—but I think it would have to be Thomas Pynchon because there's so many characters.

But it's not normal people that are attracted to film co-ops: it's little dreamers, dreamy would-be artists. In some cases, it's little, dreamy, Napoleonic power-hungry bureaucrats. In other cases, it's really worldly-wise, level-headed people that can steer an organization like this—through the grant application process, through a membership growth stage—and it's really interesting to watch those people. I was on the board once, and I'm terrible on boards.

Crisis on the Board

KN: When was that?

GM: The board had Larry Desrochers and Len Pendergast on it. And that was when there had been a horrible mistake somewhere and the Winnipeg Film Group had lost its charitable tax credit status, so it could no longer give tax receipts to donors. We had to get it back, to stand a chance of surviving. And we were also on such thin financial ice.

It was really intriguing, watching two really smart arts administrators. Len had this kind of strategy, like it was time to start wheeling back and throwing long bombs into the end zone, and maybe some flea flickers, some trick plays. Larry said: "Let's just lie down on this thin ice and be as still as possible, and think about it for a while without even moving an inch. If you step back and throw a Hail Mary pass now," he would argue, "you're going to just fall through the ice and that's it." It was really interesting, listening to them argue it out. I slowly came around because I'm by nature very impetuous and would always like to throw the long bombs—but I began to see the slow wisdom, and it was really wonderful watching Larry, who did prevail, in very slowly and carefully piecing together some stability for the group. And I think, by the time he left for the Manitoba Opera Association, he'd gotten the charitable tax number back and worked really hard, filling out a million forms, and got us back into a position where we could start gambling more. But that was really fascinating—just a titanic battle between those two titans. I loved that. Then I quit the board because I knew it would never be as dramatic as that. Things tend to get petty on arts boards. I'm sure arts boards are the same everywhere. It's full of all sorts of Machiavellian intrigues and with so little at stake, and so exhausting.

Dave Barber: You once poked your head in my office, I remember, during a particularly stormy era, and said: "Welcome to Bosnia!" How did you maintain your relationship with the Film Group, in this family of strife?

GM: Well, I always kept myself out of those civil wars at the Winnipeg Film Group. Even though Paizs and I probably had quit talking to each other, I probably still had his attitude of, it's best to just concentrate on your own films and just not worry about what's going on in the office. I was friends with everyone in the office—but God, there'd be someone who would get himself elected to the board by paying people off the sidewalk to come in and vote for him. Then they would attempt to turn this not-for-profit organization into some sort of right-wing, capitalist, moneymaking enterprise. No one's going to make money off of locally produced films from a film co-op. I'm one of the more distributed filmmakers from the Film Group and no one's made any money off me, except through tax write-offs and things like that.

So, there were these weird, misplaced bloody coup attempts frequently, every few years, just when everyone forgot their history. Determinism would cause one of these bloody coup attempts again, and they'd inevitably be quelled. I think even if they'd successfully completed a coup attempt, they would look around at what they'd just taken and realize it was worthless to them, as profit-motivated people. The Film Group is not there to make anyone money; it's there to make some films and to supply services for people who want to make movies and to give them some freedom and teach people stuff. I really like what's going on there now. It seems to have a healthy attitude. It seems to understand itself. I'm sure all the same crazy, self-romanticizing dreams are going on inside every filmmaker's head, but I don't *feel* it when I go in the office. I see sensible approaches. Actually, I'm sure it's just as Balkan as it's ever been.

KN: So, part of the inherent thing in the Film Group, or any arts organization, is this amnesia over time?

GM: I stay out of it. But these kinds of intoxicated administrators can really do a lot. They can kill an organization. The fact that the Film Group still exists—it's survived wave upon wave of these crazy-assed, evil, quixotic types—is amazing. It's testimony to something. It's testimony to probably the foolhardy dream almost everyone has of being a filmmaker. There'll always be someone to sign up, no matter how messed up the organization gets at times. The worst a filmmaker can do is make a boring film that you can just ignore or walk out of.

The Winnipeg Film Group as a Guy Maddin Film

KN: Okay, so if you were going to make a film about the Winnipeg Film Group, as a dramatic film. . . .

GM: As a dramatic film, yeah.

KN: What kinds of scenes would you imagine have to go into the film about the Winnipeg Film Group?

GM: Okay, if I were to make a film—based on a true story—about the Winnipeg Film Group, I think the first thing I'd do is just pull my Euripides off the shelf and just start looking through Greek tragedy plot devices. Maybe read up on the Borgias a little bit. Then I'd also read up on the surrealists and early Hollywood. I would try to infuse the film with as much romantic myth about the feelings created *by creating*. The hope, the intoxication, the self-intoxication—it's mostly self-intoxication. If only you could intoxicate your audience one hundredth as much you intoxicate yourself while making a movie, we'd have some amazing masterpieces on our hands. There'd be a lot of betrayal and love affairs. I don't mean just heteronormative or sexual love affairs—I mean crushes and cults within any group. I guess there'd be elements of *The Godfather* [1972] in it, with alliances and betrayed alliances. And there'd have to be one of those nights of the long knives where all enemies are murdered in their sleep, just to clear things up every now and then. I see the movie of the story of the Winnipeg Film Group—we have to work out a title yet—I see it being a cross between a Metropolitan Opera production of *Electra*, maybe, lots of big expressionist shadows, and you can just sense, off stage, the blood getting ready to drip—but filled with all that sort of early Hollywood romanticism.

KN: In the Film Group melodrama, one scene must begin with Greg Klymkiw walking in?

GM: Enter Greg Klymkiw.

KN: What would that moment look like in your film about the Film Group?

GM: Yeah, we'd have to heighten Greg Klymkiw's entrance considerably. I can't remember the day—I know he always needed a job and he was willing to work hard. But all he had to do was get a normal job or something. I don't know what he was qualified doing. He'd been reviewing movies on radio since he was twelve, or something like that, and then working at a racetrack since he was eleven. He was precocious and he really knew his movies. I don't know how he knew so much about movie history. He got a book of David O. Selznick memos, and he memorized memos. This is all before he was seventeen.

I knew him, but I didn't know he was applying for a job at the Film Group. One day, he just was there—at a desk. I don't even know who he replaced. I think he created a position. He talked himself into it! He had decided that he was going to be a distributor. But he actually was the first Winnipeg Film Group distributor that used long-distance, probably. He was thinking big right away, I'll give him credit. I don't think he himself had travelled much, but he knew that the Toronto Film Festival existed and he built up relationships with everyone there, with a lot of bluster. Greg has so many contrary and mutually incompatible characteristics, just thriving in him and at war with each other, at all times. Wherever he goes, whatever is going on inside him starts happening outside him, and there's a lot of action, a lot of excitement, a lot of agitation. Blood pressures rise to his level, but things happen and things get done.

Tales from the Gimli Hospital

KN: Talk about *Tales from the Gimli Hospital* [1988], with Greg Klymkiw.

GM: I was just working on my second short film, *Tales from the Gimli Hospital*. I was doing my own editing and it just ended up being a lot longer than I'd originally intended. I think I was going to make it fifteen minutes long, and it just kept getting longer and longer. It didn't help I had written a script on three or four Post-it notes and then decided to shoot this thing. Still, to this day, it isn't much longer than a fifteen-minute film. I was a practitioner of cinema-slow, apparently, right off the

bat. The scenes had no conventional drama or suspense. They just had atmosphere and just happened. There was no conventional Hollywood involvement in the narrative for anybody. I showed Greg a cut, which was forty-seven minutes long, and I thought it was finished. I was so relieved and so I chose this friend to share it with because I didn't feel like waiting the two or three months for the neg to get cut and the release print to come out. I just wanted to show it to someone.

I showed it to him and he said something I did not want to hear. He said: "I think you should go back, Guymo"—he's always called me Guymo—"and shoot some more, and make it a feature." And I went: "Oh man, Greg, this thing does not have the structure of a feature. It's barely got the structure of a short. It's just one scene after the other, and you could jumble the order of them and it wouldn't make any difference."

But he convinced me. I thought I'd never be ready to make a feature for another four or five years, or four or five pictures. I was determined, [coming] out of that screening, that I'd emerge on the eve of having made my first feature, years ahead of schedule, thanks to Greg. Then Greg just started acting like not only its distributor but its producer, even though he hadn't been there for most of its shooting. I think I'd already given the producer credit away to Steve Snyder, in exchange for two Salisbury House Nips and two chocolate donuts. He [Greg] got the producer credit. As it turns out, I needed all those credits. To get it up to feature length, I needed about three and a half minutes of end credits. It was a movie that I made basically by myself, so I started to sell credits in the movie.

Greg became a very loyal and ardent champion of *Tales from the Gimli Hospital*. He tried to get it into the Toronto Film Festival, then known as the Toronto Festival of Festivals. My first movie, *The Dead Father*, had already played there in some Canadian shorts program. Geoff Pevere

---

Steve Snyder and Guy Maddin, second day of shooting *The Dead Father*, 1982. Courtesy of Guy Maddin.

was on the jury, and he knew about *The Dead Father* and had said nice things about it. And he really liked *Tales from the Gimli Hospital*, but the other two jury members, who've since become very close friends—Kay Armatage and Piers Handling—said, "This movie is terrible." They may have been right all along. Geoff was sneaking out to a pay phone every now and then, during these jury deliberations, and telling Greg, "I still haven't convinced them that this is intentionally bad. The acting is intentionally primitive." They had voted to just turn it off after a few minutes, but Geoff really championed it. And he's championed me for decades now. So, it was kind of exciting getting these landline jury leaks, but the news finally came out that Pevere had not succeeded in convincing Piers and Kay that the movie deserved to be in the festival. And that was great: I was determined to make my next movie so good that I wouldn't let it play at the Toronto Film Festival. It really fired me up. I'd composed a letter in severe terms, which I wanted to read from a tree stump—if I could find a tree stump in downtown Toronto—full of all the anger that rejected filmmakers are full of, all the time.

Greggy, not to be deterred, just packed a suitcase full of VHS copies of the movie and just, samizdat-style, circulated it and started a rumour himself that this was the best movie at the Toronto Film Festival—which it wasn't. But he did succeed in getting coverage in a film magazine of the Toronto Film Festival. [Greg's rumour mongering] always seemed to lead off with a story about how the best film at the Toronto Film Festival wasn't programmed—it was just circulating on a bootleg VHS tape. So, he was probably the most inventive and ferociously loyal distributor I've ever had, and I've had some beloved distributors. But Greggy was just full of that fire that you can only have at the very beginning of anything.

I obsequiously accepted the invitation of my next film, *Archangel* [1990], to Toronto, which was like, just giving me a lot of rope to hang myself with because the movie was despised by everybody at the Festival. But Greggy got it there—and Greggy and I suffered alone, the two of us, after that screening. Maybe 80 percent of the people walked out and some of the people that remained did so because they were asleep. Then Greg and I just walked that walk of shame that so many filmmakers walk after a premiere. Premieres are not meant to feel good; I didn't know that yet. And I just remember Greg just swearing. The people in front of us and behind us, walking with the flow, didn't recognize us as the filmmakers and they were just complaining about how horribly bored they were and how much they hated the film. Greg was just muttering obscenities—and that guy can coin obscenities. We were really welded together at that point. And we worked together for quite a while after that.

DB: I would start to internalize that and go, oh, maybe I'm no good at this. And yet, you were getting great critical reception, from New York and Paris.

GM: Yeah, it was exceptionally depressing, that first screening of *Archangel*. After premiering *Gimli Hospital*, I'd already vowed never to show a film in Winnipeg at Dave's Cinematheque, as I was treated like a serial killer at the reception afterward. Allen Schinkel, an old filmmaking colleague of mine, asked if he could sit beside me. He always seemed to have ulterior motives. He was part of [the film's] cast of characters, and he came in early. I sat near the exit, in case I had to faint, or barf, or run out, or something, but he made a point of sitting next to me and just crossing and uncrossing his legs and sighing for the entire duration of the movie. God.

People had weak bladders during that movie. The movie was only sixty-eight minutes long, or something like that, but of the hundred people packed into that theatre, everyone went to the bathroom at least three times—I guess maybe just to pound some feeling back into their guts or something. It was horrifying. I got to know the rhythms—of the squeak in the door and the click of the door handle. I memorized it, almost metronomically closing, and a little shaft of light would wash on to the screen with each departure. Occasionally people came back.

I vowed, okay, no more screenings in Winnipeg. And then, after Toronto treated *Archangel* that way, I knew the problem lay with the film, for sure. But then I started to get these really surprising appearances in magazines, months later, with really nice notices, and from writers I didn't know about, but Greg knew: Jonathan Rosenbaum and [Jim] Hoberman, two early champions of my stuff. I'd read this really beautifully written piece that seemed to find something to talk about in the movies and, all of a sudden, that just re-empowered me in an us-versus-them kind of megalomania. But that's the kind of megalomania you need to keep going, when you're making stuff that apparently was increasingly marginalizing me more and more. When you're in the middle of your own history, it's impossible to tell where you're going. You know where you think you're going.

Procrastination

KN: As you're getting this kind of coverage, what's it like at the Film Group?

GM: Yeah, while I was working in 16-mm, I could still work through the Film Group—and I still work at the Film Group, to rent equipment now and then. I need to use the studio. I always had the same quiet confidence. I liked to call it quiet confidence. But I remember John Paizs calling me out on it a few times. He said: "You just have this look on your face, you just have this look." I kind of default to a . . . Scandinavian brooding, but apparently Scandinavian brooding had formed an alloy with a smugness—a smug smirk that needed to be wiped off my face. It's a miracle no one just punched me in the face!

But I became increasingly comfortable around there as a way of procrastinating, which is also one of the major reasons for film co-ops to exist: to provide a venue for procrastination. At one point, John Kozak and I, instead of editing these features we'd each shot, just spent about six months perfecting our ping-pong game in there. I'd literally get up at five in the morning, go in to edit from 6:00 a.m. to noon—and, for a while, I did that. But then, I was just getting up at five in the morning and just playing ping-pong from 6:00 a.m. till 6:00 p.m. or something. I got really good.

KN: So, maybe in the Guy Maddin dramatic film about the Winnipeg Film Group, ping-pong is a very important element. . . .

Still photo from Guy Maddin's *Archangel* (1989). Courtesy of Guy Maddin.

GM: Yeah, no, ping-pong is very important. When I get obsessed with something, I throw myself into it, whole hog. So, I'd become obsessed with film and then I just threw myself into film, and lived and dreamed film, and got up and wrote my dreams down and then filmed them. But then the ping-pong table came in, and I just got obsessed with that instead. Finally, Greg Klymkiw told me, listen, you've got to edit this movie you've been sitting on for six months.

KN: Lay off the ping-pong.

GM: Yeah, lay off the ping-pong. It was not easy, asking someone to give up an obsession. I'm just wondering what other successful endeavours have involved a ping-pong table. Did the Los Alamos project have a ping-pong table in the middle? Would the bomb have been dropped, three years earlier, had it not been for the ping-pong table? Or, if only they'd had a ping-pong table, maybe the bomb would never have been dropped? And, in all seriousness, one of the most horrible tragedies of the twentieth century could have been averted.

PLAYIN
FESTIVAL CINÉMA
20 ANS
SHOW CASE
1999

DAVE BARBER

Dave Barber was the senior programmer for the Winnipeg Film Group Cinematheque from its opening in 1982 until his death in 2021. He worked tirelessly to develop an audience for the works of both emerging and senior Canadian filmmakers. He received several awards for his efforts including the Winnipeg Arts Council's first ever Making a Difference Award in 2007, an Individual Award for Outstanding Support of the Arts in 2004 from the Manitoba Foundation of the Arts, and a Special Jury Award in 1999 at the Blizzard Awards for Outstanding Achievement for contributions to film and video in Manitoba. He created several short films, including the short film Will the Real Dave Barber Please Stand Up? *(2014). Dave also co-directed the documentary history of the Winnipeg Film Group, titled* Tales from the Winnipeg Film Group *(2017).*

11 OCTOBER 2015, WINNIPEG

Kevin Nikkel: Was there any hint you'd end up where you are now?

Dave Barber: I grew up in Winnipeg, but we did a lot of travelling around the world when I was younger. My father taught economics at the University of Manitoba and often went travelling on sabbaticals.

Dave Barber in his Winnipeg Film Group office, Artspace Building. Courtesy of Winnipeg Film Group.

My father took us to the movies and I am quite convinced that going to movies from a very early age was an important influence.

I was always interested in film. I ran a film club at Kelvin High School, in grade ten. I made the posters and sat by the entrance, selling tickets. This was based on finding out how to book films from distributors, as well as the NFB, which were available for rent for free. We showed films from filmmakers such as Arthur Lipsett. So, right from very early on, I've been doing this kind of thing.

I went to the University of Manitoba and took a lot of film courses. I got a BA in psychology with a minor in film. I made a bunch of Super 8 films in my film classes, as opposed to doing essays. I loved editing Super 8 films. I was ruthless in the editing room. I curated some film programs at the University of Manitoba and for the University of Winnipeg. Later, I went back to school to get a communications degree from Red River [now Red River Polytech], and so writing has always been one of my skills as well.

Canadian Film Symposium

KN: What was your first introduction to the Film Group?

DB: When we were students in film studies at the University of Manitoba and made our films, we went down to the old Film Group, in the Bate Building, to premiere them. I think Leon Johnson was the coordinator. I remember it because I brought my projector down one night and turned it on, and the bulb burned out. I had no spare bulb, so I couldn't show my film. I joined the Film Group because they had a great film library of books to borrow. Of course, I quickly realized nobody was really overseeing that library. You could take a book out for a year and nobody would notice.

KN: Who was around?

Dave Barber acting in a Winnipeg Film Group short film. Courtesy of Dave Barber.

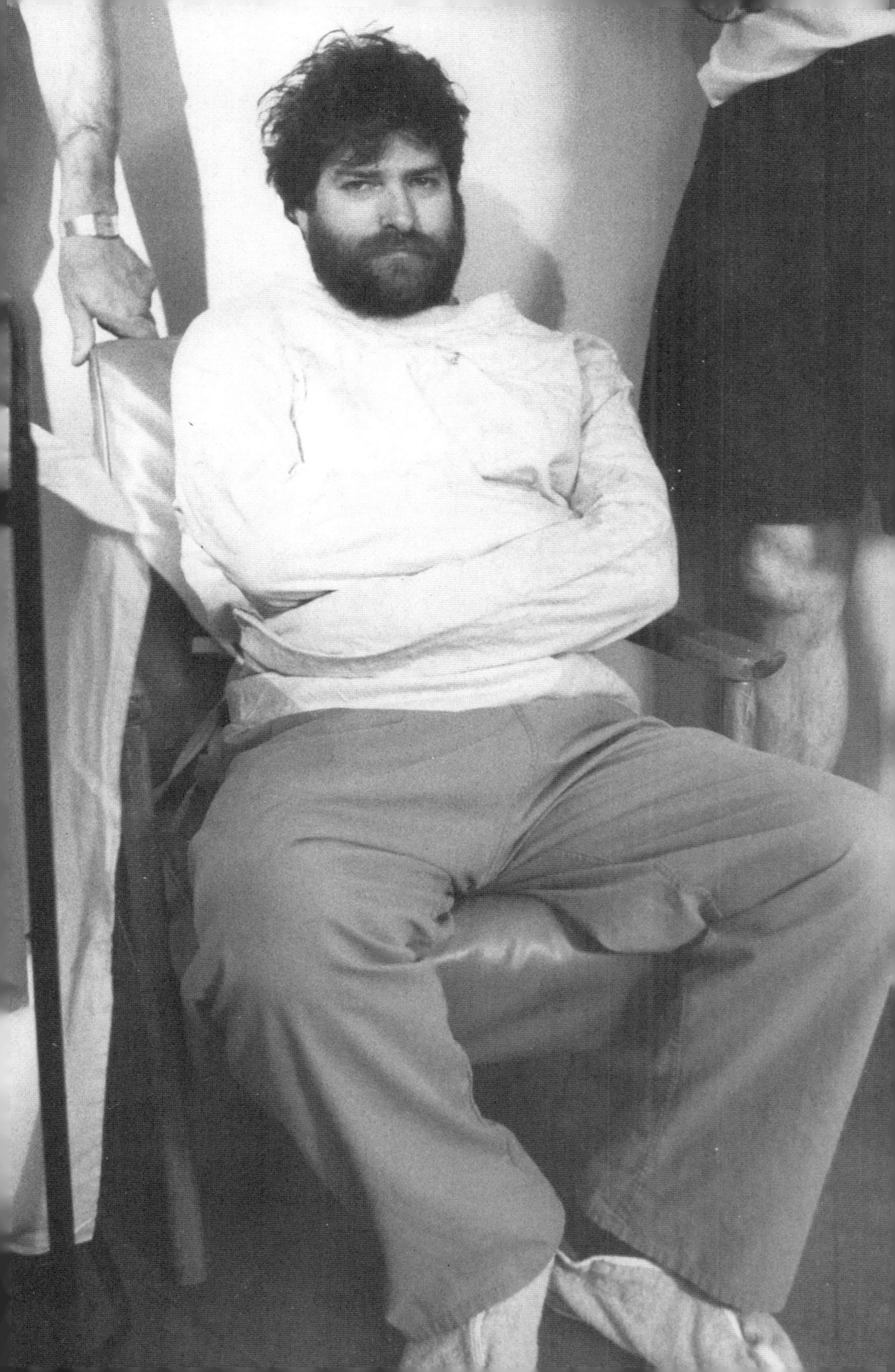

Francis Ford Coppola's
ONE FROM THE HEART

DB: I remember Merit Jensen and Ed Ackerman being in that old office in the Bate Building. I was always aware there was stuff going on in film, in Winnipeg. *The Mourning Suit* [1975], by Leonard Yakir, was shot here, which involved a lot of crew people. Then, at the University of Manitoba, there were some film symposiums that Len Klady organized, where he brought in a lot of Canadian filmmakers. I went to those.

Winnipeg Film Group

KN: What did you do before you ended up at the Winnipeg Film Group?

DB: In the late seventies into the early eighties, I did a number of odd jobs. I worked in a record store for nine months. I worked for a real-estate magazine, writing stories about how to fix up your house—even though I didn't know what I was talking about. Then I went back to school because I decided that writing was one of my best skills. When I graduated from Red River in the summer of '82, a job became open at the Winnipeg Film Group: "Wanted: Part-Time Cinematheque Coordinator."

I thought it was a long shot for me to get the job. I was pretty green. I had a lot of skills in certain areas, but I knew that probably every significant film person in the city was applying to that job and, subsequently, I do know some people who applied. I didn't hear back for a month whether I got the job. I'd long since thought they were not going to hire me. Then they did hire me and I heard, later, that they thought I would work hard. I was a bit astonished! I had to learn a lot. It was a kind of baptism-by-fire for me. It was very stressful.

KN: Tell me about that.

Dave Barber in the Winnipeg Film Group office at 88 Adelaide, 1983. Courtesy of Dave Barber.

DB: When I started at the Film Group, I thought I was walking into a highly structured job. I wasn't. I had to bring my own chair and, I think, a desk. We had meetings. What will we show? What's important? Should we bring in this filmmaker? Should we do this? Meanwhile, we had a very small amount of money and sometimes I would delay paying myself because I'd be terrified we were going to lose a lot of money. Luckily, we never lost enough money.

I quickly realized I could save money if I did the box office. I sat at a card table selling tickets. I sometimes did the projection. I could save money by not paying a projectionist. However, that was a recipe for a nervous breakdown because you're going back at night to do projection, you're there in the daytime to program films, and then you're selling tickets. I did it myself to save money, probably for a year or two. Then I did it, as well, when we went to 35-mm. It is a very stressful job, doing projection, if something goes wrong. After a while, we started to hire somebody to be projectionist.

KN: What was it like for you in the house on Adelaide?

DB: I thought it was great because I had an office upstairs, with a window. It was located in this old historic house, on 88 Adelaide Street. They had a screening booth on the main floor. I think Ed Ackerman helped wire the projection booth in the living room. They would screen films right in the living room and filmmakers loved it because it was a home.

A young Guy Maddin would wander in and out; he was working on *The Dead Father* [1985]. There was a Steenbeck editing machine upstairs. John Paizs was working on stuff. John Kozak, Greg Hanec, and John Paskievich would wander in and out to get equipment, and then they'd notice I was there and then we started talking. Norma Bailey was around. The Markiw brothers were quite active making films. They made a feature, *Mob Story* [1989], and some shorts. Allen Schinkel, and a few others.

I remember I once asked Leon Johnson: "How do you get into the equipment room?" He said: "Simple! You just reach up, take these hinges off, and climb in over the top." He was showing me how to break into the equipment room to take out equipment, which I thought was pretty funny.

Local Cinema Culture

KN: Tell me about the timing of the creation of the NFB theatre.

DB: We used the National Film Board's Cinema Main theatre on weekends. It was very important access to a screen because we had a theatre with seats and the projection booth. So, had we not had that theatre, the question becomes: where would you show our films? So, that was very important. I kept worrying that maybe they'd say, "You can't use the theatre anymore." I remember them criticizing me because I would put up posters all over the walls and they said I made it look like a church basement.

KN: You're in the middle of Winnipeg, on the prairies, far away from other centres.

DB: Basically, we would see how films would do. We'd set up an experimental series. There were a lot of significant filmmakers, like Michael Snow, David Rimmer, Patricia Gruben, Kay Armatage, and Chris Gallagher. We screened those on Tuesday nights and we started to get an audience. I started to learn a lot about marketing and about how the press perceived things. The fact that I was in a cooperative of filmmakers slowly became very important to me, when we screened their work. How important it was to them—because there wasn't any place to screen their work! So, as years passed, you could see the impact on their careers.

The Cinematheque

KN: Did you have freedom to pursue some of your own ideas in those years?

DB: Yes. The thing that I did the most was show a diversity of films—documentaries, shorts, animation, older classic films. I've always mixed

Cinematheque in the Artspace building lobby. Courtesy of Dave Barber.

it up. We did incredibly well with early Buster Keaton and Charlie Chaplin. We'd get a huge range of audience members from very young to very old. I remember being astonished one night, when we were showing a very obscure film by a silent comedian, and the attendance went through the roof. I thought, these people have never seen this film before but they know they're going to laugh and have a great time. I thought, this is great!

Some films did well. Some didn't. But there's so many films that never get proper distribution or proper marketing, and that was always the purpose we served. That was very important to me because what we did had meaning.

KN: These were formative years for you.

DB: Absolutely. I quickly learned how much work was involved in programming and running a theatre. You can never be complacent. You're constantly multitasking. You're constantly worrying about the money, programming, marketing, and technical problems with the equipment. I would jump between all these areas and I quite enjoyed it. It was great! And I think I did turn it into an obsession. Luckily, people felt I was doing a good job, so I stayed.

When I started, Bruce McManus, a playwright, was working part-time as a distributor. He was always worrying all the time, but he had a great sense of humour. I'll never forget once, after I'd just started, he wrote up a pink memo slip, that I have somewhere, that said: "Good luck tonight on your first screening. Remember, Gandhi's cool in all circumstances. Otherwise, there's razor blades in my drawer."

KN: And there were people that weren't exactly getting along?

DB: There was always tension. When I started, I walked in and I saw a lot of disagreements all the time, with filmmakers. Filmmakers are very bullheaded, very strong-minded. All they care about is making independent film. They'll walk into a room, grab whatever's around, and put it in the film. There was an old moose head in my office, which disappeared because somebody put it in their film. I always admired the independent streak of filmmakers.

I don't know if I did this consciously but I was moulding the Cinematheque around the Film Group, to serve the needs of the Film Group members. There are often tensions between independent theatres and independent filmmaker organizations. There's a lot of things I've done in programming that a lot of theatres would never do, like showing short films or running an independent filmmaker's film for a few days—or give it a serious marketing effort. We would get reviews because we would nurture the reviewers in the papers. And we would get reviews. That was very important.

Winnipeg Film Group Members

KN: Do you remember when the media first really started to pay attention, not just to the films but the Film Group itself?

DB: The reviews were often focused on individual films. I'd say the Film Group got put on the map by people like John Paizs and Guy Maddin. Their work didn't look like anything else that anyone had ever seen before. John Paizs's films had a strong influence from pop culture and they didn't resemble other Canadian films. It got noticed in larger cities like Toronto. But there are also people like Richard Condie, who had crazy animation, and that again puts a mark on it. He was on the board of the Film Group in the early days, although he graduated over to making films at the Film Board. That brought the media. Something is going on in Winnipeg. There is something in the water, or something strange or funny going on. Although, not all filmmakers like to be lumped in with making wacky, crazy films. There were serious dramatic films or documentaries, by filmmakers like Elise Swerhone and John Kozak.

But people would come and go. Somebody would hang around the Film Group for a year or two, make a short film, decide that it wasn't for them, and then disappear. Others would slowly develop a career. It's amazing to me how very few people consistently built their careers because it's such a tough thing to do—to survive as an independent filmmaker and make a career at it. To get paid for it. You always have to have a sideline that you're doing. And you're always trying to find money to make your film. I look back, now, at all the filmmakers that I know and there's not lots I can think of that made a huge career out of it.

KN: I totally agree because I'm living that life. It hasn't gotten easier. Was the era at the house on Adelaide unique?

DB: People loved it because it was a house. You're in a home—it was very important to why people gravitated to it. People would come in to use equipment and go up, upstairs. You'd have a party and lots of people in the arts community would come to that party. I'll never forget: once, I came in to work on a Saturday and there had been a party that went until five or six in the morning. I opened the door. The floor was covered with cigarette butts and beer bottles. I went, my God! So, I had to clean up some of that because nobody likes the cleanup after a party.

KN: Did John Paizs and his films mark a threshold for recognition, when his films went to Toronto?

DB: I think his films are very important because people said, wow, we've never seen anything like this before! Where did he come from? He came from Winnipeg? Where was he making his films? Where was he getting equipment? The Winnipeg Film Group name came up and then distribution became very important. Distribution sent films out to festivals, where they started getting noticed—and there was a tour of Winnipeg Film Group films. The films just did not look like films from other cities. I remember Shawna Dempsey and Lorri Millan's film *We're Talking Vulva* [1990] was on a tour and—wow! There is a great, original work that doesn't look like anything else! But also, Winnipeg generally became important as a . . . place for independent art. Richard Condie, who was involved in the early days of the Film Group, graduated to the Film Board but was still doing original work. I think the Film Group benefitted from that.

But what astonished me about John Paizs was, when I first met him, he was quiet, mild-mannered, but he would pore over a cinematographer's manual. He was quite meticulous on how to frame things. He shot some

CINEMATHEQUE

of *Crime Wave* [1985] inside the Adelaide house and just a block or two away from the house. I remember observing him on shoots and I was astonished at his resourcefulness. One example would be, one day, he came in with some white shirts and some suits. He grabbed everyone in the office and dressed them up, but he didn't have enough white shirts. I didn't have a shirt. He grabbed a white piece of paper, shoved it up my arm, and then that becomes a white shirt in a scene in *Crime Wave*, where mob-type guys are shaking hands. That's resourcefulness: when you don't have enough money to do things, you invent things.

KN: Did you feel like you were treated as an outsider, as you weren't initially an artist? You are a filmmaker too, but more recently.

DB: I don't think so—because I'm a very friendly person. I didn't know any of these people when I started. I would talk to them when they'd come upstairs. We'd yack about their films or whatever. I got to know them and we would set up a premiere. I was like a friendly face in some ways. I had an ideal position in that I wasn't an authority over them. I wasn't renting equipment. I didn't have to yell at them if they hadn't paid their bill or whatever. So, I'm in an ideal situation, when you think about it. I'm showing their work—of course they're going to be happy.

Artspace

KN: Tell me about the move into Artspace.

DB: It was a very stressful time period for me personally because a lot of the responsibility for designing parts of the theatre fell on my shoulders. I wasn't really articulate enough to go to the board and say, look, this is crazy—I don't have time to be researching how to build a theatre! What I would do is I'd run down to a company called General Sound, that had technicians who would repair theatres. I'd pick their brains. Then I'd say:

Dave Barber with the Dave Barber Cinematheque shirt. Courtesy of Winnipeg Film Group.

"What's important in a theatre? What's important in the sound system?" I'd write all this down and go back. Then there was an architect attached to the Artspace project, and I would give it to him and say, here—here is what to do.

There was one day where I had to meet with the person installing the sound system, the person putting in the chairs, the person putting in the screen—who all had impossible time schedules—and, all the while I was doing this, I wasn't feeling well. I thought it was the flu. I went to a walk-in clinic, who give me some pills. I went back home, felt weaker and weaker, and then I realized something must be wrong. I phoned the hospital. I said, this didn't seem right that I have the flu and am feeling weaker and weaker and weaker. Eventually, I passed out. I was lying on my kitchen floor and I grabbed the telephone and I phoned an ambulance. It turned out I had a bleeding ulcer. The ambulance went racing down to the Misericordia Hospital and it turns out I had lost ten units of blood. Here I was, trying to be at the Artspace building meeting with these people, and meanwhile I should've been in the hospital because I'd been losing blood. I was in the hospital for about three weeks. I thought, should I go back to this job? I just went through a very stressful experience. But before long—ha ha!—I was meeting with the person who did our posters from my hospital bed and working on the program guide. It's crazy.

KN: Were there any other stressful times at the Film Group?

DB: Twice, over the years, people have tried to fire me. I came in one day and there, sitting in a typewriter, was a letter basically saying: "Dave Barber, we just hired him. It's not working out. I think we should let him go." I thought, here I am working myself to death to keep this thing alive and I'm reading a letter saying I shouldn't be there anymore. This board member was phoning up other board members and saying "The others agree we should let Dave go." Then the board started talking amongst themselves and discovered that what he said wasn't true. The board met and decided that, no, we think he's doing a pretty good job and we're not going to let him go. Had it not been for other people supporting me, I might not have been here.

KN: How did things grow, with the move to Artspace?

DB: Once the Film Group moved into Artspace there was a definite place, with the theatre. Distribution grew a lot. The Film Group got more equipment—all of that became very important. In the early days, it was all more ramshackle. There wasn't as many staff, so the identity was not as strong. The body of work grew, over the years. The reviews of people's work grew, over the years. Films got into film festivals—this all became very important. There wasn't a huge body of work at the Film Group, at 88 Adelaide Street—there were only a few films on a shelf. It's hard to conceive of that now because we have so many films now in distribution; but back then, there was barely any.

It is a very difficult thing, I feel, that we are doing. It is something very complex, that's changed radically over the years. There were time periods where the technology changed radically and we had to adapt with new technology or we would not have survived. I can't take credit for the person who went out and did the fundraising [or who brought in the] equipment to go from 16-mm to 35-mm equipment. Then 35-mm became outdated, with the rise of digital projection. Somehow, we have to keep this thing alive through all that. That's tremendously difficult. I feel I have some good skills in that area. I have been helped tremendously by executive directors and staff.

I'm pretty proud of the fact that we've shown a lot of Canadian films and a lot of Winnipeg films. And a diversity of shorts and animation. It's very eclectic programming. And a highlight on Winnipeg Film Group films—that's not something, when I started, that I consciously was doing. It only came later because I could see the importance of showing work to people's careers.

KN: Filmmakers across Canada thank you!

JOHN KOZAK

John Kozak studied film at the University of Manitoba and New York University. An active member of the Film Group for many years, he sat on the board and made several dramatic films. John teaches film production at the University of Winnipeg.

1 SEPTEMBER 2016, WINNIPEG

Dave Barber: How did you get interested in film?

John Kozak: I was a latecomer to being interested in movies. As a kid, my interest in movies was pretty pedestrian. I just saw the Hollywood blockbusters from the 1960s: *The Battle of the Bulge* [1965], *The Great Escape* [1963], and James Bond films. For some reason, when I was in high school, in grade eleven, myself and some of my friends were talking about a Fellini film being screened in the multipurpose room at the University of Manitoba. Probably my brother had seen it. A friend of mine and I decided to take the bus to the U of M and watch it. We got there and it was packed. We couldn't get in. They announced they were going to have a second show at 11:00 p.m. My friend said, "I'm going home." But for some reason, I stayed—I don't know why. *Satyricon* [1969] blew my mind. I had no idea that films like that could exist. I was just sitting there, stunned. After that, I started to investigate. I started

---

John Kozak, 1989. Courtesy of John Kozak.

going to the Park Theatre and seeing Buñuel films and Bergman films. I was the perfect age. I was probably seventeen—it's when you're really inquisitive and you want to learn new things. I became fascinated with foreign films: Kurosawa, Bertolucci, whatever I could find.

I heard about this film program at the U of M. I figured, well, maybe I could make films, learn something about films, and watch films. Suddenly, I was a fan. So, I started taking Art of the Film, in 1973–74. We saw all sorts of great films. This segues into the Film Group—I didn't know about the Film Group being formed, in 1974. I wasn't part of the original ten members that formed it, but, in '75, I was taking a course from Frederick Edell. You were in it too, I think, Dave. You were allowed to make a film and the screening was in the Bate Building, the first Film Group location, and that's when I first found out about the Film Group. I went to that screening and we showed our films that we made that year.

I was introduced to the Film Group. This is fantastic—they make films here! You can join. You can make movies. So, the next day, or the Monday [after the Bate Building event], I phoned the Film Group and said I wanted to join. And they said: "Sorry, we're full." "Oh?" "Yeah, we're not taking any more members. We're all full." Click. And that was my first introduction to the Film Group. So, for the next two years, I didn't go there.

It wasn't until I started working at the Film Group, when Leon hired me to do that summer job—they were investigating, cataloguing, and charting archival film shot in Manitoba—that I asked Leon about that. I said, "You know, I tried to join two years ago and somebody said that you were full." He laughed and he said: "Well, that's ridiculous. It was probably just some clown picked up the phone when you called and thought they were being funny." So, I finally did join.

Kevin Nikkel: Tell me about this history project.

JK: The summer job was me and Marie Buchok—she was Roman Buchok's wife. Roman Buchok, of course, was a filmmaker and assistant

John Paizs and John Kozak. Courtesy of Dave Barber.

Howard Curle with Super 8 camera and John Kozak, 1976. Courtesy of John Kozak.

director for many years. Leon had gotten some money from some government initiative, and he created this job where we would go around, all over Manitoba, and we would seek out any old footage shot about Manitoba prior to the 1950s, the thirties, forties. We found original footage that showed the building of the Port of Churchill. We found footage of the first hip surgery operation of a certain type ever performed, at the U of M. Other stuff like that, too.

The problem was, when we found this footage, our job was just to catalogue it: here's where the footage is, here's what it is, here's when it was shot. And here's who currently owns it, here's the contact info. But most of them insisted: Here, take it! But we had no setup for it. We took it, when they insisted we take it, because I figured, well, it will be stored at the Film Group. And it was, for decades. But it's gone—the footage went missing one day.

KN: Wow. That Churchill footage?

JK: It's probably one-of-a-kind. Gone now—obviously.

DB: That should've gone to the archives.

JK: I have no idea. I left the job and I left the city. I was in New York for three years. I know that David Demchuk was taking over that, and was trying to keep working on the job. When I came back, though, I know the footage still existed because somebody pointed it out to me. It was in that room that was basically just a dump closet for years, up on the third floor in the Artspace building. And somebody said, this is all that footage. This would have been '92, '93, or something like that. And then, one day, that room was empty and turned into something else. What happened to all those boxes, nobody knew. That's how it happens. Unfortunately, all our records were gone, too. All the notes we took and everything we created. A catalogue of where the footage was and who had it—that's all gone, too.

KN: You didn't come across any reference to James Freer? He shot the first film in Canada, in the 1890s in Brandon.

JK: We didn't come across that—a lost film, obviously. There could still be stuff out there that exists in people's basements, in their attics—that's all possible. We did take trips and I know we did drive out to various places. There was a guy—I can't remember his name—who worked in the film industry in Winnipeg and in Montreal for many years, and he retired to West Hawk Lake. And we found him. He worked with John Grierson. It was detective work and we finally tracked him down because his name kept coming up in some of this old footage that we were seeing. All he talked about was John Grierson and his socks. He said: "You know, the man never changed his socks. He would come in one day and I would say, 'John, are those the same socks you were wearing yesterday?'" We didn't get very much, but he had some films.

The other thing I remember from that job was answering the phones because the Film Group at the time shared the same phone number, except for the last digit—or the last two digits were reversed—with the

Crew of John Kozak's short film *Dory*, 1989. Courtesy of John Kozak.

Venus Massage Parlour. And so, 90 percent of the calls that came into the Film Group were somebody asking how much we charge for a massage.

DB: So, you made some Super 8 films at the U of M and then went to New York.

JK: One of the things I liked about the U of M: it was film studies. They didn't have filmmaking classes, but most of the instructors there would allow a student to make a film in lieu of an essay. So, in Art of the Film, we made films. In Film Comedy (that was Gene Walz's class—you were probably in that class, Dave), Howard [Curle] and I made *Two Men in Search of a Plot* [1985] in that class. By third year, I was investigating graduate studies for film. There still wasn't a lot of a real industry base in Winnipeg and there wasn't a lot of training. The Film Group wasn't doing much. There was no Manitoba Film and Sound, no Film Training Manitoba—none of those things existed. So, if you were going to get more training, you were going to go somewhere else. For some reason, I selected NYU as the best bet. Surprisingly, got in.

DB: And you took film production there?

JK: Yeah, film production.

KN: What was it like, going from a small city to the big city? Being a Winnipegger?

JK: When you're twenty, it doesn't mean anything. You know you want to travel and you want to see things. I didn't get a sense of culture shock. I was talking about films and making films with fellow students at the U of M, and that's what I was doing in New York. There was more going on in New York. There were more theatres that showed old films. Here, we had the Park, the Highland, the Kings, Cinema Three—they were bringing in some old, classic comedy films and foreign films. But in New York, there were more.

KN: During this time, were you thinking about coming back to Winnipeg?

JK: I'm not exactly sure. I was keeping my options open and saying, let's see what happens. I did stay in New York on a student visa, and the student visas had dates . . . and you're there to go to school and you're not supposed to work, etc. I know, in my last year, I stayed in New York long enough to get a letter from the Department of Immigration that said, get out! My options were given to me. I did have to come back [to Winnipeg].

But I came back, and it's not like I felt bad about it. I thought, let's see what's going on here. When I did get back, there was more going on. The NFB had more of a presence in Winnipeg in '81 than they did in '76. They started doing a lot of stuff: they were making feature films, they moved to Main Street, and they had the theatre. Everybody was talking about making movies here.

DB: Did you go back to the Winnipeg Film Group?

Winnipeg Film Group

JK: Sure, I went to the Film Group in '81. I joined the board. I got more involved. I started putting out the newsletter.

DB: Did you see many changes?

JK: There were more members. There were more people around—it was busier. They were still in the Bate Building, but they had to move because, I think, they'd expanded too much. They'd gotten more equipment. They just got a Steenbeck. There was no place to put this stuff. Now, moving to Adelaide was a great thing. The house gave the Film Group an incredible profile, not just in the arts community but in the city. That building became known. It was kind of known to people: this is where the film guys hang out. This is where film stuff is happening. And our membership expanded drastically, between '81 and, say, '86.

Also, we were inspired because there was more funding: there were agencies talking about funding local filmmaking. A lot more people were joining the Film Group. There was more equipment. That's when people were saying, hey, I'm going to make a feature too. I'm going to make a low-budget feature. And, one after another, filmmakers started making low-budget 16-mm features—which, prior to that, I think people would not have thought that. That would be foolish. You're dreaming! You can't do that; or, we're not in that league.

DB: What sparked that?

JK: It was a number of things. There is no doubt that Paizs had an influence—or, if nothing else, his successes encouraged people. People like Paizs came along—and it's not so much because of what he did, but he was just so determined. He would just come in and work every day and had no doubt in his mind that this is what he's going to accomplish. *Billy Botski* [1980], it's a good film and it inspired people. It's not like one of those things where it's a low-budget film made by local people in Winnipeg, and you excuse it and say, it's not bad for where it was made. It was a *good* film—good enough to hold its own anywhere. So, people started to be a little bit inspired by that.

KN: And features like Greg Hanec's *Downtime*?

JK: They were all happening around the same time. I think *Crime Wave* [1985], *Downtime* [1985], Laurence Mardon's *Marquis de Sade* film [*The Sad Fate of the Girl, Justine, at the Hands of the Marquis de Sade*, 1989], and my film *Celestial Matter* [1988]—everybody was making their feature around the same time: '85, '86. So, everybody's kind of inspired at the same time. It actually helped. We talked to each other. Nobody was competing. Everybody wanted each other to be successful in their venture. Guy Maddin at the same time, too. I think *Gimli Hospital* [1988] was right around that time, too. It was a new attitude: sure, we can do this. Why not?

KN: Was there enough funding to go around?

JK: Well, there's *never* enough funding to go around, anywhere, ever. It's an attitude thing: if you want to do it, you make it happen. You look around at what the resources are and you say, well, these are my resources. This is what I want—I want to make this happen. You just do it. When it doesn't happen, I guess there's just not the will. So, I guess it kind of goes in waves. Even in the bad times, somebody always finds a way.

SHEREEN JERRETT

Shereen Jerrett is a Winnipeg-based filmmaker and educator. She has taught filmmaking at the University of Winnipeg and the University of Manitoba, and is active as a showrunner. Shereen is a regular contributor to workshops at the Winnipeg Film Group and is a past chair of its board.

23 APRIL 2017, WINNIPEG

Kevin Nikkel: How did you stumble into filmmaking?

Shereen Jerrett: Well, my dad would say it runs in the family, but I never knew my grandfather. My grandfather was a photographer and he shot little, tiny films. My father, rebelling against his father, never touched a camera. We didn't really grow up with a lot of family photos and movies or anything; we just sort of knew Granddad took pictures.

I was going to be an animator. I could draw and was interested in theatre and puppetry. It wasn't until grade eleven, I took Dave Dueck's filmmaking course. It just seemed to me to be the perfect synthesis of drawing, theatre, and photography. Everything just came together so beautifully for me in film that I thought, oh, this is what I want to do. Dave Dueck saw how enthused I was and said: "You should join the Winnipeg Film Group." I was seventeen. He took me down to the Film Group to sign up.

Shereen Jerrett on location, shooting for her short film *Horsewomen*, 1989.

Back then, you had to get approved by the board—it was a co-op. You had to apply and you had to prove that you were going to contribute back into the co-op. The idea was: what you took out of the Film Group, you'd put back into it.

Winnipeg Film Group

Dave Barber: Was that the Bate Building?

SJ: Yeah, it was on the second floor of the Bate Building. Merit [Jensen Carr] was the coordinator. Bruce McManus was the distribution person. They needed a summer intern and they offered it to me. That was the summer they got that first Steenbeck, the bright-blue one. I remember the day that arrived. I see that now—I go in and I'm so nostalgic about it. I take pictures of it.

KN: What's your first impression?

SJ: I remember Merit so well. She was so kind to me. Actually, everybody was really sweet to me. I remember John Paizs coming in, making his movies. We used to talk. I remember Merit—she drove me home one day. She said: "I was thinking of starting a cinematheque. I'm trying to think of a good name. We could call it 'Cinematheque,' but I think we can think of a better name." We both sat there and thought for a few minutes. And then she said: "You know, I've always loved the Dew Drop Inn. But I don't think that would work for a cinema." She kept driving. And it's the Cinematheque. That was my moment—I could have named it, if I'd thought of something else. In all those years, I've never thought of a better name for the cinema.

But that summer, I just remember knowing fucking nothing. I'm working for the Film Group—I had no idea what was going on or anything about filmmaking. But we watched all the movies, Saul Henteleff and I. Saul

---

Shereen Jerrett. Courtesy of Shereen Jerrett.

worked in distribution as a summer student. I worked for Merit as a summer student.

Meeting Leon, the Markiw brothers, John Paizs, Greg Hanec. Doug Culliford was starting on *Blown Ice* [1987] back then. I remember all these people just coming in through the doors. Elise Swerhone and Robert Lower were on the board. They just seemed so knowledgeable to me.

John Paizs

I remember John Paizs walked in and said: "I want to make movies the way I want to make them. I have this vision of a movie." At the time, other members of the Film Group were saying, you can't do it that way. You can't make movies like that. You can't make these wild visions. John just had this fuck-you attitude. He created these weird little worlds. He explored how to use miniatures, rear-screen projection, and paint on glass. He was just like, yes, you can do it! He was full of all sorts of pithy sayings like: "Cinematography is all about the lighting first." And he always said: "Never, ever neglect your credit sequences because it will make your film really professional." His cockiness was infectious.

People like Leon, Bob, Elise, Len, and John Kozak brought this work ethic and this sense of co-operative filmmaking. They're the ones that just had a real belief in the community. John Paizs brought in that cocky auteur attitude: "We can do it." There's nothing stopping us. I think he pissed people off, but he also balanced them out. He brought in a certain sense of independent flair, cheek, and daring that is a hallmark of the Film Group now.

First Film Fund

KN: There must have been, then, tension between the administration the filmmakers?

SJ: Oh, the filmmakers *were* the administration back then, so it was a discussion of ideals all the time, definitely. People would discuss what kind of films we should be making and how they should be used. I was part of the first group to receive the First Film Fund. It's an amazing program. You had to apply and it was rigorous. You had an intensive interview, where you had to justify your script and your treatment, and explain why this is a worthwhile film to be made. I don't know—is it as rigorous now? I'm not sure.

KN: When I got the First Film Fund, there was still an interview. But I don't think that continued.

SJ: The whole logic was that you weren't experienced enough to write a proposal that would make sense. They had to talk to you. I think it was good. I did *The Waltz* [1985]. Actually, it was Merit who started me off making movies. She always pushed me to the next level. Merit said: "You know, we have this new program called the First Film Fund. You should apply for it." So, I did. I wanted to set it in a period and I remember them asking me: "Do you have to do it that way?" And—classic stubborn filmmaker—I said: "Yes! Yes, I must!"

This was the Film Group, back then. The co-operative feeling was so amazing. I can't believe how kind people were to this nineteen-year-old kid that was just saying, "I want to make movies." Ian Elkin shot it and he said: "Well, what camera were you going to use?" And I was like, "Well, I was going to use the Film Group camera." "We'll use mine. It's a better camera—and I just bought a new lens," he said. "It makes it look like 35 [mm]." So, he brought in his beautiful camera to shoot with, with his own lens package. And then he said: "Well, how much film do you have? Two rolls? Oh, that's not enough. I have some short ends. We'll just keep shooting until you get what you need." And that's how I shot my first film. Remarkable kindness!

Ian, at the time, was Winnipeg's best cinematographer. That he would give everything to this kid that didn't know what she was doing was really amazing. Again, I think that's very much the roots of the Winnipeg Film

Group. That original group of people that was making movies all had that sense of "give it back, pay it forward."

It was all volunteer. They ran the Film Group and made their movies. And they taught all the workshops. It's funny that even from back then, I still have that sense that I owe the Film Group: I take from, I give back to. If I have the time, I'll still teach workshops. I'll still come in and help out. I did decades of dedicated service to the Film Group. I also chaired that board at least two to three years.

KN: Was it different, with the move to the Adelaide house?

SJ: It's funny how my history of the Film Group goes building to building. I started out, at seventeen, in the Bate Building, as a summer student. And then, I really learned to be a filmmaker in the building on Adelaide. I cut my first film upstairs, in the Steenbeck room. I remember getting my print back on my first film the night of a Film Group party. I'm holding the can in my hands, walking around saying: "See my new film, see my new film, look at my new film!" And Ed Ackerman said: "Congratulations! You've done your first film. Now you're going to spend the rest of your life trying to make a good one." And I'll never forget him saying that. It was true. He was right.

So many stories about that fucking house on Adelaide. They had amazing parties, back then. They used to have members' screening night. We still sort of do, but back then it was so raw because everything was spliced-together film and it was really hard to screen anything. Rough cuts would fall apart in the projector and people would spend so much money just to get that stupid thing to a point where you could actually screen it. Back then, film was so expensive.

The Board

KN: How did things change, with the move to Artspace, for your filmmaking?

SJ: I made my first film at Adelaide. Then we moved to the Artspace building. I couldn't get any traction to get a second film off the ground. I'm at this party and I'm talking to Grant Guy, and said: "Grant, I can't get any money to make another movie. I don't know what I'm doing." He said, "Well, you want the truth?" I said, "Yeah, absolutely." And he said: "Well, you're short, you have a squeaky voice, and you laugh a lot. Everyone thinks you're a flake. You have to get out there and volunteer, and show people you have a brain." And I'm, like: "Okay!" And that's how I got on the board of the Film Group.

KN: Talk about that experience.

SJ: I got on the board of the Film Group and then worked my way up to chair—and that was amazing. Omigod, I really did discover a lot about myself—and *Robert's Rules of Order*. I discovered a lot about how to work with a group of people, create policy and a vision, and how to do it in a way that is accountable. That was probably the biggest lesson.

I was chairing the Film Group right when it started to take off. Bruce Duggan was the coordinator at the time. I guess they finally started calling it an executive director, which always seemed kind of sad to me—but okay, fine. He was the executive director and I was working with him. And he was brilliant—but he was like a rocket ship, so my job was to work with the rocket ship because he would just have these crazy ideas and fly with them. At the time, John Paizs was working a lot. Guy Maddin was suddenly exploding into the stratosphere. Greg Klymkiw was creating this whole brand for the Film Group and hitting all the festivals with his very aggressive marketing. Greg Hanec, John Kozak, and all these up-and-coming filmmakers—just blasting with movies.

Bruce was taking that sense of cocky auteur-ism to the wall, saying, "We are the best. We are a force to be reckoned with. People should be watching for us." And he just blasted out with it. And it offended some people because it was so shameless. But you know, fortune favours the brave, and they were very brave times. My job was just to keep things on an even keel and make sure it didn't run over people on its trajectory. It was great. It was beautiful! Through years of service on the board, I was finally figuring out how to get money to make movies. And then I started making my documentary films.

Media Attention

KN: There was a surge of publicity, culminating with the CBC *Journal* piece.[56] What was your sense of the expectations that came out of that?

SJ: The problem with that kind of attention is people from the outside had a skewed view of what we were. John Kozak said: "They expect us to be all zany, with arrows through our heads." It was hard to explain the kind of offbeat movies coming out of Winnipeg in a way that was accurate. Then there was pressure to make those kinds of movies, which isn't everybody's vision. The film industry loves to pigeonhole. They love to stick a label on it and then that's what it is. It became a very narrowed view of us, which was a problem.

The other thing was certain people were having great success, so the Film Group became a place of haves and have-nots. The problem, when you have that, is resentment starts to grow—because not everybody has the talent to be a great filmmaker. Anybody can make a movie. Not everybody can be a really good filmmaker. The resentment that grew was significant because we had never had that kind of adulation before. And the haves and the have-nots were being split, and it did get rather ugly there for a while. Things are calmer now. There always will be an undercurrent of that. It's very hard for people to realize they're not good at something they really want to be, and, unfortunately, the Film Group is that rock that dreams break on. And that's a tough job to do and a tough realization for some people. Some realize they might not be a film director but they're really good in a crew position. Some people just boil and finally just grumble away, full of resentment.

DB: Why didn't that golden era last?

SJ: You might debate that it *did* last. Its zeitgeist—it's beautiful. It's the moment. I think about that sometimes. You have to have the right

---

Shereen Jerrett and Cookie Roscoe in the Winnipeg Film Group's Artspace offices. Courtesy of Dave Barber.

combination of talent and then you have to put them in an environment where there's opportunity and energy to develop that talent. And then you need that extra something to boost it out. I think different eras require a different mix. If we were to create exactly that same mix now, it probably wouldn't take off the same way. It changes. You can't keep going back to an old formula and expect it to work. One of my favourite quotes is: "The object isn't to make art. It's to create an environment where the making of art is inevitable." And I think that's the job of the Film Group. You have to create an environment where art becomes inevitable—and that's harder than it looks, to create that. It takes so many subtle, little factors. If everybody knew what it took to make a hit, we'd all be making hits.

The one thing I've learned, in my years with the Winnipeg Film Group, is you just keep swinging. That, and ride the change—and not to be afraid of it. I think the worst thing that can hit a filmmaker, an artist, an organization that works with artists, is that you don't keep changing, you don't allow evolution. You have to let go. I did what I could do for this organization and now I've got to let it grow because I am holding it back. I've watched all these executive directors, and coordinators, and staff, and visionaries, and boards come and go, and they all have made it grow. But you all hit a point where it's like, I've done my bit. I think the organizations that don't develop, don't stay light and flexible, they're the ones that stagnate.

Women in Film

KN: You started to do a lot more documentaries.

SJ: I never wanted to make documentaries. I still don't want to—I never did! I never studied them. I started wanting to be an animator. But documentaries were simpler, at the time, to do. Cheaper—drama was expensive. I think documentary rises up when people don't have the budgets for drama. It also is a more collaborative medium. In the early years of the Film Group, it was a very collaborative place. People liked

Shereen Jerrett working on her proposal for *Taking a Walk with Dad*. Courtesy of Dave Barber.

to work together, so they did more documentaries. John was the one that really brought in the influence of drama. Then Guy just took it. Jeff Erbach, Lorne Bailey, and Greg Hanec all just started to pour in with their dramatic films. That's where I was heading. My first film was a drama.

I would say the muse punished me for being so cheeky about documentaries, by giving me ideas for documentaries. I just went bang, bang, bang, and made three documentaries in a row because I had three strong ideas for documentaries and I just got money to do them. But one of the worst moments of my career was after I finished my third documentary. Somebody asked me: "So, what's your next documentary going to be?" And I was like, "That's it, I'm fucked. I'm totally fucked. I'm pigeonholed." I've spent the rest of my career trying to claw my way back out of that pigeonhole.

That's the problem with the film industry: it will put you in a little box really fast. Try to get out of it! Also, documentary is a ghetto for women.

Women are allowed to make documentaries. It's very hard to make dramas when you're a woman. It's very easy to make documentaries when you're a woman.

KN: Did you experience anything like that at the Film Group?

SJ: Oh, fuck yeah. I remember I raised a lot of money to do *Horsewomen* [1989] and I remember somebody saying to me: "A hundred thousand dollars, Shereen, for a film about girls and horses? Get real." I was always one of the very few women making movies, with an awful lot of white men. It's always been that way. There were a few people trying to break those barriers, but not a lot. Anybody who was a woman, a visible minority, Indigenous—they were struggling. It was so hard to break in. Winston [Moxam] would say the same thing, if he was around.

It's subtle—it's a subtle pressure. It's very hard. I always feel like I had to work twice as hard to prove I was able to do this. I always thought, if I was a foot taller, my life would be easier. It was the truth inherent, what [Grant] Guy said to me: it's very hard to prove that legitimacy. You just have to work harder. I had to get very aggressive. There were a few years, there, where people would probably describe me as a bitch because I just had to be very firm. And now I'm just tired of the fight. Still now, after three decades making movies, I'm trying to prove myself. I still have to argue constantly that I am capable, and watch people that I taught get opportunities that I don't get. Mary Walsh said: "Women are fifty percent of the tax base, twelve percent of the funding." It can't just be that I'm not good enough, you know?

Evolution of the Winnipeg Film Group

KN: Can you talk about the further growth of the Group over the years?

SJ: The problem with very tiny organizations like the Film Group is it starts to create its own energy, which can be very powerful but doesn't let anything new happen. A bigger organization is stronger and braver, and allows for exploration because it expands, it stretches. It allows for multiple visions. And that, to me, is beautiful. I don't have an issue with that. It was a pretty amazing time to be around the Film Group when Guy was just starting to take off, and John was a darling of the Canadian cinema circuit, and Greg Klymkiw was pissing on everybody. It was great—I loved it. But at the same time, it needed to expand its vision—even back then, that [era which] some people call the "golden period." Even back then, it needed to expand its vision and let more people in.

KN: The question has to be asked: do we try and follow what was done previously, or do things need to be different?

SJ: It's really hard to be heard. It's very hard. The market might not allow the meteoric rise of another Guy Maddin, but something else will happen instead. You can't apply old models to new situations. This is what I'm trying to teach my students: do not admire old models of filmmaking. Your job is to break moulds and think of new ways to tell stories. You've got to look at new platforms. You've got to have that same kind of flexibility and openness. You look at what's in front of you. You hold the hammer in your hand—whatever camera you have—and you say, how can I smash this? How can I break this? How can I retell a story? In this way, filmmaking is as exciting as it's ever been, as open, as amazing—even more so.

I just think that while you can pay tribute to the past, you can't be a slave to it. And while you can see how it was created, you can't use it as the model for your future. I cannot believe that Hollywood, more than anyone else, is trying so hard to hang on to its old models—and the Canadian film system, in copying Hollywood, is also trying to hold on to old models. I think therein lies death. And for anyone to be successful as a filmmaker, you have to look at how people want to hear stories and then figure out how to tell them that way. Stop it with the distributors, and the feature films, and the red-carpet galas. We grew up to worship the idols of cinema, whereas instead we should be burning them. But that's just me. What do I know? I'm just a little old lady with a camera.

CARMEN LETHBRIDGE

Carmen Lethbridge is a past executive director of the Winnipeg Film Group during the years when John Paizs transitioned from short films to his first feature. She oversaw the organization's transition from the Adelaide house to Artspace. She left the Film Group to work with various production companies, including Lank Beach and Credo Group.

28 MAY 2016, WINNIPEG

Winnipeg Film Group

Kevin Nikkel: Do you remember your first day on the job at the Film Group in distribution?

Carmen Lethbridge: I was really overwhelmed. Everything was so strange! The people were unbelievably supportive. It was an incredibly friendly place. People were very welcoming. I was really appreciative of that. Merit [Jensen Carr] was executive director at the time. Grant Guy was there, and he's a filmmaker. John Paizs was there. Guy Maddin was there. Shereen Jerrett and Leon Johnson were around. Derek Mazur. Norma Bailey and Elise Swerhone.

Carmen Lethbridge at the front entry of the Winnipeg Film Group offices at 88 Adelaide. Courtesy of Dave Barber.

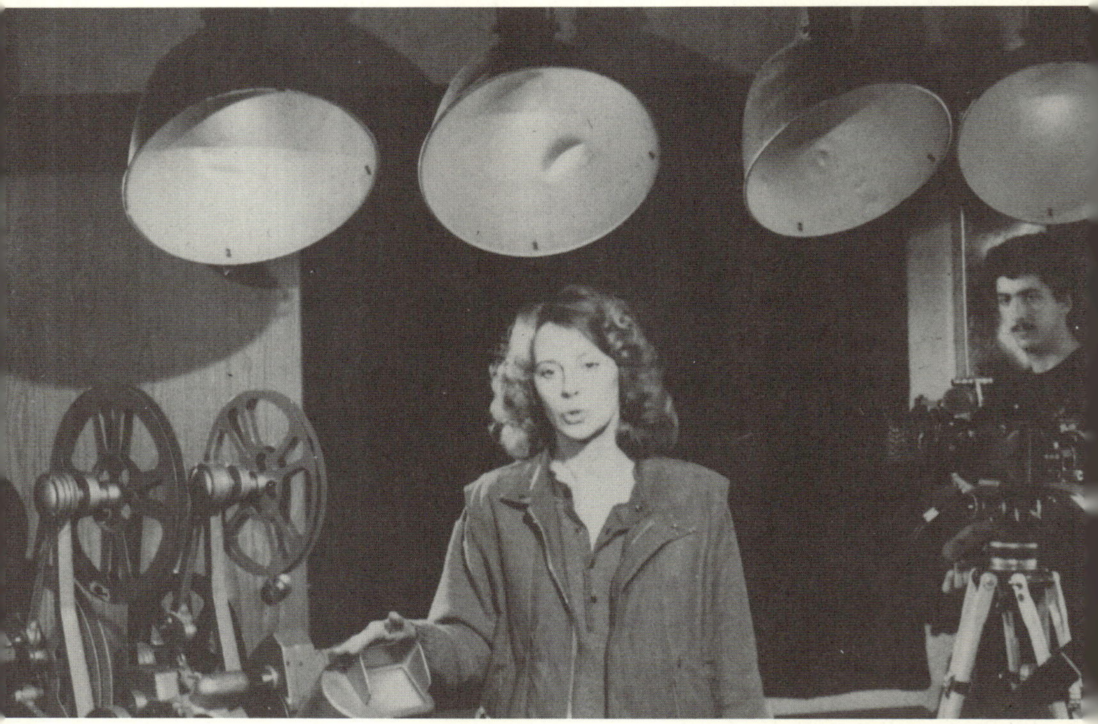

KN: What was a typical day for you?

CL: I don't ever remember it being typically tense there at all. It was just really relaxed. A typical day? A bunch of phone calls, inquiries. It just had a really nice feel to it. Grant application time was a little different, getting that ready—preparing the right language, because you're dependent on the Manitoba Arts Council and the Canada Council for support. I think with any arts organization, that's always a tense time. The Film Group was an anomaly within the country, in terms of the artist-run organizations and non-profits. It was, like, this interesting little niche in Winnipeg, where we had been around for a really long time. It was really well established and respected by other organizations around the country.

KN: What was unique about it?

CL: I guess the size of it and the proliferation of the product that came out of here from filmmakers, for such a small community. I think it was against all odds. We had a really vibrant membership. It was active and vocal, and did really good work.

Crime Wave

KN: When you were executive director, Paizs was trying to finish *Crime Wave*?

CL: People were pretty excited to see it finished. It took quite a while. Some of the scenes were shot on the side of the building, with a sort of mock-up of a Winnipeg transit bus. In one shot, I had wedding gloves on; he needed my hands. He was like, "It'll just take five minutes. Put the gloves on. I need you to do something." I think this one time, I had his sister's wedding dress on—to do something. It might have been in the can by the time we moved

---

Jim Pomeroy, Carmen Lethbridge, Shawn Wilson, and Ellen Rutter attending the Festival of Festivals, Toronto, 1990. Courtesy of Dave Barber.

Carmen Lethbridge on set of Winnipeg Film Group shoot. Courtesy of Dave Barber.

over to Artspace, because that film went to the Toronto Film Festival and that was before we moved into Artspace, because I was still in distribution.

KN: He was a typical relentless filmmaker.

CL: Oh yes, hyper-focused. He made a particular kind of film. Guy Maddin made a particular kind of film. Shereen Jerrett made a particular kind of film. I don't recall there being jealousy, in my view. But we were pretty good at getting everybody's films out. We had these summer programs. Tracy Traeger was around one summer—she was also a friend of mine—and she had packaged up all kinds of films and she would approach different organizations and go out with the projector and show films in all different kinds of places. She did a really good job of that.

KN: Did you travel with the films?

CL: Toronto, one year, with *Crime Wave*. It was very exciting. Kevin Sullivan was a distributor and the producer of *Anne of Green Gables* [1985], and he was a huge supporter of John Paizs. He was really looking forward to *Crime Wave*. There was quite a bit of buzz about *Crime Wave* prior to its release in Toronto. It was well received. John got a little bit shy after the screening. Sullivan was waiting to meet him; he eventually did. After *Crime Wave* was shown in Toronto, John came back and shot the ending over again.

Artspace

KN: Let's talk about the transition to Artspace because you stepped up to executive director with the move.

CL: We went through a process of restructuring and part of the restructuring was, shouldn't I be that person? I wasn't seeking it out. We were going into a bigger space and I think our membership was growing. We needed to be able to organize our management, and the running of the organization, slightly differently.

KN: Was Grant Guy grooming you for the position?

CL: He didn't want to be the director.

KN: So, he said, why don't you do it?

CL: It was a sort of groupthink. What if we do this with our current staff: we plug in here and plug in there. It was decided they should ask me if I wanted to do it.

KN: If you could summarize the Winnipeg Film Group in these years, what was the difference with the transition to Artspace?

CL: We just got bigger when we went over there. There seemed to be a little bit more formality. Not that it was formal in any way. It was a different space completely: it was bright and newish. It was a really handsome space, actually. At Adelaide, it had an intimacy and a kind of funkiness, I think, that people liked. I think the filmmakers understood what we were here for. We didn't need to be reminded that it was our job to support them, what our mandate was. We knew what our mandate was. We always recognized that it was about the filmmakers. That's why we're here. That's what it's about—they all knew that. I think we were really good at doing that for them. I think that they felt that we provided them with an environment where they could create. And whatever it was we could do for them, we would, because they were the priority. I was always acutely aware of that. I don't know if other organizations responded the same way. I think that was a really important element.

The Washing Machine

Dave Barber: Do you remember the grant for $20,000?

CL: I remember there was a big uproar over that. Was it Leon? I believe Norma Bailey got it? Or no—Gene Walz? *The Washing Machine* [1988]—that was in Artspace that that all happened. There was a lot of unhappiness [regarding] the way the money was handed out. Some people were really angry, but I don't recall the details of why. Who dispensed the $20,000?

DB: Bruce Wescott was the producer, at one point, but the money wasn't being spent. A year would go by and the money wasn't being spent. The story I heard was that Norma Bailey got it, but then Leon said, she is not a paid-up member. *The Adventures of Cookoo Gee* was Leon Johnson's script; I think he did it with George Morrissette. But he didn't get it, for whatever reason—I don't know why.

CL: Yeah, it is one of the uglier moments—because people were screaming, literally. It really caused an uproar. People eventually got over it. Leon has worked on Norma's films many times. It takes so much energy to be mad for that length of time, so I think it's kind of dissipated, I guess. But that was *The Washing Machine*.

Leaving the Winnipeg Film Group

KN: Where did you go after the Film Group?

CL: I went to work for an independent production company that produced corporate commercials, as an in-house producer. What I really wanted to get into was the production part of it, as opposed to the administration. I wanted to get more involved in shooting.

KN: In hindsight, how does it feel, looking back to those years?

CL: I loved those years. We had a lot of fun. I met some wonderful people. And those same people I worked with later. I eventually became a location manager. That's where I sort of landed, which was a perfect job for me. There is a huge link between the people that used to be present at the Film Group back in the day, when I first started in 1983, to when I finished up my career in film, around 2005. I knew all those people. I knew them well and I worked with them. I did a couple pictures with Norma. I loved working with her. Leon was usually the sound department—and I'm missing out some people. I did some pictures for Credo, when they were still active. I worked for a Barry Lank, of Lank Beach Productions. I was his in-house producer for a number of years. Barry used to be a member of the Film Group. I thank the Film Group for launching me in this direction. I learned so much there. It was a really great time.

Artspace Building, 2017. Courtesy of Kevin Nikkel.

Part Three

ARTSPACE 1986–1990s

GREG KLYMKIW

Greg Klymkiw was born in Winnipeg and attended the University of Manitoba, where he wrote film reviews for The Manitoban, *the campus newspaper. He programmed films for Winnipeg's Festival Theatre before joining the Winnipeg Film Group as distributor. He moved to Toronto to work for the Canadian Film Centre, as producer-in-residence. He returned to Winnipeg to serve as executive director of the Winnipeg Film Group from 2017 to 2021.*

12 SEPTEMBER 2016, TORONTO

Dave Barber: When were you first aware of the Winnipeg Film Group?

Greg Klymkiw: I was first aware of the Winnipeg Film Group through John Paizs, and this is when the Winnipeg Film Group was in this old house on Adelaide. I think it was probably during *Springtime in Greenland* [1981]. I had the honour and pleasure to be the producer of it—my first credit as a producer. I think we wandered in there and then John explained to me, this is a place where I can get really cheap equipment. It seemed pretty cool at the time, but I never went into the Winnipeg Film Group after that time, until they moved over to Artspace.

DB: When did you first meet John Paizs?

Greg Klymkiw, 1988. Courtesy of Guy Maddin.

GK: I first met John Paizs when he had just finished the film called *The Obsession of Billy Botski* [1980]. He and I were sort of like two ships passing through the night at the *Manitoban*, the University of Manitoba newspaper. I was doing controversial movie reviews and he was doing this amazing comic strip, with Nick Burns—it was a film noir thing with dogs in it. It turned out to be a very controversial item. So, he and I knew each other by being these rebel guys. He just called me up, out of the blue, and said, "Look, I've got this film—would you mind looking at it? I'm looking for a venue to premiere it." At the time, I was the program director of the Festival Cinema, at Sargent and Arlington, where we used to run all kinds of cult films. That's how I first met John Paizs. I actually went into his dad's construction building, and John had this little screening room set up in there and I watched *The Obsession of Billy Botski*. That's where I first met John and I first I saw that film. I said, this guy is out of his fucking mind!

DB: Then you got a job at the Winnipeg Film Group, as a distributor.

GK: It was a really interesting point in my life. I'd actually turned down producing *Crime Wave* [1985]. I turned down acting, in the lead role, of *Tales from the Gimli Hospital* [1988]. I thought I needed to do something with my life, and I applied to all these law schools and was making my decision as to what law school to go to, and then I heard about this job at the Winnipeg Film Group, in distribution. I thought, I will apply for that, just for fun, and see what happens.

DB: Did you feel comfortable at the Winnipeg Film Group?

GK: I have to admit, I always felt like I fit in at the Winnipeg Film Group. It seemed like it was a job made in heaven for me because it revolved around movies, which I loved. It revolved around friends who made movies, friends who I love, friends who made movies I love. It was in a wonderful building, the Artspace building. I had this wonderful corner cubbyhole that had a great view of the Old Market Square district of Winnipeg. And the people who worked at the Winnipeg Film Group were wonderful. I loved working with the executive director at the time, Bruce Duggan, who was also an amazing filmmaker in his own right (as MB Duggan). Bruce and I were fire and water. That made for a very volatile and successful combination. We'd be at each other's throats constantly, but it was good. Good stuff always came out of our scratching each other's eyes out.

DB: What were you arguing about?

GK: He kept wanting me to stick to budgets. "Okay fine. Well, I need this to do that," I'd say. He'd say, "Well, can you make it work this way?" I'd say, "Well, I'll try to—but really, with promotion you have to spend money." So, we would often argue about money. He'd say, "well, Greg, you told me that this was your budget." I said, "Well yeah, but you actually told me this was my budget and I agreed to it, but that's not the same as me saying that this is the budget." He'd get furious. But it was great working with that guy. He was one of the most visionary arts administrators and filmmakers I've had the pleasure to get to know.

Distribution Strategies

DB: When you started, what was your approach?

GK: There were mostly shorts at the time, and I guess my game plan was to try and treat them like real movies. But I found that there wasn't as aggressive a motivation to try to get films seen. My whole thing was to create some kind of an international profile for Winnipeg cinema. I got the films to festival programmers all over the world. I went out like Willy Loman, trying to hustle the films—to libraries, schools, and colleges. That was the game plan, but it was also trying to create this mystique around the films because a lot of the movies that were made at the Winnipeg Film Group—and there were some normal films—but most of the films at the Winnipeg Film Group were pretty fucked. So, coming from a background of programming cult films, loving cult films, but also a background of being a film seller of regular movies to theatres, I tried to apply the principles of basic film marketing and distribution to these wacko films—but also to create this sense of what these films were, in the international world of filmmaking. Here's these wackos, in the

middle of nowhere, making films that can find themselves internationally because they are so insane.

DB: What was the reaction by audiences?

GK: Generally speaking, the reaction was always phenomenal. There was a lot of laughs. I went on this incredible tour that was put together by Nancy Gerstman and Emily Russo, with Zeitgeist Films, called "Tales from the Winnipeg Film Group." I must have gone to about twenty American cities in twenty days. It was the most surreal experience I ever had in my life. City after city after city, the response to the films was almost identical. People laughing uproariously and just being blown away by this new vision, that seemed to come out of this place most might not have even heard of. Of course, there were the usual jokes that I would throw at them, about there being asbestos in the pipes of Winnipeg, which affected the water, and the minds, of most filmmakers. They'd laugh, but they'd take that seriously too. Part of that was creating mythologies about Winnipeg, using the old Hollywood hutzpah from the studio period and making things up. Lying about what Winnipeg was like, and why Winnipeg films were not just wacky but just totally off the beaten track. That was one of the really cool things about it, was being able to use my imagination and mythologize Winnipeg—which definitely is a city that gets only better when you mythologize it.

Marketing Paizs and Maddin

DB: At what point did Guy come into the picture?

GK: I was roommates with Guy Maddin. Everyone just knew each other. I can't remember the very first time John and Guy actually met. I'm sure I was there. What I do remember is that Guy absolutely loved the idea

---

Greg Klymkiw and Guy Maddin production still for *Tales from the Gimli Hospital,* 1988. Courtesy of Guy Maddin.

Greg Klymkiw attends a film premiere. Photo by Morley Walker, 1990. Courtesy of *Winnipeg Free Press.*

of how John was making movies. John was very gracious and generous with his time, with Guy. Very often, they'd be sitting there and maybe watching films together, or talking about films together. John would be giving all kinds of pointers on how to make a movie with no money. How to make the films have a kind of production value, by making the lack of production value a virtue. I remember, at one point, there was a preview screening of *Springtime in Greenland* and I was at that screening with Guy. It was soon after that that Guy agreed to act in some of the other shorts. I'll never forget Guy telling me, on the ride home from the screening, "Wow, did you see all the babes at that screening? So many gorgeous women. I really want to make films because, wow, what a great way to meet girls!"

DB: What can you remember about *Tales from the Gimli Hospital*?

GK: What I remember most of all is that Guy made this forty-five-minute film called *The Gimli Saga*. He was working on it in the editing suite upstairs at the Film Group and, at one point, he just said: "I think I've gone as far as I can possibly go with this film. I wouldn't mind if you take a look at it." I went up to the edit suite. I watched the first cut of *The Gimli Saga* and I just was blown away by it. I remember, at the time, the whole notion of cult films was still a big thing. It was still foremost in my mind, and I said: "Guy, you can't actually go out of your way and make a cult film. But what you have made has the potential to be a cult. The problem is, it's forty-five minutes long and it's called *The Gimli Saga*." I just said: "Can you think of some way of making it longer? We can put really ridiculously long credits on it to max out the running time, but we really need more footage." Guy put two and two together. One of the elements of the plot was that Gunnar and Einar would be telling stories to the nurses. Of course, they had this rivalry of storytelling and Guy got this brilliant idea: I've got a million stories that I can tell. I'll just have the stories come to life! Hence: *Tales from the Gimli Hospital*. Coming to that title wasn't quite that easy. That was what expanded the film. It was an amazing experience because one of my heroes was the legendary Ben Barenholtz, the impresario of cult films, who, in my pathetic little

Winnipeg way, I tried to model myself on when I was running my movie theatre. I took Ben's credo of "if you show it, they will come"—but you've got to keep showing it, and showing it, and showing it.

I found that with the black-and-white, dreamlike vision of Guy's film, that there might be a way of capitalizing on that weirdness. Lo and behold, things conspired in all the most delicious ways. The film eventually found [its way] to Ben Barenholtz, who eventually turned it into a huge cult hit in the United States. It played for a year or so, non-stop, at a Greenwich Village movie theatre every Saturday at midnight.

DB: What happened when *Tales from the Gimli Hospital* was submitted to Toronto?

GK: When *Tales from the Gimli Hospital* was submitted to the Toronto Festival, it seemed like a no-brainer. It'd be a pretty good place to launch it. I knew it was going to play Montreal, but I really wanted it to play the Toronto International Film Festival. I just assumed the film was going. Guy's short had played there. It's a great film. Then I started getting these phone calls. Geoff Pevere, who was one of the people on the selection committee, was saying, "You know, this might not be a slam dunk. There are people here, on the committee, who are not quite getting the movie." At one point, there were even complaints about the bad sound. Now, we're talking about optical hiss that Guy laid on lovingly. This is not supposed to be just a film that was from the talkie period, but with odd little anachronistic touches, here and there—like a Big Gulp cup in one of the shots.[57] But the Toronto Festival ultimately decided not to invite the film. It was really disappointing, but I decided that that wasn't going to stop me from promoting the film at the festival.

I was able to create a buzz in Montreal and get people out to see the film, including a number of important American film critics. I remember, one of the big supporters of it was Gerry Peary. I wasn't going out of my way to tell them it wasn't in Toronto. Then what happens is, I'd run into Gerry Peary in the hallway at the Toronto Film Festival and he'd introduced me to some other journalist, and said: "This is the producer of *Tales from the Gimli Hospital*, one of the best Canadian films of the year." He'd say: "When is it playing, Greg?" I'd say: "Oh, it's not playing Toronto. It's been rejected. They don't want it." He replied: "What? That's a disgrace!" One thing would lead to another. There was this whole raft of journalists that, all of a sudden, wanted to see the film.

The Toronto International Film Fest, at the time, was not as regimented and compartmentalized and *bureaucraticized* as it is now. I was able to actually use the Toronto Film Festival to promote the film. I was having private screenings for buyers, distributors, and journalists—in the screening rooms where the film had been rejected! It was fabulous. I'll never forget it. Actually, David Chute did a report on the Toronto Film Festival, in *Film Comment*, and said: "Well, the best Canadian film there was not even actually playing there, which is too bad, because it's not like the usual dour, NFB-styled Canadian film." That really got the ball rolling. It was a lot of fun to be able to use a festival that had rejected the film, to promote the film.

DB: What was the reaction in Winnipeg?

GK: I think people in Winnipeg were kind of scratching their heads over it. I think the good citizens of Gimli, Manitoba, were scandalized. That was just the local publicity, anyway. It did help the film. I'll never forget: Guy and I held a private screening of *Careful* [1992] in the Cinematheque, and it was mostly for friends and family. I remember my mother and Guy's mother were at the same screening. Guy and I were nervously waiting in the lobby of the Artspace building for people to pour out. When the film was over, my mother and Guy's mom didn't come out. We were like, where are they? I found out later, my mother, who was quite scandalized by the film, and Mrs. Maddin walked out the side door onto the street in total shock. They were talking about the film and Mrs. Maddin was saying, "There is no incest in our family!" My mom was saying, "Yes, Greg and Guy are such nice boys. I don't know

Greg Klymkiw, John Kozak, and Lorne Bailey attending the Festival of Festivals, Toronto, 1990. Courtesy of Dave Barber.

CCCP
FESTIVAL OF

how they could make a film like this." So, our mothers didn't even come out and say hello to us. They left the theatre in shame, to commiserate with each other.

DB: You later went on to make *Archangel* [1990]. Can you tell any stories about that one?

GK: I have to admit, it was a pretty good gig, having a regular job working at the Winnipeg Film Group, but also producing movies—especially movies that were being made through the Winnipeg Film Group. It was a lot of fun. *Archangel* was a really fun and exciting film to do because we were recreating World War I and the Russian Revolution. We built all these amazing sets. I made sure there was lots of garlic sausage for people to eat because my dad knew the guy who ran Manitoba Sausage. Getting garlic sausage and rye bread from City Bread, and French's mustard, was our craft services.

I have to say that making *Archangel*—Guy will corroborate this—was probably one of the most magical experiences either of us ever had. There was a point where Guy and I had gone down the street to eat at Pat's Lunch, and we were walking back. He was going to go up to the edit suite and I was going to go up to the office. We were stopped at the streetlight, at one point. We looked at each other. I remember saying: "We're actually doing this, aren't we? We're doing this for a living." "Yeah, it's kind of weird, isn't it?" Guy said. Then we went back to it, with the taste of Pat's gorgeous butter-and-onion perogies in our mouths. Having the opportunity to make that movie was a dream come true.

Winnipeg Love Hate

DB: Can you explain what it is about the uniqueness of Winnipeg, having had to live in Toronto?

GK: What strikes me about those films, and that city, is that it's a city caught in some kind of a time warp. It is supposedly a modern city. You have people saying, "world-class, world-class!" But it was kind of stupid because there were these local promotions from the city fathers like,

"Love Me, Love My Winnipeg." Or: "A Hundred and One Reasons to Love Winnipeg." And there'd be these stupid billboards that would each have a different reason to love Winnipeg, but it would be: Pickles. Bread.

Yet, you are living in a city that was full of history. Recent history. The history in Winnipeg was so recent, you could almost touch it. It wasn't just the old buildings, even though it was a hundred years ago or eighty years ago—it felt like it just happened yesterday. There was this remarkable sense of being in a place where time stood still, and you could *live in* that time that stood still. But we, in a pretentiously postmodern way, could create works that commented on it and commented on cinema, but also commented on the way in which we lived in Winnipeg—which was living in a past that we wished we'd been a part of.

DB: At what point did you decide to leave Winnipeg for Toronto?

GK: I decided to leave the Winnipeg Film Group in early '92. Tracy Traeger and I set up a company called the Greg and Tracy Film Industry—this was in 1990. Tracy worked as a line producer, associate producer, production manager on *Archangel*, and we hit it off really well. We decided to work on stuff together and we had an office on McDermot Avenue, which we rented from Plug In gallery. I was still working at the Film Group, but I was spending so much time in Toronto anyway. Most of the stuff I was doing in Winnipeg was the stuff that I was now starting to work on in Toronto, and so, eventually, I had to cut loose and leave Winnipeg. When I left Winnipeg, there wasn't a day that I didn't hate Toronto for making me leave Winnipeg.

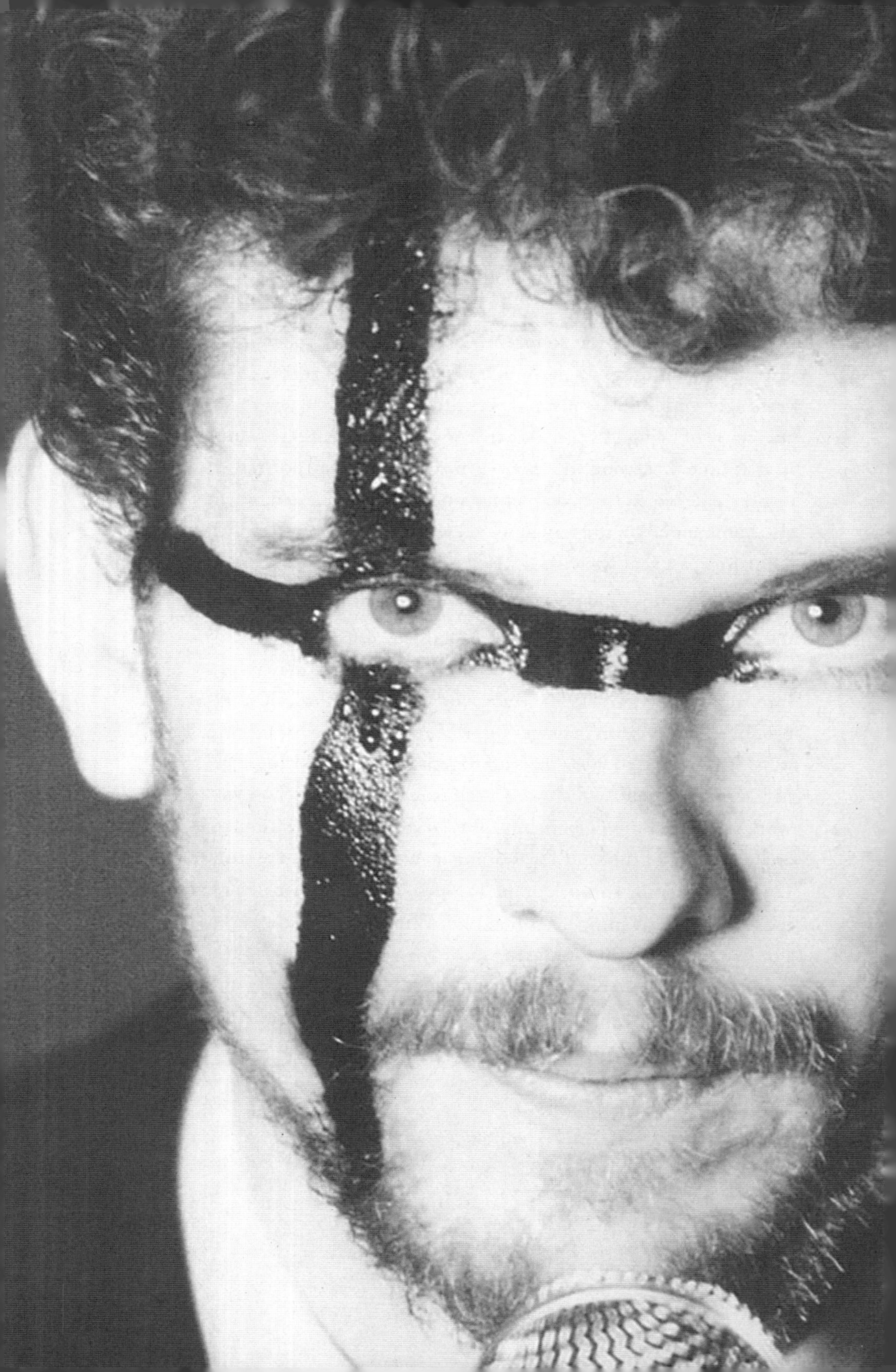

BRUCE DUGGAN

Bruce Duggan, working as MB Duggan, is a poet, musician, filmmaker, and administrator. He moved from Vancouver Island to Winnipeg to attend the University of Winnipeg, where he studied biology, religious studies, and psychology. While working in childcare, he began looking for ways to share his poetry with new audiences and found his way into filmmaking at the Winnipeg Film Group. Bruce eventually became the organization's executive director, while still pursuing his filmmaking. He continued to work in arts administration after leaving the Film Group and eventually completed an MBA at the University of Manitoba. Bruce teaches at the Buller School of Business at Providence University College and Theological Seminary, in Otterburne, Manitoba.

24 AUGUST 2016, WINNIPEG

Kevin Nikkel: Describe the start of your creative life.

Bruce Duggan: When I was in my early twenties, I was doing quite a lot of poetry and getting stuff published in magazines. No one reads poetry magazines; you drop them in and they just disappear into obscurity. Then I thought, "How can I get more people to actually pay attention?" This was right in the new wave/punk era, so a couple of my friends and I started doing poetry performances. We would do them in

---

Bruce Duggan. Courtesy of Bruce Duggan.

restaurants, in galleries, on the streets, and anywhere we could. They got more and more elaborate. Still, there was hardly anybody there.

I thought, I'm doing all this stuff and it all just evaporates after the performance, so maybe I could film some of it. I looked up film in the Yellow Pages—and there was the Film Group. I think it was actually Dave that I wandered into. He said, "Yeah, you could learn how to make films here." So, that's how I ended up in the Film Group.

KN: Take me a few more steps into that.

BD: I took the Intro Film course, a twelve-week course you could take, and, at the end of it, I think they would give you a little bit of film. I remember we shot a little, short two-minute film and then had fifty feet of film stock left. I said to somebody: "Am I allowed to make more than one film with this?"

The first couple of films were really just poetry performances put on film. Then I still had a little bit of film left over, so I got a quick lesson on how to do the animation table and did a one-second film, *Bite* [1986], which only lasts—including head and tail credits—one second. I think that is actually my best work. The conceptual part of it is that your eye can only take in fifteen frames a second. There's twenty-four frames there, so, every time you see it, it's actually a different film because your mind just randomly picks fifteen frames it can process. I thought the highest praise I ever got was from John Paizs, who put a little review in one of the Cinematheque things: "Worth the time it takes to see it." How many films can you say that about?

Winnipeg Film Group

Dave Barber: Were there any issues you had to deal with, when you were on the board?

BD: It was just as we were moving over from the house on Adelaide into Artspace. I was on the board in Adelaide, but I think Carmen [Lethbridge] made the move. Then I took over.

Right away, there was this huge struggle about Artspace because it was a communally owned building: even though the government owns it, they rented to the arts groups in there for a dollar each. A dollar a year, and they're all expected to figure out the costs. The Film Group had, far and away, the biggest amount of space: Cinematheque, half of the third floor, and then a bunch of editing suites.

I'd been executive director for three or four months. I'm on the Artspace board. I end up being the Artspace board president. Three or four in the morning, I got a phone call: "Hello, this is the Winnipeg Fire Department. Are you the president of Artspace?" I couldn't figure how to lie. "Yes I am." "You need to come down right away." I come down and go up into the big lobby, and there is a curtain of water pouring out of the drywall above the elevator onto the floor, through the floor, and down into the space below.

It turned out that water freezes on the roof. In the spring, that melts. There were little channels that were supposed to take the water away. They weren't really well designed and the maintenance people weren't told, "You have to keep these open at all costs." The water built up and then poured down through the channel where the elevator is. Fortunately, it wasn't crazy amounts of money. It was one of those moments where you go: "Holy cow! We're not just a little Film Group anymore. We've got responsibilities. We better not screw things up!"

Mike

KN: Let's talk about your film *Mike* [1990].

BD: I'd been working, before joining the Film Group, in childcare and then ended up working with teenagers and then young adults who were moving out on their own: out of assisted living or out of the child welfare system. I'd made these little short films—people seemed to like them—so I applied to the Manitoba Arts Council to make a half-hour film. The commercial film support program had just come on at that time, so I got twenty thousand bucks—huge money to make a half-hour film.

I had a dream—actually, a nightmare—that was very close to what the film ended up being, and that's what I actually wrote down and submitted as the script. Then the filming was largely a matter of trying to capture that. One of the things we worked really hard at was not making the usual clichés about someone who is in mental distress—the wacky camera, none of that stuff. I just tried to capture their sense of disconnection and alienation from the world, the sense that the world treats them as completely invisible, and their feeling that things skip. You have moments of clarity and then it's gone. It comes back and it's gone.

Film Group Films

KN: Who were some of the others making films of significance, at the time?

BD: *The Three Worlds of Nick* [1981–82], Paizs's trio, was just finishing, and he was struggling his way through making *Crime Wave* [1985]. Greg Hanec, a year or two before, had made *Downtime* [1985], which I think is a really valuable Canadian film. I remember seeing it the first time. It was shown at the NFB because it was made before we moved into Artspace. It's a very slow film, with single camera shots, very slow fade-up, and then this long, difficult-to-watch scene. Then a slow fade-down and it's black for a little while, and then it slowly fades up again. I can remember, after the seventh or eighth time that happened—me, anyway—and a couple people in the audience groaned, "Isn't this over yet?"

One of the things he was doing in that film that nobody else in the Film Group was doing was playing with the audience's sense of time—which is much more a tool and technique, at that time, that video makers over at Video Pool were doing. A lot of experimental videos, at that time, were trying to make the audience members aware of the passage of time as they're watching.

KN: Did that have an impact on you?

BD: I think that the big impacts that that had, and *The Three Worlds of Nick* had—and then there were some other films at the same time—was a realization that you could actually make a sustained narrative piece. I didn't start in thinking, "I want to make a sustained narrative." By then, I'd made five or six experimental films. Then this nightmare came along and funding came along, and it's essentially a narrative film. It was realizing there are two or three different ways of making a narrative film, but they're all achievable here—with the resources we have, with the actors we have, with the equipment we have, with the stories that are available in this place.

KN: *Mike* [1990] is released. You're the executive director of the Film Group. What is going on in your mind?

BD: I knew enough about the films, and the attention they were getting, to realize that our profile and size in Canadian film could be a lot bigger than it was. We weren't anywhere in the media. Premieres didn't get covered. Occasionally, things would go to a film festival, but there'd be no local notice or national notice that we're at a film festival—nothing like that. One of the things I noticed was that once a month or so, one of the films would get accepted at a film festival and no one really talked about it. It just seemed normal.

Every time a film got accepted in any festival, anywhere, we wrote a little press release saying, "Film X got accepted at place Y, and here's where else it's been accepted in the past." We would put it through the fax machine to all the local media. We did that for probably twenty films, twenty times, over a six-to-ten-month period. Then the local media started phoning us because it was unusual. It was surprising.

And Winnipeg, because we have such an inferiority complex, is much more convinced by outsiders saying good things about us than we are about *us* saying things about us. So, the fact that these films made here—that they'd never heard of and never seen—were getting attention seemed like a news story. Then we started packaging new films, every six months or a year, into a premiere and making a big deal about the premiere. I remember one year, for the premieres, we had Klieg lights!

It was a very conscious, deliberate strategy to raise the profile locally using external validation, and that worked. Then the longer films, especially Paizs's films—but not only his—started getting national and international attention. And we just kept riding that attention.

Media Attention

Probably the peak of our PR attention was—remember when Knowlton Nash was around? He had *The National*, and they would have twenty minutes of news and then forty minutes of documentary. They sent a crew out to do the Winnipeg Film Group. They were pure Toronto. Underdressed for the cold, really expensive haircuts, never heard of Winnipeg. They had the same question over and over again, which was: "How on Earth is it possible that this is happening in Winnipeg?" For a lot of culture in Canada, unless the CN Tower shadow touches it at some time during the day, it doesn't really exist. And we were really out in the hinterland.

They were totally baffled by why this was happening in Winnipeg. But it was a fun and absurd thing. They kept looking for wacky backgrounds. I think, for my little segment, I'm in front of one of the elks at the Manitoba Museum and the elk is wackily lit. That seemed to be what they were after. They filmed John Kozak in his apartment, smoking a pipe. They were so desperate to look for wackiness.

They kept saying: "So, why is this happening in Winnipeg? Why is this happening in Winnipeg?" I gave them two or three of what I thought were honest answers, and they kept asking. I finally said, "I think it's the water. There's a lot of lead in our water and I think it affects the brain."

KN: Pigeonholing the Film Group into something.

BD: Into a wacky narrative. I think there were a bunch of reasons for that. One reason was almost everybody was making narrative films. Very few people were making non-narrative or experimental films. Part of that was a real failure, on our part, to figure out how to join with Video Pool. We were very much a boys' club and a ghetto, frankly. Right across the hall is a whole other group of people, with a whole bunch of other interpretations and approaches to putting images on screen. We didn't share equipment, didn't share editing suites, didn't share premieres. One of my big regrets is we never figured out how to amalgamate. I think we would've been stronger and more sustainable because we would've been more diverse.

KN: CBC covers the Film Group. What happens next?

BD: At that time, Paizs had done *Crime Wave*—one version of it—and it had gone somewhere, maybe the Festival of Festivals. And I forget the name of the critic, but the critic said, "Look, the third act doesn't work."[58] So, Paizs came back, crushed as he always is, and redid the third act. It nearly killed him—and it was way better. Then, Guy Maddin had been hanging around Paizs and basically trying to extract every piece of knowledge and information he could get out of John, and made *Tales from the Gimli Hospital* [1988]. We lied about how long it was. We said it was longer than it really was, on the submission form, so that it would count toward feature film awards. And darned if it didn't get picked up by festival after festival.

Sustained Success

KN: Are you able to sustain that energy?

BD: No, it doesn't sustain. People get really frustrated that their films get less attention than Guy's and John's. John couldn't figure out how to make another film. Guy could. I think Shereen's film about her father is one of the ones that happened in there that should've been much more noticed. I thought it was a very smart and interesting film, both very personal and sweet, and very sad. Beautifully restrained.

I really do think that the biggest problem we had was we were too insular. We were too tribal. There were lots of other people making lots of other art in Manitoba at the same time. The music scene was exploding at the same time. The Crash Test Dummies were supported really intelligently by CIDO.[59] Video Pool was doing really interesting work. Floating Gallery—that photography place—was doing really interesting work. Writers were really taking off. McNally Robinson upped its game and really pushed local and Canadian writers.[60] Partially because we were dumb young men, we just hung out in our own little world and it wasn't a deep enough pool.

KN: Was there a sense that this success would just continue?

BD: Yeah. I was only there for four years. I left partially because I wanted to make *Smoked Lizard Lips* [1991]. I knew I couldn't make a feature film and be executive director at the same time. Also, there was lots of resentment and frustration with some things I was doing. And four years is long enough to manage something, I think.

DB: Did you ever perceive tension between the needs of the administration and the needs of filmmakers?

BD: Not so much because our administrative expenses weren't really high and we had funding to cover things. It wasn't like we were saying, "It'd be great to buy a camera but we just can't afford it, because we have this training person we hired." There was a sense that "all the other stuff isn't really necessary because my film is what's going to sell. Just get my film to that film festival. They'll realize how unbelievably brilliant it is and I'll win all those awards—just like Richard Condie, or whoever else—and I'll be launched, too."

Because most films aren't very good. Most things aren't very good. If it goes to a festival and doesn't get in, or doesn't win an award, it's way easier to say, "Oh, it's because the distributor didn't push hard enough or didn't send it to the right festival" than it is to say "I guess that was a limp effort." But things are fluky—you get a streak, and then you don't. Why is that? The Who had about four years where they had great songs, and then they didn't. Why is that? It's hard to know.

I think, now, the Film Group's product is much healthier: more diverse people working, more diverse styles, not so much emphasis on feature films. Feature films are a big risk. They're a three-year investment of your time. Either it works or it dies. A group of a dozen people can make a lot more short films than [they] can make feature films.

I don't think of ours as the golden period. I just think it was a chunk. It had certain qualities that went away. There was certainly lots of bumps and struggles and sharp elbows, but I wouldn't say it was more dysfunctional. On average, it was more functional than most. Because film is a Calvinist art form, you have to work. It's not something you can just toss off. And having to work imposes a lot of discipline on all the other politics. You just have to get the work done.

Smoked Lizard Lips

KN: That's great. I want to come back to this idea of the four-year era—a window—around the time when you wanted to make your feature, *Smoked Lizard Lips*.

BD: Which bombed, by the way.

KN: Tell me about that.

BD: So, *Mike* does really well. Canada Council, the local film guy at CIDO, and one of the local film distributors come to me and say: "So, you got a feature film?" I'd been working on that for a while, so I said yeah. And darned if money didn't come. We had started filming without Telefilm money. Everybody on the film had a two-part contract that said, if Telefilm doesn't come in, this is what you get paid: forty bucks a day or something; and if Telefilm does come in, this is what you get paid: it was like, eighty bucks a day or something. About the third day of filming, Telefilm said, yeah, we're in.

So, suddenly, we had craft services, extra lights, and people could have a living wage for the time that we were filming. It was a fun, interesting, cool process. In the editing process, not so much fun—but in the filming process, tons of fun.

DB: Why not in the editing process?

BD: It wasn't fun in the editing process because I wanted to make a different film than the other two producers wanted and a different film from what the distributor wanted.

Movie poster for *Smoked Lizard Lips*, 1991. Courtesy of Bruce Duggan.

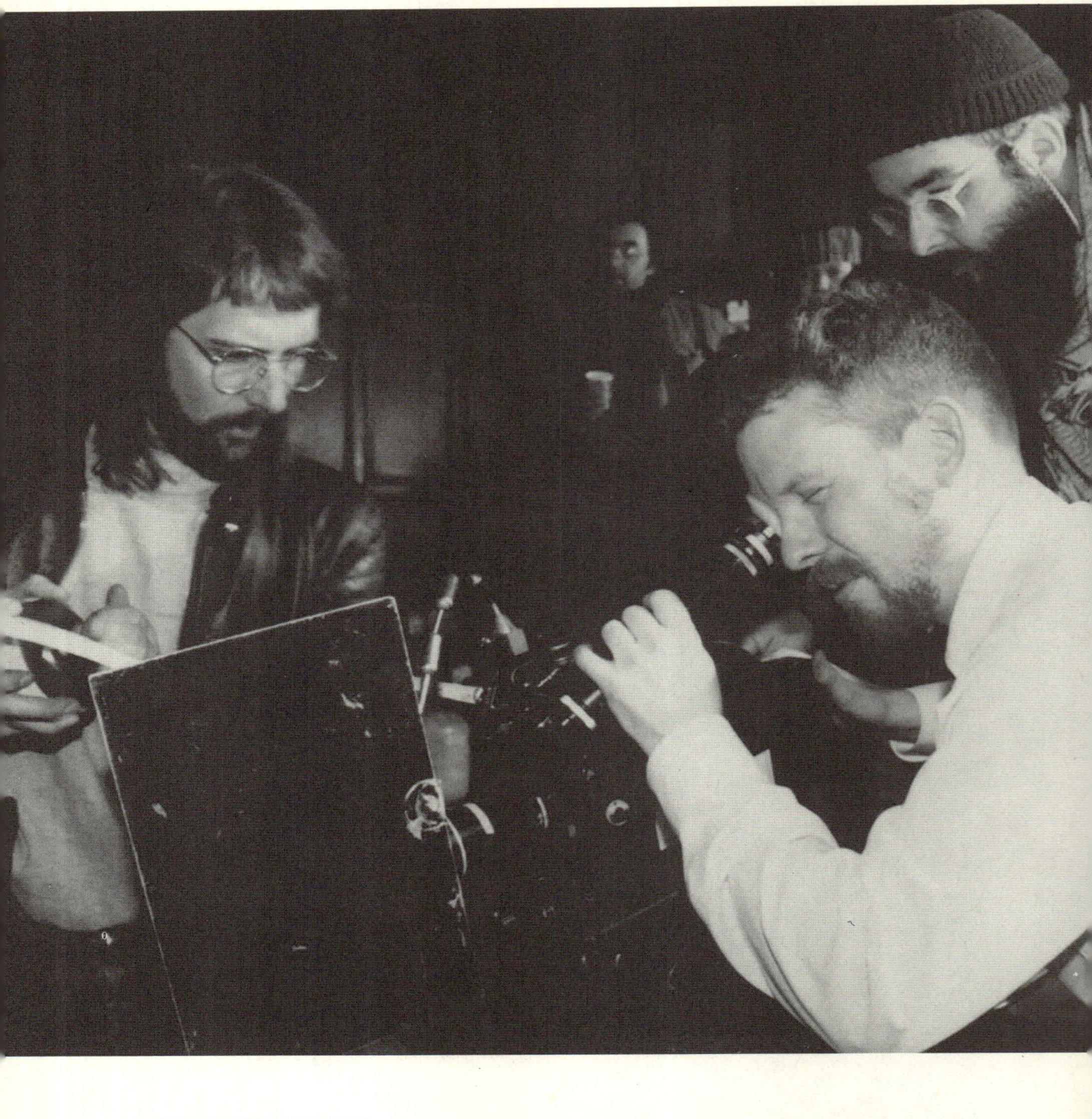

Crew on set of *Smoked Lizard Lips*, with Bruce Duggan checking the camera, 1990. Courtesy of Bruce Duggan.

KN: Was it obvious, in the script and at the shoot stage, what you wanted?

BD: Yes. We shot the film script. It takes a very sharp turn, into the third act, from wackiness into sadness or seriousness—that was always there and always the intention. The distributor never read the script. The other two producers, once they saw the film, it was not what they were after because it's not commercial.

But I was trying to make something that nobody in the Film Group was making, which was political satire. Nobody did anything about politics at all. I was also trying to make an affectionate film about a small town, and nobody did that either. Everybody was trying to be really hip and cool and urban. Both of those things, while it has some stylistic resemblance to other films—both of those things don't fit the Film Group mould or the image constructed in the media.

KN: What were the influences on the script?

BD: I really wanted to portray a kind of mythical Manitoba—a very mythical place. One of the things I really, really admire about Paizs's work (and also about Guy's, as well) is the mythologization of place—that Paizs's films are clearly set in Winnipeg, but it's not an un-skewed Winnipeg. When we were first marketing one of his films, he and Greg [Klymkiw] invented a film company—I think in Gimli or somewhere north of Selkirk that been there since the '20s—and this is a film homage to it. There was this whole mythical construction of place.

For me, the film I was trying to do was an affectionate, but not soft, portrait of Manitoba. You can't do that without the presence of First Nations and the struggle for power. As soon as you get into a struggle for power, then you have to take that seriously. They actually win the struggle, so that is partially why it is a fantasy. They come out better than the town.

DB: Were you happy with the distributor?

BD: No. The distributor hated it and didn't distribute it, and went bankrupt. Most first feature films in Canada disappear without a trace. They drop into the world and then they're gone, and that's what happened to that. That was really painful but—so? No one promises you it's going to be pleasurable, or not painful.

PATRICK LOWE

Patrick Lowe was born in Kenora, but moved to Winnipeg to begin making films with the Winnipeg Film Group. His dynamic film work includes animated shorts and a trio of independent documentary portraits of local Winnipeg artists. He has contributed cartoon segments to CBC*'s* Sesame Street *and has written extensively on the subject of local and Canadian film.*

5 DECEMBER 2015, WINNIPEG

Kevin Nikkel: Introduce yourself. What's your background?

Patrick Lowe: I am Patrick Lowe, a Kenora-born filmmaker wannabee. All my life, I've been struggling to get films finished, when I'm not at my full-time job as a market research interviewer at Ipsos-Reid. Like many filmmakers, I've struggled with the pathetic day job, just to try and get movies made.

I'm an animator, partly. I had a desire to join up with the animation wave that was sweeping Winnipeg in the eighties. At that time, Richard Condie had just come out with *Getting Started* [1979] and *Pig Bird* [1981]. When I got involved with the Film Group, he was just finishing up *The Big Snit* [1985]. John Paizs was finishing up *Crime Wave* [1985] and Greg Hanec was finishing up *Downtime* [1985].

You had the earlier group—they included everyone from Derek Mazur, who would later run Credo Productions, to Brad Caslor, Richard

---

Patrick Lowe acting for Bruce Duggan's feature film *Smoked Lizard Lips*, 1990. Photo by Jeff Solylo. Courtesy of Patrick Lowe.

Condie, and Leon Johnson. They started out at the Winnipeg Film Group, but they eventually moved on to more industry-based jobs. Robert Lower and Elise Swerhone would go on to the National Film Board to make their films. But the independents, as I call them—the John Paizses, the Greg Hanecs and, later on, the Guy Maddins, and even other filmmakers like Bruce Duggan and Shereen Jerrett—they were the new generation popping up. I like to think of myself as part of that generation, but part of the problem was I did independent animated films. Talk to anyone who's worked locally on an animated film without the NFB's backing—with your own money, with grants and everything on your own time. It takes a lot longer! It's a long process because you're spending years trying to perfect something in your spare time. At least guys like Cordell Barker and Richard Condie had full-time money. They had the NFB backing, full-time. Independents—their funding is dependent on the seasons and who's on the grant jury. I came in at that period.

There was this realization, I think, with a lot of people—that with the Oscar nomination, both for *The Big Snit* and *The Cat Came Back* [1988], with *Crime Wave* making a hit at the Toronto Festival, *Downtime* being a hit at the Berlin International Film Festival and, of course, the success of *Tales from the Gimli Hospital* [1988]—encouraged a lot of people to say, yeah, there is something happening in Winnipeg, in the centre. This is not just a flash in the pan, but a real film culture. I say film culture both in the sense of the industry, the financial aspect, the business side—and the artistic side. They cannot be separated. They interact with each other in very strange ways. I think filmmakers like myself are still struggling to deal with the business side of filmmaking.

Winnipeg Film Group

KN: Do you remember when you first walked into the Film Group?

PL: It was the summer of 1983, when I went into the Winnipeg Film Group. I'd gone to the National Film Board and presented a project to Michael Scott, who was executive producer there. Being more of a senior producer, he recommended I go to the Winnipeg Film Group. He suggested they would be more of an organization to my leaning, for the type of films I wanted to make. At that time, I had stars in my eyes and the idea that there would be a place that was making actual movies—like, real 16-mm movies—in Winnipeg, just two hours away from Kenora, that was the cat's meow. There was a film community.

The way it worked out was in 1983, Michael Scott agreed that the NFB would sponsor my first independent movie. They got me animation materials and they directed me to the Winnipeg Film Group. I got to use their Bolex animation stand. It was a primitive thing: just a windup Bolex on an animation stand, in what was the bathroom. Without a clue in the world, I just made this little film, *Going Ape* [1985], my first attempt at cell animation. I thought it would end up as a Manitoba vignette. It got to play with *Downtime, Two Men in Search of a Plot* [1985, dir. John Kozak and Howard Curle], and *In Search of Something Different* [1985, dir. Doug Davidson and Wil Paton]. It was a premiere that was held in the spring of 1985.

I got my first good review in the *Winnipeg Free Press*, so this went to my head and I went to the CBC, asking if I could animate some segments for them for *Sesame Street*. They gave me two segments and, later, more segments. I think my most productive time as a CBC animator was between 1991 and 1995, where I did fifteen segments on the cheap. I had my own recurring character on the show: Enviroman. One of the things that animators had in Winnipeg to their advantage was there were two studios: Neil McInnis's Audience West and there was Kenn Perkins's own animation studio.

I came from what I call the Peter Bogdanovich school of filmmaking, which was: you hung around filmmakers, you watched filmmakers, and you read every book available. But hanging around John Kozak, Guy Maddin, and John Paizs—God knows they hated me. They probably thought of me as this annoying kid who would wander around editing rooms, looking over shoulders. But I have to say, I thank them for their patience because that was how I learned. I'm hoping with what I have learned with the Winnipeg Film Group, through osmosis, that I have been able to develop a style.

KN: Was there a shared sense of idealism at the Film Group?

PL: For me, the Film Group, at the worst of times, became like an example of the shining city on the hill—our utopia, if you will. It's not a utopia. The Film Group can never be a utopia. There are too many warring people and too many people with huge egos, or people who are hungry for a break, or people who just want to use the Film Group as a springboard to something better. At its best, the Winnipeg Film Group acts as a kind of a magnet to get people together. As a result, you find these waves, or these eddies, and these currents of things happening at the Film Group.

So, you get things like the postmodern wave of filmmaking that came after documentary, or what we call *prairie postmodernism*. It's funny because we're known for *Crime Wave*, we're known for *Tales from the Gimli Hospital*, and we're known, always, for the prairie postmodern films. But after Lorne Bailey, Bruce Duggan, Guy and John had their day in the sun, all of a sudden, the one filmmaker that came out of that was Guy Maddin. The two filmmakers that were only able to really follow him in terms of his career were Sean Garrity and Gary Yates because they got more than one project to do.

Guy was hireable because people would want him in Paris. They'd want him in Toronto. But the group that came after that, like Jeff Erbach, with

---

Patrick Lowe on location, shooting *Gavin Alcock*, 2004. Courtesy of Patrick Lowe.
Patrick Lowe on set shooting *Gavin Alcock*, 2005. Photo by Peter Vesuwalla. Courtesy of Patrick Lowe.

HOOK

his with films *Soft Like Me* [1996] and *The Nature of Nicholas* [2002], didn't get quite the same response. People like Paul Suderman, Gord Wilding, and Jeff Erbach had their own group because they were people largely who had studied at Confederation College. You could call the wave that came after the prairie postmodernism wave the Confederation School filmmaking group. Then came Sol Nagler, with his hand-processing, which became very big time at the Film Group. You get all these changes, in all these waves. Trying to navigate those waves is really trying to tell the history of the Film Group.

KN: You talked about ebb and flow. What are the effects of erosion on the Group itself? Is there a danger of the shore becoming too unstable?

PL: Christ, yes—but I would say the survival of the Film Group often came down to financial issues more than anything else. I generally have found that whenever the Film Group became too much of a top-level organization, often what happens is that there is a chasm between the membership and the board. This has happened a number of times throughout the history of the Film Group—so many times it's hard to pick one example.

I was on the board the time when they put forward the twentieth anniversary program, which was a complete disaster. It needed to be better organized and needed to be centred around one event, as opposed to a number of events over the year.

The classic example is the great story of when a group of students from the University of Manitoba Students' Union came into the Film Group, around 1994. During the annual general meeting, they purchased memberships and voted themselves onto the board. They had a completely different board that had no clue as to what the members were doing. They just thought that the Film Group would be a great place to make cheap rock videos. I'll never forget, it was the very same day that O.J. Simpson's verdict was released. I remember I was out on the set of a film called *My Mother's Ghost* [1996], as a lowly PA guarding the honey wagons at night. I got a call from Dean Naday saying that, apparently, the board had just found out that they had a $50,000 deficit and that Grant

Guy was threatening to resign. A number of other board members were threatening to resign. We had a general meeting to deal with it and it was one of the most historical turning points of the Film Group. That was a kind of a make-or-break thing.

A year later, a major MAC [Manitoba Arts Council] grant for distribution got turned down, in '96, because the distributor did not do a very good job for an application and was let go. A year later, Larry Desrochers became executive coordinator. I cannot emphasize how important that was. It looked like the Film Group was going to shut down, in December 1996. But Dave Barber had such a wonderful program of commercial features—he had *Truly Madly Deeply* [1990], he had *Secrets and Lies* [1996]. There was so much money coming in from the Cinematheque that Larry was able to guide the Film Group through to the next year.

KN: Any other notable Film Group history moments?

PL: For me, the highlight of '97 was the premiere of *Rapture*, *1919*, *Gerald the Genie*, *Good Citizen: Betty Baker*, and *Question of Reality*, which was a successful bunch of shorts. Most of them went to Toronto—except mine.

KN: What do you think of the current era of the Film Group?

PL: I think the potential for another wave is there. Recently, Winnipeg has become a bit of an analog centre. Aaron Zeghers was interviewed in the *Globe and Mail* about all the camera equipment, the Steenbeck, and equipment that he's been buying himself. I think there's this need for old analog technology. It's like a love for a particular guitar; you think that with the synthesizer, why would people want to be still playing with guitars let alone blowing oxygen into metal instruments? Why do they want to do that? I guess because it's the style, and people would rather see their jazz in a club as opposed to listening to it on a CD.

Resilient Filmmaking

KN: Has the Film Group been able to shed the insecurity of being from Winnipeg, always looking over their shoulder to Toronto for approval?

Patrick Lowe, 1996. Courtesy of John Paskievich.

PL: I don't think filmmakers are really conscious of the forces that they're up against. I think a lot of Canadian filmmakers come in thinking that they are God's gift to the industry: "I'm not going to make shit like those other Canadian films." In fact, a lot of filmmakers will put down the competition in order to build themselves up, not knowing the realities of distribution, or the tension between regions, or who is at Telefilm Canada. It means they're essentially setting themselves up for failure.

I can't tell you how many filmmakers have cried on my shoulder. Inevitably, at some point, some filmmaker is going to feel really let down by the distribution system or by the funding jury. It's a disappointment that they've got to face. I think most filmmakers face those insecurities, down the line; and, when they do face them, if they aren't broken by them, they come out stronger. Look at Guy Maddin. Whenever Guy Maddin made a flop, he would rejuvenate himself. After the failure of *Careful* [1992], he made *Odilon Redon* [1995]. After the failure of

Twilight of the Ice Nymphs [1997], he shifted down to a lower gear and made *Heart of the World* [2000]. After the failure of *Keyhole* [2011], he shifts another gear and he makes *The Forbidden Room* [2015]. I think the rule is, you gotta be prepared to shift to a lower gear when you don't get up that hill the first time.

Dave Barber: It struck me over the years, despite all these disputes, filmmakers generally keep on working on their project. I remember Guy Maddin coming in and hearing an argument, and saying to me: "Welcome to Bosnia!"

PL: Given the civil wars that the Film Group has been involved in, it often comes down to people who want to make their movies and their ideal of what the Film Group should be. They always get ticked off if it doesn't fit that ideal. If it's like Bosnia, yeah—Hell hath no fury like a white filmmaker scorned.

But even someone like Winston Moxam could have been described as an angry filmmaker because he'd move hell and high water to get his films finished. I don't think he was as good a filmmaker as he could've been; but the fact was, like Barry Gibson, he kept on no matter what. Those filmmakers, God bless 'em—you gotta have an ego the size of Mount Everest. That can put you on collision courses with other filmmakers, with other egos.

KN: Are you an angry filmmaker?

PL: Christ, I'm pissed off! I've been working on this *Gavin Alcock* project since 2004. Finally, we get the animation stand done and, all of a sudden, people are saying: "You could've done the animation digitally on this." I'm thinking to myself, no—we wanted an animation stand because we could work on it the old-fashioned way. I guess sometimes I ask myself, why didn't you choose simpler projects? Why didn't I choose projects that could have been done faster? Then I started doing MTS TV docs. Then, all of a sudden, I realize how much fun it was just to see stuff you've always wanted to do on your computer screen, in a much shorter period of time. I vowed my next live action film is going to be digital. I'm going to shoot it on RED, but I'm going to keep trying to make 16-mm films. I'm going to try and keep making them as long as I can.

NOAM GONICK

Noam Gonick was born in Winnipeg and studied at Ryerson, now Toronto Metropolitan University. He acted for the stage before beginning his practice in film. He was the program coordinator at the Winnipeg Film Group and has also served on the board. His work focuses on queer sexuality, uprisings, and cross-cultural expression playing with genre.

23 OCTOBER 2016, WINNIPEG

Kevin Nikkel: Tell me about how you got into film.

Noam Gonick: I started out as a precocious theatre brat, actually. I used to direct a little theatre company with my friends. I was a child actor. I did some television as well—Shakespeare at RMTC. I went to a high school for the arts in Toronto, for drama. It was there that I was introduced, through Reg Hartt and Cineforum, to underground film. He was showing a lot of expressionist films and French surrealist films. This was around grade ten; I was about fifteen years old. I came back to Winnipeg for grade eleven and met Guy Maddin; he was the media desk guy at the University of Winnipeg Collegiate, where I was a student taking film classes with Lionel Ditz. Guy and I talked a lot about films like *The Cabinet of Dr. Caligari* [1920] and things I had seen the year

---

Noam Gonick. Courtesy of Gregoire Nicod.

before. He encouraged me to come to the Film Group. We did a little, collaborative filmmaking workshop. I was about sixteen at the time.

I think, though, a few years before—I might've been fifteen or fourteen years old—I went to the Film Group when it was at the house on Adelaide. I showed up for a rough-cuts screening afternoon. I remember Kyle McCulloch was showing a film of his walking around Winnipeg, and there was jazz music and shots of a coffee pot bubbling. I sat on the floor and took it all in.

KN: Tell me more about what it was like, going into Adelaide at that age. This is a different group—you're not their age. What's that like?

NG: I was trying to put myself back in that feeling. I think Dave Barber might've been there in the crowd. I don't think Guy or John Paizs were around. These were older guys, mid-to-late twenties, and, at that time, I was in my mid-teens. I was just a very quiet fly on the wall, just listening in, thinking I was not too impressed. I really didn't appreciate the project that was screening. I just couldn't see the point in it all—the kind arrogance of youth.

I knew about the Film Group from that point and I came back to it a few years later, when I met Guy. He asked me to do that participatory workshop. A bunch of younger film students got together with him and we all told him our dreams and nightmares. My contribution was the memory of being kidnapped in Toronto in 1977, the summer of the Emanuel Jaques's murder.[61] I'm still making a film about kidnapping to this day. He'd made his first short, *The Dead Father* [1985], and he was editing *Tales from the Gimli Hospital* [1988]. We went to his apartment and he had a Bolex, and we filmed little selected sequences. I think, in the end, whatever project came out of that went into that pile of endless, forgotten Film Group workshop films. By now, there must be hundreds and hundreds of them—and that in itself would make a fun film.

1919

KN: What stands out to you as you moved toward directing? Was *1919* [1997] your first short?

NG: *1919* was my first short film. Prior to that, I did do some video art. I was working as the program coordinator person at the Winnipeg Film Group. I was very immersed in the film community. Interesting people came in the door, all the time. I was starting to think: I need to make my first short film. I had watched people come into the studio and make things.

The inspiration for *1919* must've come from actually going to Bill the Barber and the sauna that was underneath there. When I worked at the Film Group, I would go there to get my hair cut and there was the sauna in the basement—and the sauna on the main floor, too. In the basement, it was "men only"; on the main floor, you could bring your girlfriend, too. It was so old and so decrepit that you couldn't really relate it to contemporary gay culture. It really felt like it was steeped in history. I remember being in there and thinking, "This place was here during the 1919 General Strike—it's that old. Just a block away is where the streetcar was tipped over, the RCMP were charging up and down the street killing people." I was just ruminating on that. What would it have been like? What would've happened if the whole strike was planned from here? Merging what was, at the time, the nineties contemporary sexual liberation ethos with early twentieth-century labour radicalism and the issues of that day—putting them together, trying to make something new of it.

Guy Maddin

KN: You made the documentary *Guy Maddin: Waiting for Twilight* [1997], which is really about the backstory of Guy. Where did the idea for that come from?

NG: When I started working at the Film Group, the acting director was Laura Michalchyshyn. We crossed paths—literally, her last day of work at Film Group was my first day of work as the production coordinator. She was going to move on, to Toronto. Eventually, she moved back to Winnipeg to work with the Women's Television Network, in the mid-nineties. For a few years, it was a national TV channel based in Winnipeg—the only national channel based here until APTN [Aboriginal Peoples Television Network]. It was a bit of an anomaly. A lot of people from the film community got work there, myself included. Laura and I reunited.

We put together short-film programs: "Shameless Shorts." I was the director. She was the producer. It was while working there we decided that we liked working together, and a real producer-director relationship was created. It was her idea to do a film about the Guy Maddin movie *Twilight of the Ice Nymphs* [1997] that was coming up. She pitched the idea to me—and this is something that she's consistently done. In our recent documentary about the Russian Olympics in Sochi, again, it was Laura (and Elle Flanders) coming to me, as the producers, saying, do you want to direct this? So, that relationship started at the Winnipeg Film Group and continues to this day. I think there's a lot of great collegial film relationships, historically, that have originated with the Film Group, and continue.

KN: Anything else you can say about *Guy Maddin: Waiting for Twilight*?

NG: Early on in that shoot, we were going to an ostrich farm because Guy had ostriches in the movie and he wanted to see what it was like, working with ostriches. I was in the back seat with the handicam, filming, and one of Guy's producers was driving, harping on at me about what should be in the documentary or shouldn't be in the film. And Guy said: "Just let Noam do what he wants to do." And from that point on, people gave me space. I had all access and carte blanche. Caelum Vatnsdal did some shooting and helped with the Tom Waits narration. Bruce Little was the editor.

KN: How important is Guy Maddin?

NG: Because Guy is the dominant filmmaker from Winnipeg—the alpha filmmaker—we are all under his shadow, and it's a really interesting place to be. Younger filmmakers either resist, or try, to imitate. We are gifted with a very strange alpha filmmaker. He's doing something unique, that has informed the rest of the filmmaking community. It gives us the allowance to experiment, to value artistic innovation.

Hey, Happy!

KN: What was the transition from *1919* to your first feature, *Hey, Happy!* [2001]?

NG: I was lucky, with my first feature, in that I had a producer like Laura Michalchyshyn. There was a certain inevitability to the fact that an idea as out-there as *Hey, Happy!* would get made because I had such a powerful force behind me, giving me the confidence that it *would* get made.

Hey, Happy! actually started out as another project when I was at Ryerson, as a student. It was a Super 8 film that fell apart. By the late 1990s, I was doing my shorts and I was doing a book on Bruce LaBruce, and a documentary about Guy Maddin. In those projects, I was researching and getting ready. I went to Mykonos to do a writing residency. Here, I thought I was going to some Hellenistic Greek resort island, but actually, it was November and I was the only one there. I didn't realize there was a season and November was *not* the season. It was miserable weather and I had to wear all my clothes for warmth. I got a lot of writing done and actually did what I had intended to do. I came back with a full outline. Then I went away to Gilles Hébert's cabin at Lester Beach, and I wrote the script that was *Hey, Happy!*

It wouldn't have been made if we hadn't gotten the Canada Council grant. We got the full $60,000 Canada Council grant—and the jury was comprised completely of women from Quebec that I'd never met. I don't know what happened on the jury because I proposed to make a madcap movie about a DJ who sleeps with two thousand guys and causes an apocalypse. You would think that that was a long shot; but, somehow, we got the money and that's how we filmed it. After fifteen years of the AIDS pandemic and the anti-sex fear that came with it, I wanted to turn that

upside-down while also looking satirically at same-sex marriage which was gathering steam.

There was a brief period where we thought we'll film it on a zero budget, but then, out of the blue, we got that letter saying that you've got the grant. We could actually fly in a special 16-mm Cinemascope lens from London.

We did a rave on Garbage Hill[62] that people still complain about. I guess the City of Winnipeg hadn't quite put in all its rules and regulations about filmmaking. We said that we were shooting a movie, but actually got a permit to have a rave. It was a two-day, non-stop music festival on Garbage Hill. I have since met people, who were studying for tests, that lived around Garbage Hill and said that I ruined their grades. Mind you, they went on to become filmmakers, so I think they have a lot to thank me for. Full disclosure: this person has gone on to be the executive director of the Winnipeg Film Group, Leslie Supnet!

KN: Was there anything to do with the Film Group, in the making of that film?

NG: On *Hey, Happy!*, we rented some equipment from the Film Group, and lost and damaged a lot of that equipment, I remember. I think the next generation of Film Group apple boxes were purchased with an insurance claim against *Hey, Happy!* There were some really expensive cables lost, big lightbulbs broken—it was really difficult on the equipment.

Regionalism

KN: Let's talk about the My Winnipeg Exhibition. What was that whole thing and what was your role?

NG: I was the story consultant on *My Winnipeg* [2007]—the "forks beneath the forks" was something I'd heard about over late-night coffee with a pair of queer mystics. We had a visit from an artist from France,

---

Still photo from Noam Gonick's feature film *Hey, Happy!*, 2001. Courtesy of Noam Gonick.

Hervé Di Rosa, who was fascinated with this city and its culture. Not just Guy but the Royal Art Lodge, too. He came to me, at the time I was the chair of the Plug In board, and asked if we could help put together a show of Winnipeg artists for France. What eventually transpired was a huge museum show: over seventy-five Winnipeg artists, from Group of Seven members all the way up to today. I curated the basement section of the show, which was all Winnipeg erotic art: about thirty different artists in all mediums, all different aspects of sexuality in Winnipeg. Kent Monkman had a huge installation, and then Guy's *My Winnipeg* was playing on a loop. This was presented at a place called Maison Rouge, in Paris, which was one of the top contemporary art venues in France. It was a private museum owned by a collector, Antoine de Galbert, who is one of the biggest art collectors in Europe. Since *My Winnipeg*, they've actually done subsequent shows: *My Joburg* [2013], *My Buenos Aires* [2015], and other cities have had the same treatment. It was inspired by Guy's film as much as anything else. Guy did an art installation, as well. *Hauntings* [2011] was shown there, and tons of other peripheral activities. The show then toured to the south of France and then eventually came back to Winnipeg, to Plug In.

KN: Is there a Winnipeg aesthetic in terms of cinema?

NG: Experimentalism, the idea of black-and-white, low-budget level, referencing old styles of cinema, that kind of thing. Almost an Arte Povera—poverty of means—as part of your aesthetic. Historically, that's what Winnipeg has been known for. Those early Maddin films—*Archangel* [1990], *Careful* [1992], *Tales from the Gimli Hospital* [1988] produced by the impresario Greg Klymkiw—that is now getting to be thirty years ago. But has there been anything, since then, that has kind of displaced that Winnipeg idea? I don't think so.

It's about 16-mm, black-and-white, with one shaky light, off camera. Is that really what's going on here? Is that really what the hundreds of people who work in the Winnipeg film industry do? No—not at all. Mostly, it's about a B-list Hollywood actors coming here, doing Christmas movies. Right now, on the street outside Cinematheque, they're filming one of two Christmas movies that are being shot in Winnipeg. It's the Christmas-movie capital of the world and we always do at least five a year! That could *really* be the Winnipeg aesthetic, at the end of the day: it's the Christmas-movie genre. I have friends who live on this street and, all night, bright film lights are beaming in. They're hearing the assistant director screaming for the carollers to walk through the background of the shot.

But that's a harsh reality. It's an economic reality—one we might not want to really accept. So, instead, we'll look back to that golden era of the Winnipeg Film Group, when Guy was doing those first three or four features in rapid succession, in 16-mm. Winnipeg was applauded at the New York Film Festival and at Berlin, and it was really cutting its teeth, getting experience and a reputation. That's what I prefer to think of as the Winnipeg aesthetic.

KN: I want to bring in the word *regionalism*—the fact that what the Film Group is doing, and what Guy has created, has given an opportunity for us to have a bit of a voice and a presence. We're doing something here. The history of the Film Group is the Canada Council recognizing that there is something here and we need to support the regions. Thoughts on that?

Still photo from Noam Gonick's short film *1919*, 1997. Courtesy of Noam Gonick.

NG: I subscribe to the idea of radical regionalism. That's something you can really achieve in a town like Winnipeg, where the nearest place is Minneapolis, which doesn't have much effect on us. We're really thousands of miles away from large Canadian centres. So, being in the hinterland has allowed a petri dish of culture to emerge. We're the only province in confederation formed by rebellion. I call it *radical regionalism* because it opens itself up to different ideas that maybe wouldn't get supported in mainstream media. You can have a filmmaker like Guy, who was obsessed with old forms of filmmaking and styles from the 1920s; and there aren't enough gatekeepers here to control whether or not something like that gets made, saying: "Wait a minute, we can't do a silent movie. It's not the silent era anymore." Things happen because nobody's really on watch—and it's great.

Dave Barber: When you say "Winnipeg Film Group," people in the know will say, yes, it is distinctive: there is something different here, something irreverent here. When you say Toronto, nothing comes to mind.

NG: No—it's bland. When you think of Toronto, you think of a place that's very good at masking itself as something else. I remember when *1919* premiered in Toronto and afterwards, in the bathroom of the theatre, Jeremy Podeswa, a famous Canadian director, was at the urinal. And he said to me: "There's something in the water in Winnipeg." I like that. Maybe there is something in the water. Actually, if we think about the water in Winnipeg, it comes from Shoal Lake, which is very charged politically; and I think, if you talk about the radical regionalism of this zone, it is the fact that it is such an Indigenous city.[63]

I've always felt, even as a film student in Toronto, I would go back to Winnipeg. Winnipeg's Treaty 1 Territory. It's a town of "cowboys and Indians." Am I one or the other, or both, or neither? How can I ethically use my voice as a filmmaker in Winnipeg? Just a few blocks from the Cinematheque, we have a skid row that is one of the most acute in the world. Winnipeg has been called the most racist city in Canada. So, that makes for a lot to contend with, for any artist in any genre—but specifically film because so much of our ideas about race and indigeneity come from the media.

The *Winnipeg Free Press* is always casting Native issues and Native plight with a certain colonial gaze. We're filmmakers and artists in the middle of that, trying to navigate. It's a conversation, really, the entire world is having right now. But in Winnipeg it's omnipresent.

KN: And there's a bunch of up-and-coming Aboriginal filmmakers that are meeting together, as a collective, at the Winnipeg Film Group. Lots of potential there. What does the future hold for the Winnipeg Film Group?

NG: I think the Film Group has been trying to rediscover itself. I wonder where the next wave of Winnipeg *cinema* will occur? Will it occur out of the Indigenous filmmaking community? Or other groups? I know there are refugee filmmakers in Winnipeg now. And there are some established directors, like myself, that are still plotting cinematic collaborations. Guy will make another movie. I don't really know what the future holds. I don't know. I'm not sure—no crystal ball, in that regard. But I know what I'm planning.

From *Wildflowers of Manitoba* film installation by Noam Gonick and Luis Jacob, 2007. Courtesy of Noam Gonick.

JEFF ERBACH

Jeff Erbach grew up in Transcona, on the eastern outskirts of Winnipeg. He studied at Confederation College, in Thunder Bay, and then returned to Winnipeg to work on films, in the camera department. He served the Winnipeg Film Group as the organization's training coordinator, while starting his own filmmaking practice, and eventually teaching acting. Jeff has continued to work in the arts as an accomplished administrator and cultural specialist. He served as the executive director of the Art Gallery of Grande Prairie, in Grande Prairie, Alberta, from 2017 to 2022.

29 OCTOBER 2016, SHAUNAVON, SASKATCHEWAN

Dave Barber: Was there anything in your background of an artistic nature that got you interested in film?

Jeff Erbach: I was always really jealous of people who always knew they wanted to make films, way back into their childhood. I was eighteen years old and graduating in two months, and didn't know what I was going to do. So, within a ten-minute span, I had written two columns of things I was interested in, science and art. I wasn't very good at chemistry and physics, so I eliminated it. I also wasn't a particularly good dancer, or painter, or writer, or any of the other arts that I could think of. So, it dawned on me that I might try film because I loved movies. So yeah, within ten minutes, I decided that I would start getting into movies.

Jeff Erbach. Courtesy of Winnipeg Film Group.

I went to Confederation College, in Thunder Bay. It was an incredibly technical college and they really valued you making work rather than just discussing it, or all the theory behind it. So, that was an amazing opportunity for those two years.

Winnipeg Film Group

DB: When did you first walk into the Winnipeg Film Group?

JE: It was only after I graduated that we needed to figure out where our placement would be, as part of film school. I didn't know anyone in Winnipeg except the Film Group, so I decided my placement would be there. My placement was with Ritchard Findlay, who was the production coordinator at the time. Jim Robinson was the executive director. I remember going to the Film Group and saying, I'm here to work for two months, to volunteer and do what you want. And Ritchard put me to work right away, after a two-hour lunch.

DB: And what was your sense of it when you came in, compared with what you knew before?

JE: It was interesting. I think small, non-profit organizations really take their cue from the leadership of the time. Both Jim and Ritchard were the kind of people who would do a lot of meetings and would take long lunches. They would sort of keep things moving, but there didn't seem to be a strong vision for what that organization was doing. It was, the tail was wagging the dog a little bit. It felt to me like the institution was riding the success of the John Paizses and Guy Maddins, rather than supporting and nurturing the way that they could be, as an institution. So, that was a strange time. The changeover of staff that the organization went through, I think, was very positive and healthy, and has changed things dramatically.

DB: Were you making your films, once you started becoming involved?

Soft Like Me, 1996. Courtesy of Jeff Erbach.

JE: No, only *after* I became involved. Again, that's a really good example of how the organization stokes and nurtures talent at its early stages. I may not have ever made any films if it wasn't for the First Film Fund, which was an opportunity to get equipment, to put a team of people together, and to have the resources to actually make a movie. If it's not for funds like that, you'd never make anything, right? It would just be so difficult.

Transgressive Aesthetics

DB: Those films you made are incredibly transgressive—infinitely more disturbing than some films made there. Can you tell me your influences?

JE: I felt like there was a group of filmmakers, at the time, who were working under the influence of some of the films that were made in the eighties; and those films were absurdist and some of them were whimsical. Guy Maddin's work, at the time, had a bed of surrealism in it. Even some of John Kozak's work. Some of Shereen Jerrett's stuff, like *Dog Stories* [1992]—a great example of a really whimsical, strange piece.

But I felt, at the time, there was another level—a darker level—that could be talked about in the work and that artists started exploring really personal places. Winnipeg is a place where film is also influenced by other artistic disciplines and, at the time, you had people like Diana Thorneycroft making her work, which was very dark and personal. I think all of that just sort of worked to get people to start exploring other places of themselves, and of Winnipeg, and of the centre and what it meant to be there. And what it meant to be in a place that wasn't one of the major cities in Canada, and was a place that was off the map.

I know I'm not speaking too personally about where all of that material comes from. I've always had an affinity for material that pushes the envelope, is really marginal, explores personal sexuality and sexual identity—but along with the sort of grotesque nature of what it means to be a person in the world. All of that, I think, was all happening all at once. I don't want to make it about me and I don't think it was about me. I just think there was a whole line of filmmakers, at the time, that were doing a lot of that: Noam Gonick, Gord Wilding, and even Paul Suderman. And Kelli Shinfield, who didn't make a lot of films; but, I think, who was really extraordinarily talented.

DB: Do you think, then, that you were reacting against the wacky comedies?

JE: A little bit. I think there was an awareness, from the younger filmmakers, of the seminal work of the Film Group. Even *Primiti Too Taa* [1986], and Patrick Lowe's incredible animation. That level of absurdism is still always there. I remember having conversations with people, in the 1990s, about how the work needed to push into another place; and that a lot of the filmmakers, at the time, weren't satisfied making something that was jovial. They wanted something that they were seeing out of Europe. They were seeing a lot of really dark material out of the UK, especially.

Kevin Nikkel: Who were the filmmakers you were looking up to for examples, while making your shorts?

JE: I would say they were more narrative. At the time, I was really interested in Abbas Kiarostami, Hou Hsiao-Hsien, and Michael Haneke—they're making dramatic films; though, especially, some of the Hsien stuff is very loosely narrative. I mean, some of those films are only ten shots, mostly a European sort of sensibility. I've always had a love for David Cronenberg and Atom Egoyan, and the sort of old-school Canadian filmmakers. I really love Denis Villeneuve's stuff.

Under Chad Valley

KN: Let's talk about some of your short films—raw meat in the studio?

JE: When we made *Under Chad Valley* [1998], we built a meat locker in the studio and I needed meat. We had two different kinds of meat. We had fake meat, made out of Styrofoam and plastic, for closeups and things. Then we had real meat. The difficulty with the real meat is keeping it under the lights for a while.

When we were putting that film together, I wasn't sure quite how to do it, and relied on Gord Wilding and asked him: "You know, what can we do

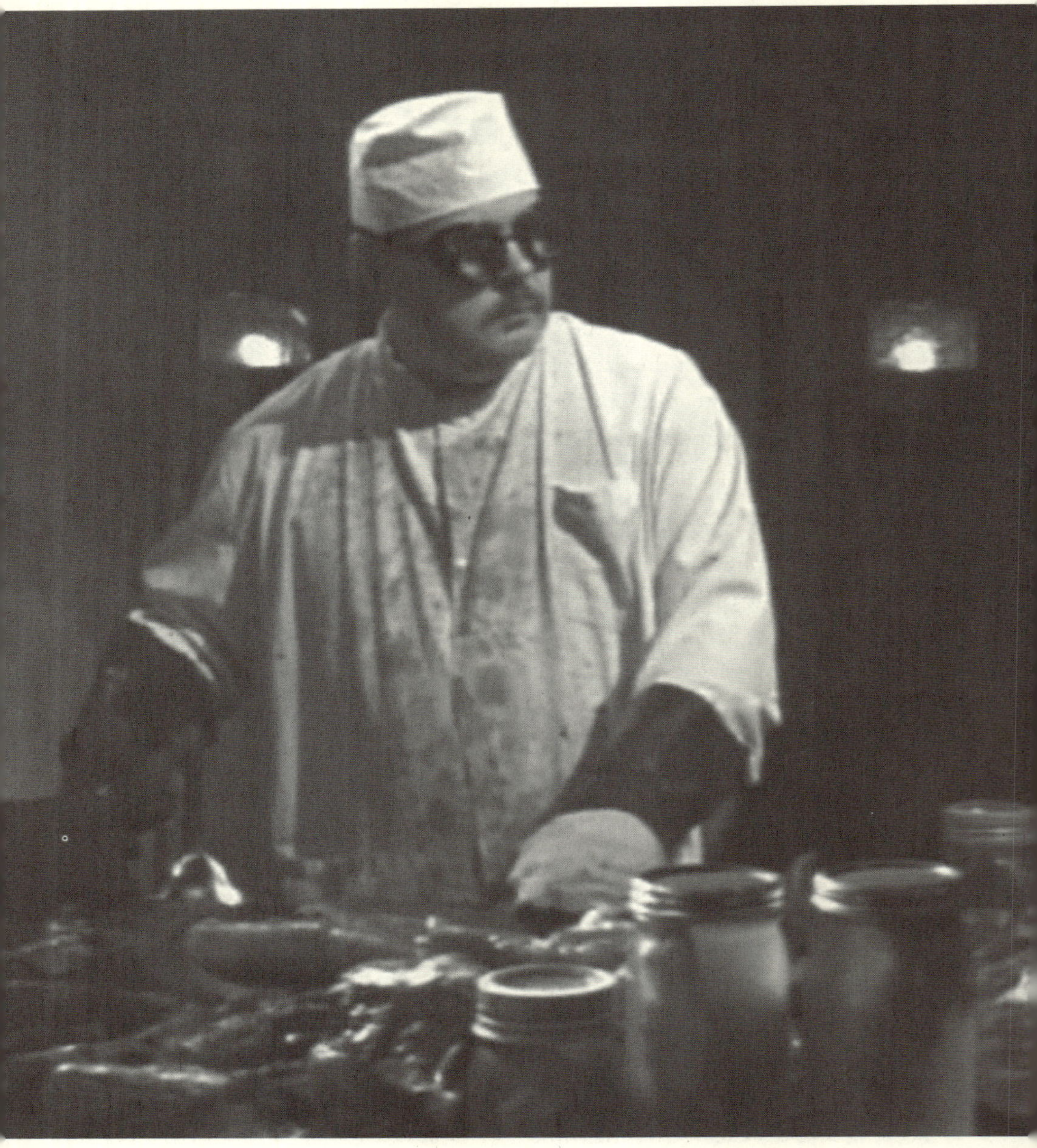

Still from Jeff Erbach's short film *Under Chad Valley*, 1998. Courtesy of Jeff Erbach.

about this? We need a lot of meat." Somehow, Gord was able to say: "Oh, I know where we can get a big pile of meat. There's this company and they put all of the stuff they're not using out in bins. I can just go steal it out of the bins." I'm pretty sure that Gord Wilding, on a late Friday night, pulled up with a truck outside of some warehouse that had bins of discarded meat that were unusable. He loaded them up. We didn't buy it—we took it.

Marriage

DB: Can you talk about the making of your film *Marriage* [2008]?

JE: I decided to make a film about a marriage that was dissolving. There's a first piece that takes place outside, where the husband comes up and she says she thinks she's seen a deer. And then, we cut to a hotel room and they've been having an argument, and clearly the marriage isn't going well. The husband goes into the bathroom and there's a corpse of a deer in the bathtub. The story that goes along with that is, we're shooting in a real hotel room. It's not a set. And we need to get the corpse of a deer into a hotel room. Illegal—not something you're supposed to do, for a million health reasons.

I didn't know how to get a deer, so I talked to the City of Winnipeg. I said: "What am I supposed to do?" And they put me in touch with someone at Birds Hill Provincial Park, whose job was to travel around the Perimeter Highway every Monday morning, collecting roadkill. That was his job. And I said: "Well, can I have one?" And he said: "No, because we compost them. But you know, all you need to do is go Monday morning and you will find a deer—because they're everywhere. You only have forty-eight hours, because its internal organs will start liquefying and it becomes a gruesome mess."

So, we go out with a truck and, sure enough, we find a deer. It was no problem. We brought it back to my house. As soon as we get the deer, I arranged to get into this hotel to do this shot.

I called Darcy Fehr. Darcy comes to my house, and I take him out and I get him a little bit drunk. We're not sure how we're going to get the

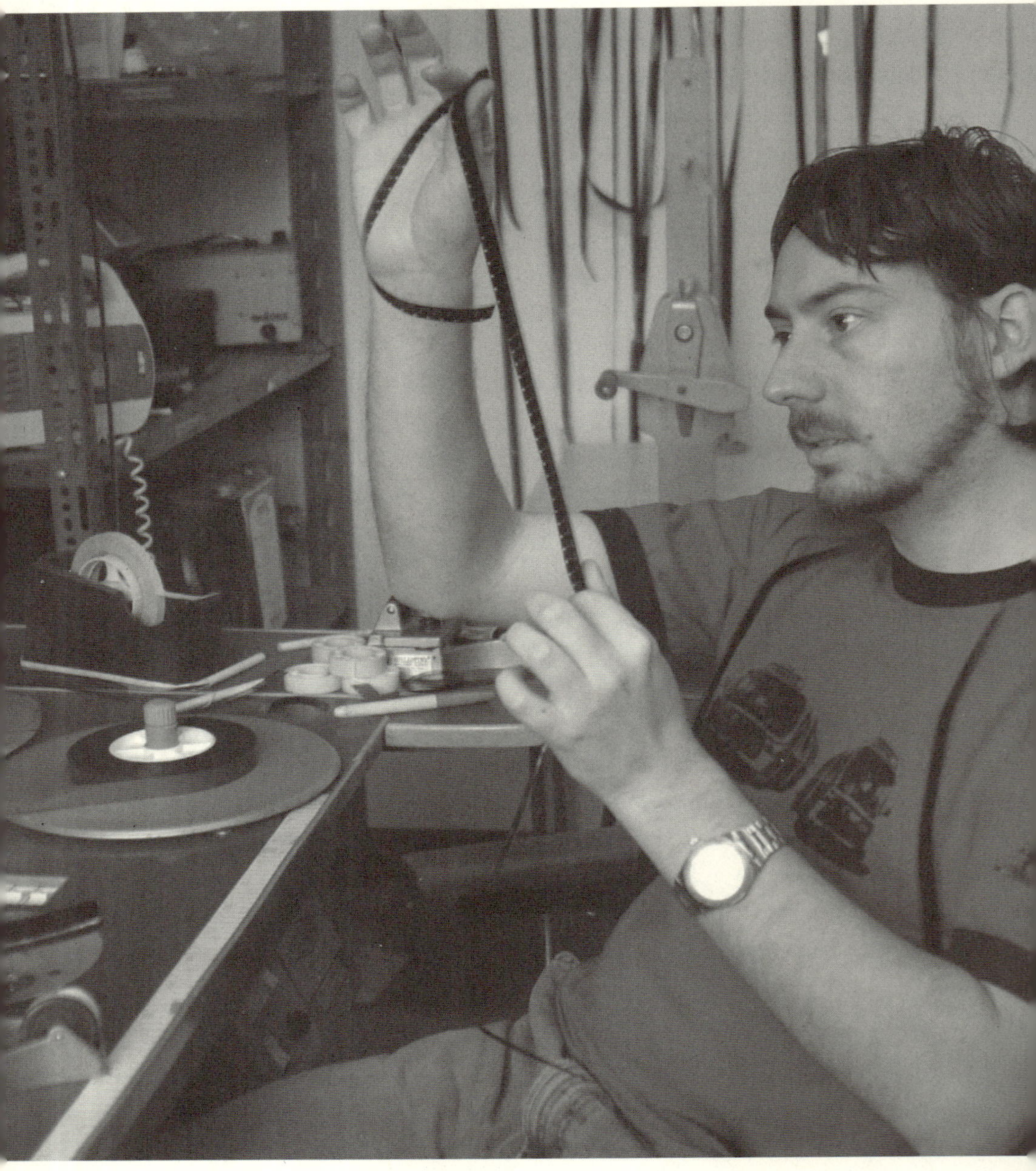

Jeff Erbach. Photo by Linda Vermette, 2003. Courtesy of *Winnipeg Free Press*, 1995.

deer into the hotel. I buy a big bin from Home Depot and we get these gloves; and he brings a saw, in case we need to cut this thing into pieces. We open the back of the truck—and blood pours out of the back of the truck. This is midnight, in my backyard, and we're standing there with a hacksaw and gloves and a truckful of blood. How it is no one called the police on us, I don't know.

We ended up cramming the deer into this tub, and we put a bunch of air fresheners in it and taped it up. The next day, we take it to the hotel and we dump the deer into the bathtub. At this point, it's been thirty hours and the deer is, well, *oozing* out of couple of different orifices. It was disgusting. Darcy was very sick—he couldn't be in the room with it. He hung his head out the window. I did the shots. Then we're done. We put the deer back into the tub. It stinks. We tape it up. The bathtub's a mess. And we say, what are we going to do? We have to clean this up! My wife at the time, Kristen, was with us—one of the strongest human beings ever—puts on these gloves, and takes a thing of bleach and just closes the door without saying a word. Like the fixer, she's going to go clean this up.

So, Darcy and I are carrying the deer out. We feel like we've won. Just as we're getting out the door, this old woman is coming in and she stops us. And she looks at the tub, and she looks at Darcy. And it stinks. She says: "What do you got in there, a dead body?" And Darcy—very serious and stoic—says: "Yeah. Yeah, it is." And she turns and starts walking to the front counter, where there's a phone. I can see that she's starting a conversation with the person at the counter. We hightailed it out of there.

The Nature of Nicholas

DB: What led you to making features?

JE: It felt like the next step. I'd made a number of short films and I was naively always interested in being a feature film director. I thought that's what I wanted to do. I had a film that I thought was good. After I finished *The Nature of Nicholas*, I felt like I hadn't executed it well. I started second-guessing my abilities, and that I probably wasn't the director I thought I could be. Pedro Almodóvar actually said something at the time, which really stuck with me, even now, a decade later; he said: "You know, to be a feature filmmaker, you have to keep making feature films. Just like anything, you have to practice it." I felt like the industry in Canada isn't set to that. People have to keep proving and re-proving themselves, over and over and over, and it can take you three or four years to get a feature film going.

I tried getting back to short films, but a switch had gone off in me. Something had changed, and I wasn't getting any feeling out of it anymore. I didn't feel like I was expressing myself. I didn't feel like it was for me. I started teaching acting, which was very immediate. I got immediate artistic gratification out of teaching acting, whereas the artistic gratification I got out of making films is not only incredibly prolonged, it's also a very vague sort of general feeling of artistic satisfaction because it doesn't happen all at once and you don't see it in the moment. It takes months, sometimes years.

One of the challenges that I had with making films is that I didn't take a really heavy DIY approach to the work. These were not hand-processed in my bathtub: these were films that had big crews, big sets, big production design, big cinematography. They were expensive. I often had to rely on public-sector funding for a lot of them. I did pretty well, until I got to the feature-film level. Once I got to that level, after *The Nature of Nicholas*, I had another feature film that I wanted to do, and I was just unable to get any support for that. I still think it was actually a good film.

It's maybe part of why I stopped making films. There's lots of reasons, but one of them is: once you get to that place where you're existing outside of funding from arts councils for artistic work, once you get to a place of working in an industry, you're having to rely on television broadcasters telling you whether that's material they'd like to broadcast or not, which was never a place that I was comfortable with. It was unfortunate, in the sense that I was naive, and it took me fifteen years to figure out that my pursuit of wanting to be a film director and make feature films was probably the wrong idea. I probably should have put my efforts into doing something else in film other than that because it led me down a path that was a dead end that I never saw, but should have seen all along.

DB: Couldn't you have just kept making shorts?

JE: Yeah, you know—I tried. I tried making a film about Tom Sukanen, actually; the Sukanen Museum [the Sukanen Ship Pioneer Village and Museum] is outside of Moose Jaw. A guy who built a ship on the prairies because he was going to sail it all the way back to Finland—it's a really interesting story. But something about getting to that dead end in the maze just broke the rest of my filmmaking ability. I wasn't able to get back to it. I wasn't able to enjoy it. I didn't like the process. I was on set making this film, and I remember thinking to myself, why am I doing this, again? What is the purpose of this, again? It doesn't feel like a passion of mine now and I don't know what it will result in. Maybe it will play some festivals. Maybe some people will see it—maybe. But I don't get any comfort out of that anymore, like I used to. I don't know whether that's just because I matured or whether I became one of the million filmmakers in Canada who make films and then stop making films. I would actually call it an epidemic.

KN: What observations can you make about the next generation coming up?

JE: I just think filmmaking in Canada is so hard. I really do mourn the loss of the possibilities of what could be. I mean, there have been so many people who've come to the Film Group and gone, who started making work—and I just thought the work was so great and, if they would've put their nose to the grindstone, stuck to it, and kept at it, it could've really amounted to something. For a variety of reasons—many of them personal, some of them professional and relating to the industry—people just stop or they move on to something else. I'm not sure who's responsible for that, if anyone. I'm not sure whether it's the broadcasters, or Telefilm, or it's the non-profit organizations, or whether this is just individual responsibility for keeping at something.

DB: What does it take to make an independent filmmaker keep going?

JE: I remember when I was struggling—this was after *The Nature of Nicholas* and I didn't know what I was going to do next—I had another feature film in mind and couldn't find any support for it. The folks from Telefilm came to Winnipeg and I met with them. I was talking about things and the one guy wasn't at all interested—he was bored out of his mind. The other guy said, maybe I should direct other people's work. Maybe I shouldn't write my own work. I'm a guy that made and directed my own work, right? This isn't me indicting anyone; to their credit, no one in the industry really thought I could direct a commercial piece, and they're right about that. I couldn't even find that level of support in the industry in Winnipeg. That was an example of where I thought to myself, okay, I'm at that dead end that I never saw coming, where I no longer can launch anything of my own. But I also can't do someone else's. Then what do I do? Well, I seek artistic gratification elsewhere. That's what I do. I think that's what a lot of people do.

What does it take? I think it takes a certain amount of steel in an individual. I think they have to be a hardened person. I have nothing but respect for Sean Garrity and Danishka Esterhazy, and the people who have been doing it a long time, and who keep doing it, and are doing well. I think that's super-admirable. I don't know if it breaks that way for everybody. I think some people get ground down. I actually am not full of answers on this; maybe it's just these kinds of conversations that need to happen more fully. Maybe it's that at the time, ten years ago, I needed somebody to kind of illuminate some path options for me, and there was nobody there to do that. So, maybe it's sort of a mentorship issue.

If you're going to make an independent artistic work, then you're talking about arts-council money and public-sector money, which has a very limited ceiling. I mean, you're going to maybe piece together $80,000, maybe $100,000. What does that path look like for people? If you're thirty-five years old, you're going to work two years of your life on this thing and make nothing? You're not going to make a dime? For all that time and effort and work—and you're thirty-five. If you're twenty-four, I suppose you'd do it, right?

You get all the young filmmakers doing it. But once you get older, once you start maturing as an artist, these are not numbers that make any sense for you—not if you've started a family, not if you have a relationship, and a house, and a mortgage, and bills. You can't do it. I want to make sure I'm clear: this isn't me venting or whining about how individual filmmakers should just be endlessly supported with money, no matter what they decide to do. Not at all. I just think we have to have a real conversation about where these limitations are and why you're seeing an epidemic of film artists who do it for a few years and then vacate it. Why is that? And let's just be clear about why it is, and not pretend that it's any different.

It would be an interesting exercise to go back to [the period from] 1997 to 2001, to the Toronto International Film Festival and the Vancouver International Film Festival catalogues, and look at the short films that they showed for those four years. How many of those filmmakers are still making films in Canada? What percentage? Five? Ten? That's a huge problem. That's a problem unseen in other disciplines. It's not the same problem in the visual arts or any other artistic discipline. That's a film problem.

Administration versus Artists

DB: You have administrative skills, having worked at the Winnipeg Film Group. What's the other side?

JE: Working at the Film Group was incredibly gratifying. It really was. Being able to help other filmmakers with their work, and especially new filmmakers. Like any small, non-profit arts organization, the Film Group needs, and has needed, a strong executive director. I mean, it needs a really strong leader to balance some of the crazy that you're going to get at the board level. And to keep the vision going, so the support is there for its membership, which is why it exists. It doesn't exist for the staff.

DB: And speaking of crazy, you were there at a time period that was very raucous.

JE: Yeah, you know, non-profit arts organizations are not always known for strong governance, or having even policies or bylaws in place to protect themselves because they just don't feel they need to. Why would they need to protect themselves? From what? There was a period there where a number of people who saw the opportunity to make use of film equipment in order to make certain kinds of work, to further their own commercial aims—they all joined the board, all at once. There was nothing in place to prevent that.

The executive director at the time, at the Film Group, didn't really push on that, so you had this funny, odd, unfortunate set of a few years where board members were directly working with staff *around* the executive director, which never should happen—directing the staff about what they should do and how they should do it. I suffered the brunt of a lot of that because I was being very protective of why the Film Group was there. And it wasn't there to be a playground for people's own commercial aims; they had to play by the same rules as everyone else. I think at some point they fired me, but then the membership sort of said, you can't fire Jeff. And then they rescinded it.

DB: Why do you think there's been such stormy politics, over the years, at the Film Group?

JE: But I don't think that what the Film Group has seen is different than any other arts organization. I really don't. I've worked with hundreds of arts organizations in different capacities in my life, and these things are really common. I just think it's a cauldron for sometimes there being explosive stuff.

My opinion is that it's not unique to Winnipeg. It's not unique to the Film Group. There is one thing that's unique to film organizations, unlike others, which is the blanket of industry that lies overtop of this. Sometimes, film attracts businesspeople, people who want to be producers, people who see that there's a currency to this, which is valued in entertainment. There's always this tension between the commercial nature of it and the artistic nature of it. I think that's a piece that is hard to navigate.

Regionalism and Aesthetic

KN: Let's talk about the Winnipeg Film Group and what makes the work here unique.

JE: I used to think that it was funding and that, in other places in Canada, outside of Quebec, the funding isn't as strong to support work as it is in Manitoba. I don't actually think that's true anymore. Looking back, and having travelled all over Canada as well, I think the Film Group deserves more credit than it gets. I think there's something about the institution itself that stokes the sort of freedom to explore films in your own regard, to pursue artistic success in whatever ways that means for you. That's a highly celebrated thing in that community.

You can transplant this conversation into Edmonton or into Halifax, and you just don't see this kind of activity, and so it isn't a funding conversation. I think it comes down to the institution itself, where the Film Group just nationally leads in ways that others are not. Related to that, and something, now that I'm here in Saskatchewan—something that I'm not seeing as much in Saskatchewan as I did in Winnipeg is this sense of cyclical renewal, which Winnipeg has in such a big way. When I started in the early nineties, the person that I emulated was John Paizs. Or Guy Maddin. What you'd see there is someone who still lived in Winnipeg, made films in Winnipeg—did it in their own way. That seemed like the height of success to me: that you could make films, still live in Winnipeg, a place that I love and still do. You could own a house, have a career, and be successful. It has nothing to do with the industry. It had nothing to do with Toronto or L.A. We emulated those people. And then, what happens in Winnipeg that doesn't happen elsewhere is that then, when those filmmakers become senior filmmakers, they, in turn, become emulated by the younger generation. So, it becomes a cycle of renewal that doesn't happen in other places because the senior filmmakers leave—they go work elsewhere. They're not there to mentor the younger generation.

SHAWNA DEMPSEY AND LORRI MILLAN

Shawna Dempsey and Lorri Millan are collaborators with over three decades of experience in film and video work, performance, writing, installation, artist books, and curation. Originally from Toronto, they moved to Winnipeg and stayed there to practise their provocative and humorous work, exploring topics through a feminist and lesbian lens. Their work is screened and toured internationally.

28 MAY 2017, WINNIPEG

Dave Barber: Where did you first grow up and how did you get involved in your artistic career?

Shawna Dempsey: I grew up in Scarborough, part of Toronto; and when I was little, I wanted to be an artist. Then I grew up and did it.

DB: Did you go to art school?

SD: I went to York University and I took a whole lot of different majors—but it wasn't art school, no. I ended with a degree in fine arts studies, which was an academic degree.

Still photo from Shawna Dempsey and Lorri Millan's short film *Good Citizen: Betty Baker*, 1996. Photo by Sheila Spence. Courtesy of Shawna Dempsey and Lorri Millan.

DB: How about you, Lorri? Where did you grow up? How did you become involved in the artistic field?

Lorri Millan: I grew up in Toronto. I guess, at a certain age, I realized I wanted to be an artist, not sure exactly when. Maybe the tween years. I worked for a while as a theatre technician and that's where Shawna and I met. We started creating performances together. That led to creating videos, as well.

DB: Was that in Toronto?

LM: No, we really did most of our work here in Winnipeg. We came at the end of the eighties. We had some collaborative beginnings, before then. We'd both been working on our own, previous to that. But Winnipeg has just the right magic. At that time, it had a low cost of living, and we could have part-time jobs, have studios, and just pursue art; whereas in Toronto, there really wasn't a possibility at all.

DB: How was it that Winnipeg was the place you came to live?

SD: I have family here and, really, we were economic refugees leaving Toronto. We couldn't afford an apartment in Toronto anymore. So, we came where we knew people who we could stay with free of charge for a while, basically.

LM: One of the people we could stay with was a practising artist. We had an entry point into the arts community here, through Eleanor Bond, Shawna's aunt.

SD: She was living on McMillan, sharing a house with Guy Maddin at the time.

Kevin Nikkel: Was that an influence at all? Guy's presence in your life?

LM: We may have influenced him. I was building this giant foam vulva in the backyard and I don't think he's been the same since. We like to take some credit.

SD: We were both doing projects at the same time. We were doing *We're Talking Vulva* [1990]. Then he was doing—which?

LM: Was it *Archangel* [1990]?

We're Talking Vulva

DB: You've been heavily involved with Video Pool. Can you recall when you first heard about the Winnipeg Film Group?

SD: We got funding to make *We're Talking Vulva*, which was our first film, when we were briefly living in Edmonton. But we got the funding through the Winnipeg NFB office. We came back to Winnipeg and we got involved with the Film Group, because we needed the Film Group to make that film.

LM: We'd never made a film before. It was natural. I guess we knew about the Film Group, at that point. How? Maybe just from our time here.

SD: Maybe from Guy?

LM: Not exactly sure. It was definitely in the water, Video Pool being across the hall from the Film Group. We'd already made some connections at Video Pool; it wasn't a great leap to walk across the hall.

KN: I like how you're describing the intentionality of what you're doing, and yet there is still this spontaneity. What was your motivation behind *We're Talking Vulva*?

SD: Could we make a music video? Keep in mind, this is 1990, so music videos are brand-new, and pretty exciting for artists. Could we make a music video and, instead of a handsome white guy walking up the hill with his torn jeans, and his guitar on his back—could we do that with female genitalia? The thing that we've all been taught to be ashamed of, not to touch, not even to say its name? Could we have a giant vulva walking up that same hill, with that same kind of strut?

LM: There was a perfect marrying of rap, a musical genre also new at that time, with the new form of music video. It came together perfectly, in terms of making something that no one really wants to talk about. As accessible as you can make female genitalia.

DB: Can you recall any of the reactions to *We're Talking Vulva*, when we first premiered it?

SD: Oh yeah! Oh my gosh. *We're Talking Vulva* was insane when it came out. It came out in 1990 and there was some press about it. The phone started ringing at the NFB office, with death threats, rape threats. It was insanity. An MLA at the time wanted to recall the [provincial legislative] house to institute an X rating in Manitoba, to ensure that no child would ever see *We're Talking Vulva*.[64]

LM: They wanted to create a rating that didn't exist in the province, just for *We're Talking Vulva*!

SD: Fortunately, it was the summer and there's no way those MLAs are coming back.

KN: What is the genesis behind the film?

SD: I created it as a performance piece, *We're Talking Vulva*, in 1986. Then I started working with Lorri. Lorri had made independent experimental films, so we hit upon the idea that Lorri could translate it to film. There was an opportunity through the NFB Studio D at the time, which was the women's branch of the NFB that doesn't exist anymore, to allow first-time filmmakers to make five-minute films. The project was called Five Feminist Minutes.

Artistic Collaboration

DB: When you collaborate, how do you work together?

LM: By and large, we brainstorm ideas. We've been working together now for almost thirty years. A long time. We have a kind of shorthand communication, at this point. We dream up ideas together. We have social concerns that usually get caught up in whatever visual metaphor we're working with. Then we proceed to either create the costume, or some of the visual material, or sometimes we start with the script, but not usually. The writing usually flows from a visual idea. In terms of collaborating, it's really all interwoven together. Shawna may go away and write some material, and come back, and we'll talk about it.

Still photo from Shawna Dempsey and Lorri Millan's short film *We're Talking Vulva*, 1990. Photo by Sheila Spence. Courtesy of Shawna Dempsey and Lorri Millan.

SD: We learned, early on, that to say who does what inspires others to impose a hierarchy on our collaboration.

LM: There is a real desire—most people want to know—who writes it? Who is the director?

SD: Who is the brains?

LM: It's just not a model that we keep to. We have no interest in it, nor does it fit how we work. However, that's how most people think of live performance. We spent a lot of time, in our career, talking about the nature of collaboration. In fact, when we talk about being collaborators, we don't talk about sharing work fifty-fifty; we each own 100 percent of the work. I think that's one of the better reflections of how we approach it.

SD: Film is so much more hierarchical, even than live performance—which, I guess, is why we've been more comfortable in video because there is not that industry model.

KN: What were other people thinking when you washed up on the shores of the Winnipeg Film Group? Not everyone there is doing that sort of thing.

SD: When we made *We're Talking Vulva*, there was a lot of consternation about who would be named what; and that's why, when you look at the credits of that film, I think Lorri is credited with the screenplay and assistant director. And that was us trying to fit into that mould, that hierarchy, because it didn't seem acceptable to simply say "by."

LM: There was a lot of tension and negotiating around how you got billed, and that was completely foreign to us. By and large, I think people didn't know what to make of our collaboration. They really couldn't understand the notion that we were creators and performers, and that these distinctions didn't matter to us; because, in the film industry, people are very aware of what they have to do to move up in the industry. That really played a role. It's not unique to film; this was also true in the visual arts world. They often don't know what to do with us, as collaborators. Once again, they thought that Shawna was the performer and I was the writer.

SD: Or the roadie.

LM: So, negotiating was a normal part of our early years. We definitely had to educate people about how we worked.

SD: Even still, as visual artists usually, we share one artist fee—a solo artist fee. Even though, as we like to point out, we both do eat.

LM: We have different houses that we live in. I guess the model is of a maverick individual creating some Zeus-like vision.

SD: Auteur.

LM: It's not as foreign [as it once was], but we don't usually get two fees.

DB: It's true. The higher up you go within the film industry, the more the issue of credit, and the hierarchy, gets stronger and stronger.

Women in Film

LM: Something that we did on *We're Talking Vulva*—and we did very consciously—was we hired a lot of women. Hired many women, in every single capacity, in every role we could think of—and, in fact, a lot of people got a first-time film credit. A lot of people were trained on the project. We're kind of proud of it, from that perspective. At the time, it was very frowned upon. Everyone thought, why do you want to do that?

SD: Because it's the right thing to do!

DB: There has been criticism of the Film Group being a boys' club, over the years. Did you have a good experience there?

LM: When we first arrived in Winnipeg, I think it was pretty clear that the Film Group was a boys' club and I don't think that's an unfair thing to say. That was the end of the eighties, early nineties. That seemed a fairly strong contrast to what was happening in the other co-op we belonged to, which was Video Pool, across the hall. It was something we heard from other women in the community—it wasn't just our experience—and I think that that is reflected in the film industry generally.

I think that it remains a difficult place for women to create work. When we got this opportunity to make *We're Talking Vulva*, when the project crossed one executive's desk, he said: "My wife's got one of those." He thought it was a Volvo! We're Talking Volvo.

SD: In fact, one of our funders, at Manitoba Film and Sound, wouldn't let us call it *We're Talking Vulva*.

LM: We had to call it *The Rap*, all through production. Then we called it what we wanted in the end, when we released it. The project itself created waves. There was a definite reaction to the film.

SD: Who did we think we were? We were new to town, we were women working at the Film Group, and we were dykes. And unapologetic about that.

LM: At a time that was very different from now—it was a very different era. It's difficult to remember that sometimes. It's not nothing that it was a boys' club, and that the film industry still remains pretty closed to women, in significant ways.

LGBTQ and Film

DB: You went on to make another film, *Good Citizen: Betty Baker* [1996], which seemed very ambitious. With great art direction.

SD: Oh gosh—*Good Citizen: Betty Baker*. It could have been better—if we had a little more experience, or a little more money, or a little more time. We took on a lot. We took on that dramatic half-hour, with an entirely fabricated, 2D, paper-doll-type aesthetic, with a big cast. We learned a lot doing that piece.

LM: We just watched it recently because we remastered a lot of work. We were expecting not to like it, but we were entertained by it. What

---

Still photo from Shawna Dempsey and Lorri Millan's short film *A Day in the Life of a Bull-Dyke*, 1995. Photo by Sheila Spence. Courtesy of Shawna Dempsey and Lorri Millan.

was amazing was how many people were involved in it. We brought in the art directors from Toronto—two artists that we knew—to design these two-dimensional sets. It looked like a cartoon set. The clothing was also two-dimensional, very evocative. There was a huge art department, creating everything in what was the basement of the WAG. It wasn't a vault then.

DB: What was the reaction to the film?

LM: *Betty Baker* was well received with the experimental and queer film-festival setting. But I think it was a little experimental for queer audiences. And a little queer for experimental audiences.

SD: I remember showing it to lesbians in Ireland, at the end of the nineties, and they were shocked by it—by what they perceived as an anti-family perspective in it. Now, I don't think that would be the case—because, now, we have the chosen family in the so-called Queer Nation. We get to make our own families now.

DB: I noticed you melded two disciplines together—the playfulness, with a strong social activism. Has that always been there in the work you create?

LM: Yep.

SD: But we don't sit around saying: "How can we do a social commentary in a playful way?" It just turns out that way.

LM: The work, even if we think it's serious, usually tends to be a little funny.

SD: I didn't think *We're Talking Vulva* was funny.

LM: That was you, Shawna. But I think that our starting point is usually a visual idea, and we are driven by the social concerns. They are one of our biggest motivators. That always ends up in there, somehow. I think the first decade, or more, of our work was pretty playful. In retrospect, we didn't set out to make playful work, but it turned out to be playful and with a political message, a social message. In the nineties, it felt very right to create that kind of work. That is what we had in us. We moved into the 2000s, and I think our work shifted somewhat—as it does, as an artist. And it's less playful, in some respects. Some of the work has more gravity to it.

SD: In the nineties, we were making lesbian-positive work. Really, that was our thing. That's what needed to be done.

DB: Your diversity of multimedia projects is amazing. From curatorial work, to books, to video, to film—do you prefer one to any of the others?

SD: Installations, too.

LM: Shawna loves to perform.

SD: I think we're performance artists.

LM: I think that that is the place we often start with. Even if what we start off with doesn't look like performance, I think the voice is present in all the work. We come up with ideas, and sometimes we think they are a performance and realize that the best way to serve these ideas is a video or an installation. That's actually not a small part of the process because we can go through all kinds of terrible combinations of ideas and media before we settle on the right combination.

SD: Of image and media and content.

LM: The whole picture. Every element has to suit the meaning we're after. The content, whether it's something more poetic or whether it's very bluntly political—it doesn't matter. Everything needs to support each other, for the piece to feel like we've done our job.

SD: And often, there is an element of creating the image first. Our film *A Day in the Life of a Bull-Dyke* [1995]—we shot it, then wrote the script, and then went back and reshot things we were missing, and then did the voiceover. But we needed to see it and see what we got on Super 8, before we knew we had a film, or even what the film was about.

LM: One whole half of the piece was created after we shot a lot of material. Then we scripted new material and went back.

DB: The film is quite seamless.

SD: Which is incredible because we edited it on three-quarter-inch, which was linear. So, once your first shot is there and your second shot is there, you're not going back to your first shot.

LM: That was a headache to edit.

DB: Have you gotten much feedback from people on how your work has influenced them?

SD: Yeah, often we meet young artists who say they studied our work at university, or they saw it on TV when they were in high school, and it meant a lot to them.

LM: The fact is that we made so much work in the nineties and we toured a lot. We performed a lot. We were on the road seven months of the year.

SD: I think we added it up once: it's over thirty performances a year. Which is a lot for a performance artist.

DB: Is it important for you to be independent, as opposed to working with larger institutions—say, the Winnipeg Art Gallery?

LM: We try to sell out all the time, but no one wants us.

Still photo from Shawna Dempsey and Lorri Millan's short film *A Day in the Life of a Bull-Dyke*, 1995. Photo by Sheila Spence. Courtesy of Shawna Dempsey and Lorri Millan.

SD: We loved working at the Winnipeg Art Gallery as curators because it was access to a huge, diverse audience and, especially, access to kids. For most of our lives, people have not let us near children. So, that was a happy change.

Winnipeg Film Group Love Hate

KN: What was your sense of working at the Film Group? Did it reach a point where it was time to move on?

SD: We started working at the Film Group in '90 and then came back when we were working on *Good Citizen: Betty Baker*. And we came back just recently because we made a hand-processed Super 8 film that was released in 2015. The Winnipeg Film Group is always there for us when we need that gear.

LM: It's more a matter of the Film Group is a resource and an environment we seek out sometimes—whether it is for gear, or for a workshop, or whether it's to connect us with people that we need to create a project. Just part of our psyche, somehow, in the background. We don't make a lot of films, for a variety of reasons, but it doesn't mean we won't be back again.

KN: Thoughts on the Film Group?

SD: The Winnipeg Film Group sometimes is a real shitshow, actually. I don't know why that is. Maybe a lot of creative people in one spot, trying to make things happen, in a culture of hierarchy. Maybe that's what makes the difference.

DB: You don't see that at Video Pool?

SD: Not to the same degree of shitshow.

LM: Chaos can happen. Disagreements. Like any not-for-profit organization, there can be rudderless moments.

SD: There is something around stress and film, and that's part of the reason why we didn't make our feature, actually.

LM: We didn't want to go there.

SD: Who needs all that stress? Any film shoot is so stress-laden, and part of that is money.

LM: It's just tick, tick, tick. The anxieties are just ratcheting up all day long, even if you fight it and try to create a teamwork approach. We've had stressful video shoots, but it's just never been the same.

SD: Maybe that's what informs the tangled knot of the Film Group.

LM: The swamp.

KN: I like what you're saying. But if we compare the Winnipeg Film Group to the broader industry and other cities as well, even though the Film Group is a shitshow at times, yet it is still quite remarkable.

SD: I think one of the incredible things is, no matter how insane things are at the Film Group, it still enables people to make work. Things get done.

LM: People still want to make work. They still want to work at the Film Group, and it persists. There's this stubborn nature to Winnipeg artists, just generally. A little drama isn't going to get between you and making your work.

DB: There is a lot of philosophy about artists working in Winnipeg and the subconscious effect of the city. What does it mean to you, to be artists based in Winnipeg?

SD: That's a really complicated question. Winnipeg is rich terrain. There's something heartbreaking about Winnipeg. We see colonization being played out—still, every day—here in Winnipeg. It's a poor city. It's a rough city. But it's got so much heart. Nowhere else could we decide to make a film, and call people the night before and say, would you show up and be revolutionary terrorists? Or be bull dykes? Or be any number of crazy other things we've had people show up and do.

LM: You'd think the poorness of this place would be a barrier to production, but here it's not. It's as if there are very few barriers between you and whatever you want to make here. Maybe we were ignorant enough to just perceive it that way, and we made a career here. But I think that there is a genuine supportive community. There is a genuine sense of *it would be great to do that*. And, as Shawna said, make almost anything happen. Here, the automatic response is yes: "I know a guy. Let's talk next week and make it happen." There is some sort of easiness about the notion of sharing a production and creating things together here.

DB: You've never been tempted to leave Winnipeg? It's a hard city, if you don't have a grant or a project on the go.

SD: Staying in Winnipeg has been good. I think that it's a great base, even if we do spend time elsewhere. Over the years, we have spent time away, making work or showing work. But I think that that's another thing that sets us apart from people who are filmmakers. We have this rather diverse practice that allows us to make work here. There is a comfort with the sort of poverty of art production here. There are a lot of us in the same boat. It's collegial in its simplicity. People have these simple lifestyles and studio practices.

DB: The cost of living is cheaper.

SD: The culture is different. I never think twice about what I'm wearing in Winnipeg. I never feel like a loser. I walk down the street carrying my things in a Safeway bag. I think that we, here in Winnipeg, value people based on what they bring to the conversation, not on the brands you're wearing. Coolness doesn't really fly here.

DB: Laura Michalchyshyn once said to me: "Do you know what the problem with Winnipeg is? They're bad dressers."

SD: We are proudly bad dressers! Because what you're wearing isn't who you are in Winnipeg.

WINSTON WASHINGTON MOXAM

Winston Washington Moxam was an African-Canadian filmmaker. He grew up in Winnipeg and attended film school at Confederation College, in Thunder Bay. He returned to Winnipeg to pursue filmmaking, persevering as a Black filmmaker in a predominantly white film industry. Winston was the head projectionist at the Winnipeg Film Group for many years.

3 NOVEMBER 2007, WINNIPEG

This interview, with participation by the audience, took place following the screening of Winston Moxam's *Barbara James* (2003), at Catacomb Microcinema.

Matthew Etches: How did you get into filmmaking?

Winston Moxam: I was at the University of Winnipeg, taking anthropology. I got bored. I wanted to do something. I have always been interested in films. I made some inquiries and sent out my resume to several schools across the country. I ended up going to Confederation College, in Thunder Bay. It took me two years. I ended up going to Toronto for my placement, and I hated it. I was supposed to work as third assistant editor on *Street Legal* [1987–94] but the editor that I was under quit. At

---

Winston Washington Moxam. Courtesy of Winnipeg Film Group.

that time, in 1989, *Street Legal* was going from film to video and, as an aesthetic thing, the editor was all upset and he said: "I can't cut on video. I need to cut on film. I need to touch the film." He quit. I was under contract with him. I walked into CBC a couple weeks later and they said: "No, you don't have a job here. He's gone. You are under contract with him." I ended up on the streets of Toronto. I got a few gigs working in industry. Then I did a documentary called *From the Other Side* [1990], about homeless minorities living on the streets in Toronto. It went to a few festivals and was shown on Vision TV. Then after that I ended up, in 1992, coming back to Winnipeg and joined the Winnipeg Film Group and started making films there. I made about twelve or thirteen shorts.

ME: Do you feel there was some value, going to film school?

WM: Yeah, I did. I got a structure, on what to do and not to do. There was someone there to guide me. Going to a place like Confederation College, it's more technical than aesthetic. They teach you how to make a film, from A to Z. If you're doing your own thing at home and you're watching videos—whatever, that's good. Go out and try it—that's good. I just liked the structure.

African-Canadian Voices

ME: Let's talk about your artistic vision.

WM: My artistic vision is always to include some sort of point of view of the African-Canadian experience: trying to tell our stories in whatever way because no one else is doing it. That's all there is to it. And I like colour. I like the historical point of view. I love history.

Each film is different, except for the African-Canadian point of view. I don't come to every film with a standard, like: *I've got to have this shot.* This is my thumbprint showing one thing, or it has to always have blue in it, or something like that. Each film is different. Like, for example, with *Billy* [2010], we shot black-and-white 16-mm and we shot Ernesto Griffith as a ninety-five-year-old man. It's exactly like *Little Big Man* [1970], where he recounts his life as an old man.

Blair Dagdick: How do you feel about the representation of Black voices in Winnipeg cinema?

WM: There is no Black voice in Winnipeg cinema. There is no Black representation in Winnipeg, for filmmakers. I think the door is open—it's there. There is no stopping anybody, regardless of if you're a man, woman, green, black, pink—whatever. You can go and make films whenever you want to. It never stopped me.

When I made *Barbara James* [2003], I tried to make it a-racial. There's no point in me trying to make a Black point because, first of all, it was written, produced, directed, and starred in by Black people—already the point has been made. There is no reason for me to bring in that issue because, as soon as you are a Black filmmaker, the first thing that people tend to think is that you're using it as a crutch. I don't want that. I want you to take my film and judge it on its own merits. Have I presented it well? Is there a connection to the audience? I tried to make it regardless of race.

BD: Did it ever affect you?

WM: Oh yeah, totally. Even though I said what I just said, I'm a person of contradictions. I'm always sitting there going, why aren't there more films of colour—from our perspective, the African-Canadian experience? I've always wondered about that. It's never-ending. It's always there. I can only do what I do for myself. If there's another Black person out there who wants to make movies, that's fine. They can come and do whatever they want. It's a medium for everybody.

ME: As a Black Canadian, do you feel like your voice is being left out?

WM: Absolutely.

ME: But there is Black film in Canada and you are making yours in Winnipeg.

WM: Yes.

ME: And there are probably no other Black filmmakers in Winnipeg?

WM: My production partner, Ernesto Griffith—he's a filmmaker.

Barbara James

Kevin Nikkel: Where did you get the story for *Barbara James* from?

WM: I was living at home and I had an argument with my mother. We were talking—she tries to get involved when I'm working. She said: "Why don't you get out and get an apartment?" I said: "This really peeves me off. You wouldn't be on my ass to get the hell out of here if I was a Black woman and pregnant!" And I said, hey! And it just clicked. That's how it happened.

KN: What has the response been from women who are pregnant or have been pregnant?

WM: It's gotten some good reviews from places around the world, where they've asked for the video for women in shelters who are pregnant. They say: "We saw your film—we liked it. We'd like to show this to our clients and to people who are in crisis. It's something that they may connect to." It's been very good that way.

Audience Member: Something that struck me is that there are a lot of compelling interpersonal interactions. How much experience have you had with suicidal people?

WM: None at all. That was the point of view of the actress [Storma T. McDonald]: she came to me and she said, "I never get a sense of dread from Barbara James, that she's about to do something really drastic. I'd like to write a couple scenes of her thinking about getting rid of the baby, or getting rid of her life." I said: "You know what? I don't have the exact experience with being a woman, or those feelings, or being suicidal. Why don't you just write it?" She got a cowriting credit.

Audience Member: It struck me that the suicidal aspects are mundane and everyday.

Still photo from Winston Washington Moxam's film *Barbara James*, 2001. Courtesy of Winnipeg Film Group.

WM: Yeah, it's just Barbara James. She just decides. That was the actress's point of view. She said: "Barbara James just makes these stupid decisions. One day she is just like, I'm going to kill myself and it's going to be great." I'm glad you picked up on that, though. It's very intriguing.

KN: Would you ever consider doing more shorts, as part of growing and experimentation? Or are you just interested in features?

WM: That's a good point. I don't know about shorts, man. I did twelve of them before and, personally, I don't know if I would anymore. Because I need time to develop my story. I need to get into the next level. That's all there is to it for me.

Resilient Filmmaking

Audience Member: When you were working on this one and you were running out of money, did you ever say: "Oh my God, I can't do this"?

WM: Yeah, I did. I started giggling to myself. I started laughing the crazy laugh. I was driving with the equipment in the back seat and I'm giggling: "I think I can't do it. What the hell am I doing?" And then, in the in-between time—like 1998 and 1999—my director of photography, Claude Savard, would take me out to get a beer every once in a while, at the Norwood. I would crap my pants. He would say: "Oh my God, you shot that film and it's in your fridge? You know, I was reading that if you leave it in the fridge too long, your film will get wet. Don't you want to get it processed?" I said: "I don't have the money. It's gone." He'd be like, okay. Then, the next week, he asked me out again and then we'd go out and he'd worry again. It was a constant process of him worrying. I said: "Don't worry about it. Just leave."

KN: What was the budget?

WM: Twenty thousand, just to shoot it. Then I raised another nine or ten thousand. To finish, it came to $100,000, for transferring costs, sound edit, cleaning up the picture, and print costs. We had gone to the laboratory to do a print and it was unusable because it sounded so bad. It

Winston Washington Moxam. Photo by Ruth Bonneville, 1995. Courtesy of *Winnipeg Free Press*.

was awful. I have a print that is really nice, but the sound is awful. Sound was a big problem. Sound cost me $40,000 on this film!

ME: What did you learn from *Barbara James*?

WM: We did a smart thing: we got some good actors. Professional actors can save you time. They can help you to condense your ideas and cut around things. They can improve the script.

Bevan Klassen: Where do you find your motivation and support from? Not that the Winnipeg Film Group is the only place to get that. You've got Ernesto, I guess?

WM: Yeah, and I've got my wife. And my mother. You just keep doing it. I know it's petty to keep talking about, oh, I don't get mentioned. You make films for yourself but also you make films to be seen. You make films to be appreciated by somebody. When it's not, you say: "I'm going to be big about this. I'm not going to get upset about it." But in the back of your head, it's eating at you. You've got to do for yourself. You've got to be honest with yourself and say, I'm upset—but you know what? I have to keep going. Something will happen for me.

Audience Member: Do you do anything else besides make films?

WM: Yes, I work as a projectionist at the Winnipeg Film Group. That's how I pay the bills.

ME: Does being a projectionist influence your filmmaking?

WM: I have a visual Rolodex in my head. I have no idea where the film comes from, but I have a visual Rolodex in my head. Seriously! Like on *Billy*, I know where the camera goes because I have a reference for all those stupid-ass European films. Let's be honest, there is a lot of crap out there I've seen over the years.

ME: You probably watch a lot of local films. Thoughts on that?

WM: I'll be honest with you: I don't understand. I think there's not enough drama going on. Straight narrative. I mean, Bevan [Klassen] does it. Everyone else is doing all that experimental stuff, and I'm getting a little overwhelmed by all the black-and-white, experimental two- or three-minute films. All those programs seem to be blending into the same image.

ME: Do you watch the films you are projecting?

WM: If I'm not interested, I don't watch them. I make sure the thing is in focus and running, and then I sit down. Then I change over. But there's a lot of stuff I do watch. There's the Iranian perspective; if you go to the Cinematheque, they've had a lot of these Iranian films that I enjoy, like *The White Balloon* [1995] or *The Story of the Weeping Camel* [2003]. Or there is the new wave from China and all the historical films from China—those are wonderful. There's a lot of great films I sit and watch, but there's a lot of crap. I have to be honest with you. There's a lot of stuff from Toronto I hate: the inane sexual confusion. The person hasn't figured out what they're doing in life, so they say, "How am going to get through life without sex?" Forget it. Toronto can screw it.

Poster for a Winnipeg Film Group screening of hand-processed films. Courtesy of Winnipeg Film Group.

Part Four

COMMUNITY AND EXPERIMENTATION 2000s

SOLOMON NAGLER

Born in Winnipeg, Solomon Nagler studied at the University of Winnipeg and at Concordia University, in Montreal. He found his way into filmmaking through the Basic Workshop, at the Winnipeg Film Group. He has served on the board of the Film Group, worked as an artist-in-residence, and was instrumental in creating the Film Group's hand-processing workshops. Solomon teaches film production in Halifax.

28 JUNE 2016, WINNIPEG

Kevin Nikkel: How did you come to filmmaking?

Solomon Nagler: The best thing that ever happened in Winnipeg is they didn't have a film school. This is coming from someone who is now teaching at a film school, although where I teach isn't really a film school; it's an art school that teaches film, which is amazing and the best way you should learn film because you learn film in the context of fine arts. From someone who's self-taught, or taught at the Film Group, I think it really suits my philosophy of what I think filming is and how it should be taught. People depended on the Winnipeg Film Group to learn about an aesthetic and a certain history, the way that people thought films should be made.

I was actually studying philosophy at the University of Winnipeg. At the time, I was dabbling in photography and was a poet as well. I was writing

---

Solomon Nagler. Photo by Jeff Wheaton. Courtesy of Jeff Wheaton.

a lot. In Winnipeg, there was this video store called Movie Village. It was this place that had the best VHS collection of the most obscure titles, and they had the most attractive people in the city that worked there. One of the people that worked there was this beautiful woman, who was a big cinephile, and I was smitten. This woman is incredible, she is brilliant, she likes film—well, I'm going to like film. I knew nothing about film. She was like, "I'm going to take these workshops at the Winnipeg Film Group." Okay, I'm going to, too. We took the basic workshop with Shereen Jerrett. She dropped out (the woman I liked) but then I immediately knew this is what I wanted to do. This is my passion.

Interestingly enough, in the studio at the time, there was a film that was being shot. It was Jeff Erbach, one of his transgressive-themed films of children doing things with meat. I think there was a freezer involved, with jars of dismembered body parts. Of course, I'm sold. I love this shit. I wrote a script around one of Jeff Erbach's sets and then I got to actually learn how to break down the script and to make a film. Weeks after that basic workshop concluded, I made my first film. It was called *M.O.Y.* [1998]. It went on to play a few festivals. I made that film and immediately left Winnipeg to move to Vancouver. I made a film there called *doc1.doc* [1999], which Dave Barber is a big fan of. My first really weird, prairie surrealist film. Then I moved to Poland and made a film there called *spadające płatki* [1999]. I made three films in the period of two years on 16-mm and, to my surprise, they were quite well received.

Winnipeg Film Group

KN: What was it like at the Film Group?

SN: The Film Group, as you know, there's a lot of piss and vinegar in that place. Jeff Erbach was the production coordinator, back in the day. I got the post-Erbach years. You'd walk in the Film Group. The first thing Erbach would do, he'd give you the finger. But it was all very fun. It was that sort of like a clashing of ideas. That was during a time when people like Gord Wilding and Erbach, Paul Suderman and Noam Gonick were making their remarkable series of very transgressive, sexually perverse films, and I was really turned on by all that. Not that my filmmaking was that style, but I just loved the fact they were making work that really pushed the envelope. Back then, things were really heated.

When I go into the hallways of Artspace, even just the smell of it—I wouldn't call it nostalgia—I go in that space and it really lights a fire under my ass. This is the shit—this is where I started, where I got the bug. This is where I thought I could join this stratum of Manitoba filmmaking, add my voice to the group of perverts that were making work back then. My work was actually quite tame compared to their work. I'm coming to realize, now, I'm actually a bit of a romantic. My work is not as ironic as everyone else's at the Winnipeg Film Group, like Mike Maryniuk and Matthew Rankin, all the people that popped up afterward. After I came in and introduced a few techniques, and whatever, then they went off and made brilliant work—far more experimental than the work that I was doing at that time. My work is very different. It's romantic. It's metaphysical. It's something that has a different poetry to it, but I still think it fits with that place in some way. Little transgression in my films, compared to other people that were making film in those days.

Experimentation

KN: So, what brought you back to Winnipeg, after Poland?

SN: What happened was I made three films and, like every good philosophy major learning to be an artist, you backpack across Europe by yourself. While I was doing it, I was making films. I went to Poland and made a short film there called *spadające płatki* [1999], which played, thanks to the graces of Dave Barber, at the Cinematheque and which gave me a lot of encouragement. Then I came back to Winnipeg, for a short period of time, and went back to Poland and shot a film called *perhaps/We* [2003], which was a film that really changed everything in terms of how I make film. Then I came back because I got a grant to make a fairly large project funded by the Canada Council for the Arts, called *A Treatise on Prairie Mysticism* [2001],

which was a very ambitious, thirty-minute film, sort of like an experimental narrative. It's a film I don't really claim anymore. I think I've changed quite a bit from when I made that work. I think we actually played at your venue. Remember you had that cinema—what was it called?

KN: Catacomb Microcinema.

SN: Yeah, we premiered it there. That was great! That was a nice little space. Around that time, I had met Phil Hoffman, who I sort of pounced on when he showed some work from his Film Farm. I said: "Hey, you've got to get me into this Film Farm. I need to learn about what you guys are doing." There was usually a three-to-four-year-long wait to get in. But for some reason, Phil liked me and said: "Okay, that's it. You are in." That totally changed my life, and then changed my whole trajectory of the way that I treat my filmmaking practice. The hand-processing, experimental techniques changed with that.

What happened was Phil's experimental handmade stuff morphed with my weird, experimental narrative stuff that came from Winnipeg. The synthesis came with *perhaps/We*. That film was my first film that really did well internationally. It played at some very prestigious festivals and won some awards. By travelling with my work through Europe, and other places, I really learned about filmmaking and learned about what people were getting from my work, and how it reached across cultures. Then I sort of went into this filmmaking frenzy. I made a film called *The Sex of Self-Hatred* [2004] and that was made through an artist-in-residence program at the Winnipeg Film Group.

That film, *The Sex of Self-Hatred*, was almost an homage to those perverts that influenced me: Erbach and Wilding, and Noam Gonick. People I respect. I love their work. Noam is someone who I think is an exceptionally important filmmaker, who has really inspired me. It was almost like a film that I thought could shock, based on the success of my early films.

Solomon Nagler with cinematographer Aleksander Schwartz on location shooting his short film *spadające płatki* in Poland, 1999. Courtesy of Solomon Nagler.

I wanted to see if I could punch people in the face a little bit with that film. It worked. That film also did really well on the festival circuit. Then I moved to Montreal and did my master's. Before I moved to Montreal, I did a film called *Fugue Nefesh* [2007], which I did on 35-mm film.

KN: You came back to town after being away. What was your plan?

SN: I wanted to start an army of filmmakers. I came back after experiencing this thing at Phil's Farm and I found, at the Film Group, there was just so much competition. People were just so—a lot of men were like—*ugah ugah!* It was fucking stupid. I longed for that spirit of collaboration and community that other experimental film communities had. I could have stayed in Europe and fucked around there and made films, but I wanted to come back. I felt like I could do something here. I needed colleagues. I needed people I can share with. I don't want to hide what I'm doing. I think that filmmakers that are so protective of their work, so secretive of their work, and what they're doing is so bloody insecure. They frankly have so few ideas that they guard every last one of them. In fact, if you put your ideas up in the air, in the ether, and just let them speak for themselves, not only do they grow into things that are more interesting but you end up inspiring other people, which is why I went into teaching. I thought: fuck this! I want other people to learn.

The aesthetic I learned at Phil's Farm fit so well with what was happening in Winnipeg. I saw so many talented people that I thought would just make better work than I was making. And that is in fact what happened, with Mike [Maryniuk] and with Carole [O'Brien]. All these people were making better experimental work than I was. They're better filmmakers at that than I am. I just said, well, here's a toolbox. Let's just hang out and talk. I take no credit for anything that they've done. I take no credit for the community that evolved out of it. All I did was just put a sentence out there: let's try this. And their talents are their own. Their talents are far beyond anything that I was able to do. I was just lonely. I wanted to make work together, and it blossomed.

John Kapitany and I started this thing called the "$225 Film Experiment," where we said: for $225, you're going to make a film. You get the stock, you get the chemicals—and we had such a good time. It was so great. The

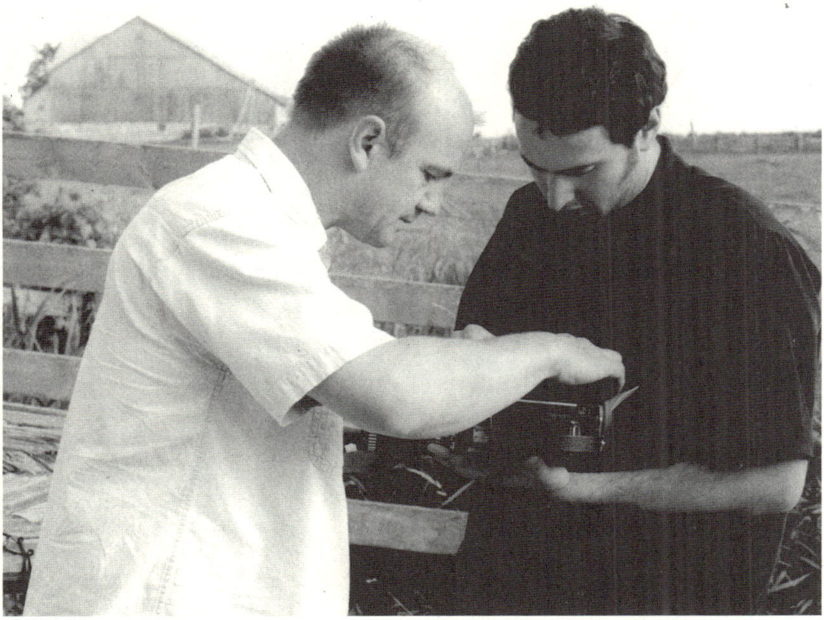

Filmmaker Phil Hoffman and Solomon Nagler at Phil's Farm, 2001. Courtesy of Solomon Nagler.

films that popped out of there ended up playing all these festivals. Fucking Winnipeg all-stars came out of that group. It was just brilliant. So, it was just out of isolation. I didn't want to make work in isolation anymore. I wanted a community to hang out with and learn from, and just make work together.

Collaborative Energy

KN: Do you think this was just waiting to happen?

SN: Yeah, I think we needed someone to say: listen, there is another way. This sort of rock star, man-with-the-camera-type attitude that was

happening was not the way it needed to be. There's a way of making film that is low-budget, that is handmade, that is intimate. There is a way of creating work collectively that can be really inspiring.

The amount of talent that comes out of this town is remarkable, both in visual arts, fine arts, and in music. Everyone here has an idea. What makes Winnipeg unique is an idea of what their stamp can be, in the trajectory of not only experimental film in Canada but even globally. Everyone that makes the work wants to make the work *their way*. How is it that their voice can be heard? That's what I felt when I first started making films. I left the Film Group inspired, thinking: What is your vision? What is your voice? How is it related to the work that's made in this town? How is it special, in the way this town's work is accepted and celebrated across the world?

There's so much talent in this town. Winnipeg not only punches over its weight, it pummels the heavyweights—with one fucking uppercut! I don't think filmmakers in Montreal really can hold a torch to the work that's being made here. I think in Toronto, as well. I think the work out here is fiercely independent and fiercely original.

Conflict and Change

KN: The Film Group has been called a boys' club. Was change coming there, too?

SN: I think that the Film Group needed a culture change. I agree that it was really a men's club, aside from Carole [O'Brien] and Shereen [Jerrett]. But I don't think it's unique to the Film Group. I was asked to do a retrospective, forty-year screening for AFCOOP [Atlantic Filmmakers Cooperative]. The work that was made in the eighties was for men. But I think, in Winnipeg and especially at the Film Group, that gender divide had to be

---

On set of Solomon Nagler's short film *The Sex of Self-Hatred*, 2004. Photo by John Kapitany. Courtesy of Solomon Nagler.

addressed. I think that the Film Group is really doing amazingly well and making sure that, also, the First Nations communities are engaged.

I just came from a co-op out east and—trust me—tumultuous is everywhere. Listen, it's an artist-run centre. The way we roll, we don't roll with logic. We're not rational people. Fuck—we're not accountants! We're people that speak from our guts. You put a bunch of artists in an administrative organization, you're going to get fucking sparks. It's exciting. It's a lot more exciting than a bunch of bankers talking about $500-a-plate meals to help the cancer society. That's boring. I'd rather be with a bunch of artists who are living close to the bone and fighting over the necessities of life, and art, and passion, and philosophy, and poetry. You're not going to get an organization that runs smoothly. There's always going to be fights. There's always going to be conflict, and thank God for that. That's why I'm in it.

It's trench warfare out there. The arts are constantly under attack by these idiots in political power. First thing they want to do is destroy the arts. We have to be advocates, half the time. I say this to my students: "Listen, half your role is going to be making your work. The other half has to fight. You have to be a fighter. You have to fight constantly because there are a lot of people out there who are very ignorant, who want to not only destroy the art but destroy the world. If you're not there to fight while you make your artwork and let it inform it, then you should just go and stop making art."

Eras of the Winnipeg Film Group

KN: Let's talk about the various eras of the Film Group.

SN: I think that it's natural and really good, strategically, to find colleagues and to find similar ideas, and to articulate that through a certain idea, or a school, of some sort. There was always a reaction against the predecessors. The first school would be the prairie postmodern school: Guy Maddin's rivalry with Paizs—brothers fighting over girls. And the incredible, self-referential way of treating the film material, which I think was an exceptional first step in terms of the experimental work that came out after that. What I find fascinating is the school that came up after that—the transgressive school. I always called it the *sensationalist school*—work that was very transgressive, very colourful and lush, taken from Maddin's school of expressionism but turning it upside-down and making it a bit more about sexual perversion and stuff like that. I love that work. That work is really controversial. After that, what may have emerged, if I may be so bold, would be the more experimental work. That step Maddin took by having the material of the film referenced in the filmmaking, through the scratches to the texture. The idea that we're watching a film that came out of the archives. I think that was a very easy segue to the experimental work, where the material itself has a more handmade quality—the destructionist scratching and high contrast. It easily fits in with the prairie surrealism stuff that I think Deco [Dawson] probably riffed off, with his influence of Maddin.

From there came the Winnipeg-eats-itself school of Forsberg and Rankin, and even Clint Enns a little bit. But Clint Enns came more off an experimental technique of glitch, moving things around. I think someone like Clint Enns, and Isiah Medina, are a part of this newer school. It riffs off of the found VHS glitch stuff, where they're learning about would-be archaeology through this material deconstruction of the Atelier—and I think Mike was involved with that as well.[65] Then you have this new school, with someone like Rhayne Vermette, whose work is influenced by architecture. I think Scott Fitzpatrick brings a glitch influence into handmade work. I mean, it's amazing—it really is because it's such a small community and people are so committed to their work. There is a line that you could trace. I think it's a fascinating thread, but it's nothing to the people who ate too many perogies one night and had bad dreams.

ARLEA ASHCROFT

Arlea Ashcroft is a filmmaker and artist based in Winnipeg. She worked as a lighting technician in the Manitoba film industry before taking a job as the Film Group's membership services coordinator, in 2007, a post she held for five years. She currently works as the Indigenous programs manager at Creative Manitoba.

7 OCTOBER 2016, WINNIPEG

Kevin Nikkel: How did you get into film?

Arlea Ashcroft: I started as an actor. I took courses at Prairie Theatre Exchange, for theatre acting. Then, eventually, I started getting cast in television commercials and some short films. One of the first film sets I was ever on was Guy Maddin's *Careful* [1992]. I had heard that there is this filmmaker, Guy. I didn't know who he was, at the time. He was making a feature film and I decided, I've taken three courses in acting. I am going to be in his movie! I looked him up in the phone book and I found out his address, and I went to his house. I just knocked on his door. Nobody was there. I had a resume and a photo, and was thinking I should just leave it in his door. Just as I was about to do that, this man was walking up the sidewalk and asked me what I was up to. I said: "I'm

---

Director Arlea Ashcroft consults with director of photography Michael Marshall on the set of *Iris and Nathan*, 1994. Photo by Szu Burgess. Courtesy of Arlea Ashcroft.

an actor and I heard there's a guy named Guy that lives here. I want to be in his movie." He said: "Well, I'm Guy Maddin. I'm the man." I asked him if I could be in his movie. He said: "Oh, okay." I gave him my resume, my headshot. A day later, he called me and said that, yes, I could be in his movie. I said: "That's fantastic! Are there any speaking roles? How many lines do I have?" He said: "Well, you don't have any because we've cast the whole film already." I said, "Are you sure? Because I'm really good. You should probably rethink that." But he didn't. But I ended up getting in the film.

It was the first film set I'd ever been on. I think it was Guy's first colour picture, and it was magical. I remember being on the film set and we were shooting in a big warehouse, and there's all the sets of mountains and coal mines and boarding schools. To me, I'd never been behind the scenes of a film before, so it opened up this whole new world of what was possible and all these secrets, of things that happen behind the camera. I got really fascinated with it. I asked some of the crew members, how do you get to do what you do? I liked the fact that they were there every single day, doing something that looked so important. They told me to go to the Winnipeg Film Group. So, I did.

Joining the Film Group

KN: What was that like?

AA: I took the Basic Filmmaking Workshop. I think, at the time, it might've been an eight-week course. I took that class and it was just, like, mind-blowing—all this cool stuff! I learned how to use the gear. I got really fascinated with being behind the camera. Then I was given an opportunity to work on a film by Maureen Devanik [Butterfield], called *Dames* [1996]. There was a program being run through the National Film Board of Canada at the time—funding specifically for women to work in stereotypically male roles, on a film shoot. They got funding for me to train as a lighting technician. I trained with Michael Drabot and Charles Lavack. Then I just fell in love with the idea of lighting. I'm an artist and a painter, so I was very fortunate to work with somebody like Michael Drabot, and then, eventually, with Michael Marshall, who are very much artists with light and stressed that you are essentially painting with light. That idea and philosophy really appealed to me. A lot of films at the time were film noir—this was in the early nineties—and had a real strong lighting aesthetic, a very genre bent. There wasn't a lot of naturalism. There was a lot of room for playing with light. I just loved the idea of playing with the light in the shadows.

I think one of the next earlier films I worked on was probably Guy Maddin's *Odilon Redon* [1995]. I did a lot of art department, as well as the lighting, and he really allowed us on the set to be creative. It was so cool because we were shooting in the Winnipeg Film Group studio and built this massive train. To this day, I stand in that studio and I wonder how we did all of that. It's like we created layers and layers of worlds. It was almost like there was no end to the room. It was so massive in our minds, what you see on screen. Guy was really generous with us. If we had an idea for a shot, he would say: "There's the camera. Go shoot it." We got to shoot our own little bits for his film. It was really all about pulling ideas and collaborating and creating together. There were no stupid questions. All ideas were given equal weight and encouraged. I felt really special to be able to be a part of those earlier films, and part of that camaraderie and that magic that we created. I was really lucky that those are some of my first films to work on.

From there, I went into working on industry pictures as a lighting technician with International Alliance of Theatrical Stage Employees (IATSE). The cool thing about our lighting crews was all of us were filmmakers. We all would encourage each other to make films. Then, when we weren't doing our industry work, we would help each other make our own independent films. And it always came back to working at the Winnipeg Film Group.

KN: Let's keep talking about the Film Group. Tell me more about how you got involved there.

Arlea Ashcroft and Shauna Townley on set. Courtesy of Arlea Ashcroft.

AA: I directed some of my own films, as well. Then I was brought in to teach part of the Basic Filmmaking Workshop. I would teach the lighting portion of it, or do special one-off lighting workshops. Eventually, in 2007, I got a job at the Winnipeg Film Group and I worked there for five years. My job title was Membership Services Coordinator. A lot of what I would do was encourage and educate young filmmakers about all the possibilities that lie within our walls. I'd show them how to use equipment, and help to make connections with other filmmakers, and problem solve. I did that for five years, while going back and forth teaching workshops. I sat on a lot of juries for the Film Group. At one point, I had taught an eleven-week screenwriting workshop. It kind of blows me away right now—I think that Danishka Esterhazy was one of my students and now she is a famous filmmaker, which is really cool. But I do find that with the Film Group, once you get into that community—and it is a real community—that people don't forget that. They are so generous with their time and their knowledge, and they want to share what they know. It always comes around. I find that a lot of my closest friends in the arts scene, now, are still the filmmakers that I met at the Film Group way back when—and even now.

KN: How would you summarize the importance of the Winnipeg Film Group to the local art scene?

AA: I think that the Winnipeg Film Group is one of the most important aspects in the whole arts and culture sector of Manitoba. It's the place pretty much every single filmmaker, or video artist, has gone to learn the tricks of the trade. It's their very first time on a film set—the very first time they put their hands on a camera, or on sound-recording gear, or an editing suite. It's the very first time they touch film. It's been intrinsic to create filmmakers whose careers have lasted thirty years. Right now, I'm working at Creative Manitoba and we're having a screening for the Indigenous Filmmakers Association. All those filmmakers are meeting at the Winnipeg Film Group, so it's also a real community hub. I think that's also a great encourager of experimentation.

Indigenous Filmmakers

KN: It seems like in the story of the Film Group, there are these eras where people come and go. It seems like there is a new wave.

AA: Is there a wave of Indigenous filmmakers? Yes, there is—absolutely. I don't think it's a wave as in being a trend; I think it's time for Indigenous voices to be heard. I think that the film and digital mediums are a very powerful way to make those voices heard. I think that it's being embraced by the Indigenous community. When you say it's a wave, I don't see it. I think it's more like a tide, as opposed to a wave. It's people coming together and going, hey look, there's another medium we can use. We can try to figure out a way to use it, to see how our voices can be heard. I think that tide is going to get higher and higher, and more and more people will get involved.

On Staff at the Film Group

KN: You're the point of contact, while you are at the Film Group. What did you bring to the job?

AA: I would usually start with: "How can I help you? What do you want to do? What are you interested in? Let's figure this out." A lot of times, people didn't know what they wanted to do. We would just sit and talk—that was my thing. I'd just sit and spend some time talking and hanging out with them. Oftentimes, I would have a chair right beside my desk. We called it my Chair of Truth. It would happen that when filmmakers would come in—sometimes I would know them, sometimes I would've never met them before—they would just sit down and they would spill their hearts out about what they wanted to do, or what they were going through, or what the big challenge was, or what their fears were. They would always spill and share what they were going through. A lot of times, through those stories and just taking the time to listen to people, you can figure out what they want. They might go about it in a roundabout way, but if you really listen, you can hear what they're saying. I think that was probably my greatest strength, working at the Film Group, is listening. Listening to people. A lot of people just needed someone to tell them: "You can do it. We got your back"; and be an advocate for them, saying: "We're here to help you. We want you to succeed. Whatever it takes, man—we got you."

KN: You were part therapist, part cheerleader, and then had all the paperwork, too.

AA: That, and also a technician. I would help a lot of people with their lighting, since my background is as a lighting technician, which I did for fourteen years. I would take people into the studio, often not even in an official class sense, to say, okay, let's play with lights. Let's recreate scenes. Tell me what you want to do and let's figure out how to do that. You don't have any money to rent lights? Okay, well, I have this whole box of things I got from Home Depot. Let's make a lighting kit. Let's figure out how we can do this for no budget. We got you, man.

Artists—whether filmmakers or painters or writers—have their own neuroses and their own fears. So, that whole thing about being the film therapist—that goes with any medium. Anytime someone is trying to create something, they're trying to pull something out of themselves, and the Film Group always felt like a safe place you can do that. It was encouraged.

Dave Barber: What's your favourite filmmaking phrase?

AA: "Don't be an asshole." That's a quote from Ellen Kuras, an award-winning documentary filmmaker and director of photography who we brought to the Winnipeg Film Group to teach lighting workshops, screen her films, and do one-on-one sessions with local filmmakers. I asked her if she had any advice for up-and-coming directors of photography and aspiring filmmakers, and she said: "The one piece of advice that I can pass on is: don't be an asshole." I agree with that, 100 percent.

WALTER FORSBERG

Walter Forsberg was born in Regina, Saskatchewan. Currently, he works as a media conservator with WET Labs, in Mexico City, and is a member of the film collective Laboratorio Experimental de Cine. From 2005 through 2008, Walter made collaborative films and art projects in Winnipeg with Matthew Rankin, Mike Maryniuk, and others as part of l'Atelier national du Manitoba. He held many positions at the Winnipeg Film Group and he co-designed the Dave Barber Cinematheque T-shirt. A graduate of NYU's Moving Image Archiving and Preservation master's program, he now works as a media archivist and is a contributing editor with INCITE: Journal of Experimental Media.

24 AUGUST 2015, WASHINGTON, DC

Kevin Nikkel: Let's start with introductions.

Walter Forsberg: I'm Walter Forsberg. I was born in Regina, Saskatchewan, in 1980. Right now, we're sitting at the temporary home of the National Museum of African American History and Culture, at the Smithsonian in Washington, DC, where I am the media archivist.

KN: Was your family background highly artistic, contributing to the road that you eventually took?

Walter Forsberg, co-designer of the Dave Barber Cinematheque T-shirt. Courtesy of Walter Forsberg.

WF: Not at all. I was born in a funeral home and my mother owned a chain of beauty salons, which she sold when she married my father. She did the hair and makeup of the deceased at the funeral home. My dad was a mortician and undertaker at funeral homes.

KN: You grew up seeing the bodies?

WF: Yeah, very normal. I followed in my father's footsteps, but ended up as some kind of mortician for old media.

KN: Caring for and doctoring and preserving the old media?

WF: Yeah, giving them new life, in a new format, and caring for the end-of-life cycles of the older formats.

KN: You're originally from Regina. Then you went to school where?

WF: I grew up all over western Canada. In high school, I moved to the United States, to the Chicago area. I finished high school in Chicago, before going back to Canada—Quebec, more specifically—for university.

KN: What did you study?

WF: I went to McGill University, where I studied history, mainly American and Quebec history, and cultural studies. Cultural studies was a stream of the English department there, wherein students were able to take film appreciation courses, semiotics courses, and cultural philosophy. A kind of namby-pamby academic stream.

KN: Tell me about how you found your way to the artistic life.

WF: I'm not really sure that I'm in the artistic life, or am comfortable being in the artistic life, mainly because I feel an aversion to that kind of taxonomy. I think one Winnipeg-related foray into filmmaking I can relate would be the 2001 Free Trade Area of the Americas (FTAA) protest in Quebec City. Travelling there on a yellow Bluebird school bus, I was playing around with a Super 8 camera, planning to shoot some Super 8 at the protests. I encountered a young man on that school bus that was in my French class at McGill. He was this "odd bird," as people considered him in university French class—that was Matt Rankin. We ended up making a film at the FTAA protests. We called it *Kino Québec*

[2002]. That was one of my initial forays into making films, although I had made a couple Super 8 films in Montreal before that.

Rankin and I had a really great time in Quebec City. When we returned to Montreal, there was a disused production facility of the English department on Peel Street, in Montreal, in an old brownstone building. I guess, at some point, the McGill English department had offered video and film production courses and they no longer offered those. So, all of the equipment was up for grabs and we were able to obtain a key to the building. We would go there at night and on weekends, and edit in Adobe Premiere on a Macintosh Performa, ordering pizza and listening to Rolling Stones albums that were randomly in that production space.

L'Atelier national du Manitoba

KN: How did you end up in Winnipeg and the Film Group?

WF: Rankin and I continued to be friends and see each other occasionally, cohabitate occasionally. I think he would sublet in a loft on Saint-Denis Street that I had, maybe while he was in between trips to Iran and the Middle East. We made some other films together. In the summer of 2003, we were commissioned by Brian Young, the chair of the McGill history department, who had been our professor in different classes. He paid us to make a documentary for a history conference that McGill was hosting. Matt and I spent the summer of 2003 making this documentary together, all over eastern Canada, which was very fun. I think it really inspired both of us with the realization that we could make films, and get money to make films. Several years later, when we no longer lived in the same town and didn't necessarily make films together, we hatched this idea to do a "year of reading," and that evolved into the Atelier national du Manitoba.

KN: Tell me about that the "year of reading."

WF: Study, self-improvement, reading books, and working some kind of menial-Joe job in order to sustain a life of personal enrichment and exploration. This idea came directly from Guy Maddin's then-recently published journals, which Rankin and I read and reread many times. I have very profound memories of being in Iraq in 2003, where Guy's journals were the only book in English available to me. Anyway, Rankin and I decided that this "year of reading" should take place in Winnipeg because Winnipeg was cheap and it was going to be easy to do projects in Winnipeg. One rationale we had was that all of the best artists were living in Montreal or Toronto or Vancouver; therefore, it would be easier to move to Winnipeg and get grants there because we would have less competition for getting grants. I think we were wrong about the quality of the artists because Winnipeg—as everyone says—has amazing artists.

Joining the Film Group

KN: When did the Film Group enter into that process?

WF: One of the first things that I did, when I moved to Winnipeg, was to go and meet Dave Barber. Dave was magnanimously generous and asked me if I wouldn't mind inspecting some 16-mm prints that were going to be screened. I believe this was John Paizs's *Springtime in Greenland* [1981]. I had seen *Springtime in Greenland* from a ghetto telecine on VHS that Matthew Etches had sent me, when I was a programmer at the Chicago Underground Film Festival, in 2003. I had programmed a series of Winnipeg films and videos, and I had met Matt Etches.

When I moved to Winnipeg, I knew to go to the Film Group primarily because of Matt Etches, but also because of the legend of Dave Barber. Dave had me inspect 16-mm prints and clean them by hand, which was really beautiful—up on the fourth floor in the Winnipeg Film Group, in the old optical printing cave. It was a very special experience because I felt immediately trusted with that important task. I had some film-handling experience from making films, but I had no archival experience, so that was a very, very important first opportunity that Dave gave me. I made very detailed report sheets for him.

Matthew Rankin and Walter Forsberg. Courtesy of Walter Forsberg.

NO SUITS. NO LIMITS.
NO SEATS. NO SUITS. NO LIMITS.
.06
VIDEO AWARDS
the Throttles
STAND TA
going to need a bigger trailer
NOKIA
JUNE 18

After that, I think the Film Group was, initially, a way to get things done—a place where you could meet other filmmakers and, perhaps eventually, a place where you might be able to have a little job. You might work a few days a week, a shift or two, or teach a workshop. Get a little bit of money, or get some in-kind services that you could use and parlay into rental for a camera to make something. Initially, the Film Group was very wonderful, and an idyllic place.

KN: What was the climate like at the Film Group in 2005?

WF: When I first went into the Winnipeg Film Group, it was on the third floor of the Artspace building, on Arthur Street. There was still this kind of sleepy office vibe going on. Victor Enns was the executive director. Matthew Etches was distributor. I even think Jeff Erbach was the production coordinator, although I might be wrong and it may have changed to David Zellis by that point. It definitely had a femaleless boy vibe going on. I can't really say that that struck me then—but now, yes, very much. It was kind of an interesting place, but I didn't quite understand exactly what it offered. I always stayed pretty close to Matthew Etches as he was my first friend and point of contact there, having known him before I moved to Winnipeg. I eventually became the assistant distributor. I worked a lot of different jobs at the Film Group.

KN: That turned out to be very useful for you, long-term-wise.

WF: I held so many different jobs at the Film Group. I worked for Matthew Etches as the assistant distributor, volunteered under Tara Walker, and subsequently got paid to work the Sunday-night box office shift at the Cinematheque for Dave Barber and Erin Childs. Eventually, I had the Friday-night-and-Saturday-night gig as Cinematheque projectionist and worked Monday, Tuesday, Wednesday, and Thursday as the box office manager—so, I was working six days a week at Cinematheque, at one point. Then I was a line producer for the 30th Anniversary

---

Burton Stand Tall poster installed at the Metropolitan Theatre, Winnipeg, 2005. Courtesy of Walter Forsberg.

Film Commissions project, in 2007—project manager of that process. I worked a lot at the Film Group, in addition to teaching various workshops there. I think it really gave me an education about the whole factory line of cinema. Eventually, when I retired from writing film reviews for the *Uptown* newsprint weekly (as Peter Vesuwalla's replacement for two years), I did write in my final *Film with Walter* column that I had effectively worked the entire factory line of cinema. I worked on showing people how to make movies, making the movies, distributing the movies, exhibiting the movies, and then writing critiques of the movies in the newspaper. I really did get an incredibly well-rounded experience in that small cinema universe.

Death by Popcorn

KN: Let's talk about the Atelier national du Manitoba. You hooked up with Matt Rankin, and Mike Maryniuk joined at some point?

WF: I think, from the beginning, it was really clear to us that Mike Maryniuk was a genius and that we needed to have him involved. I remember hanging out at his place, on Maryland Avenue, and feeling that Mike had to be involved somehow, and came up with this idea that Matt and I had talked about—having these commissions or assignments, where each of us were supposed to make some Super 8 film. That seemed like a really good way to get Mike Maryniuk involved in the Atelier.

KN: It seems like things picked up quickly?

WF: I think, initially, we had this idea of an assignment that each of us would complete: a Super 8 assignment pairing imagery shot on Super 8 with a Canadian pop song from the eighties. Mike ended up making a really brilliant film out of that, about the mad-cow disease: *Give Beef a Chance* [2007].

But in terms of the three of us working together, I think that really took place when we started to make the hockey movie about the Winnipeg Jets. I remember one evening, hanging out at Mike's Maryland Avenue apartment with some recently digitized footage from CKY-TV that we

Poster from l'Atelier national du Manitoba's feature film *Death by Popcorn*, 2006. Courtesy of Walter Forsberg.

Still photo with Paul Butler from l'Atelier national du Manitoba's *Death by Popcorn*, 2006. Courtesy of Walter Forsberg.

had dumpster dived. We made a short on right winger Paul McLean, which was very silly—very GIF-y, actually, with repetitive motion loops. We were just making it in Final Cut Pro on my laptop and we called it *Paul McLean on Anal Strain* because there was this movement that we had discerned that was very Arnoldian. Martin Arnold would've approved of this movement, which involved a hockey stick repeatedly spanking Paul MacLean on the bottom.

I think, at that moment, we realized that we could make little experimental films out of all of this footage of the Winnipeg Jets, which CKY had [destroyed]. That was really when that *Death by Popcorn* movie [2006] came together as an idea, although each of us had different ideas about what that would mean. Each of us made different parts of the movie and then kind of tried to string them together. I think Rankin, who is a brilliant editor, is responsible for much of the cohesion—maybe I'm slagging his skills by saying that—but really seeing this kind of operatic unity to all of these disparate little experimental films. That was really when Mike became involved. Mike played hockey. Mike was really into the Jets and certainly knew more about the Jets than I did. I grew up in Edmonton in the 1980s, when the Oilers were regularly decimating the Winnipeg Jets, so I was a big Gretzky fan. My interest was in demonizing Gretzky, for fun.

Winnipeg Film Group

KN: Are there parallels between what you guys were doing, with what was happening at the Film Group? A separate collective or mini-film group?

WF: I don't really see it as a parallel thing because, selfishly, even though maybe we worked at the Film Group or contributed in our own way to the co-op, it was always a resource for us. It was always primarily a resource for me, at least, even though I worked there and cared a lot about it. I'm not sure that I considered it a parallel pond of creativity. For me, it was where you could make and show your movie. It was where you could rent the video camera that you couldn't afford to own. I'm not sure I felt a strong aesthetic affinity with most of the creative output of its members at that time, although I helped many to create and disseminate those movies.

KN: You cared about it.

WF: I cared deeply about the Film Group, I think, because a lot of my friends were there and I spent a lot of my time there. The Film Group is a kind of prairie socialist ideal, but I didn't really feel passionate about it for that reason. I cared about the Film Group a lot, but also too much because, eventually, I had differences of opinion with certain people who are in charge of the Film Group—and I'm not just talking about Cecilia Araneda [former executive director of the Winnipeg Film Group] but like anyone, or the board, or even you when you were on the board—over decisions made in a vacuum that didn't necessarily take into consideration things the staff were going through. I got very wrapped up in that, and I learned a lot about myself and how I should not get wrapped up in those kinds of things. I don't know why I cared so much about it. I guess I'd seen a lot of cool stuff and opportunities happen there and also a lot of garbage that came out of there, production- and politics-wise. I just wanted there to be more cool stuff than garbage.

Leaving Winnipeg

KN: Let's talk about your self-inflicted exile. When did you feel like you had to go?

WF: I wanted to go to graduate school. Every year, Rankin and I would renew our vows of staying. I decided to stay one more year, one more year, and, eventually, in the fall 2007, I thought I should really apply, just to have an option. I knew that I wanted to get a master's degree, so I applied. I had met a couple different people who had gone to this program at New York University, for film and video and media preservation. I applied. When I got in, it just seemed like it was the right thing to do. Curiously, that fall of 2008 proved an exodus moment for nearly a dozen of my close Film Group friends, who all relocated to Montreal and Toronto.

To address your nostalgia question: I think, as I grow older, I can look back at my time in Winnipeg as very formative in learning about the whole factory line of cinema—production, exhibition, distribution, preservation—and really see its critical importance in the narrative of my adult life. It was where I learned about making films from a technical standpoint. And I was also thrust into this position—with the Videon/VPW archives and with the CKY-TV Winnipeg Jets tape material—where I became a conduit through which videotapes could be preserved and history could be written.[66] In Winnipeg, I think I realized that was a niche that needed to be filled in a lot of different universes outside of Winnipeg—all the way from going to New York and working with artists like Cory Arcangel and Lillian Schwartz, helping them to start thinking about the long-term life of their artworks, to here in Washington, building a new national collection of memory of the African-American experience and collaborating on how those memories need to be preserved. Really, all of that came from getting a phone call from my landlord about the CKY dumpster being full of Jets tapes. In that way, it's not really nostalgia for my time in Winnipeg as much as it is an appreciation that I was open to it, and that it happened. It's really funny, but I joke with my parents about how they had this moment of fear, in their parental lives, when I had moved to Winnipeg. I was living in Chinatown, in this former grocery store with mice and no bathroom. I tell my parents that if it were not for that, I would not have done any of the other things in my career that I've done and really enjoyed.

One thing that I saw lacking at artist-run centres is this self-documentation process, of marking time. Whether it's through a documentary, which would be far more predictable, or doing it through a book project, where people are able to look back. I remember for the 30th Anniversary Film Commissions project, where the five filmmakers were commissioned by the Canada Council, we were putting together the DVD booklet and we wanted ephemera from the different periods of the Film Group. It was really sad to see how only around certain dates, or events, or executive directors, were there publications made that had colour photos. And I think that that really taught me about the importance of documenting that kind of stuff. That eventually inspired me to edit and publish the *STARVATION YEARS* scrapbook, about all of our Atelier projects.[67]

KN: What are your thoughts on the impact of the Film Group on the Canadian film scene?

WF: I think that my thoughts about the import of the Film Group on the international movie market or filmmaking scene would be more cooperatively oriented. I think that the Film Group is very influential in giving a wide array of people a certain experience. Maybe they learn to hand-paint Super 8 film there with Mike Maryniuk, or maybe they learn optical printing from someone, or maybe they learn how to use Final Cut Pro. Maybe some of them never become filmmakers, or maybe some of them never drink the Kool-Aid that is the feature-film dream. But at least they had this experience and a lot of them will go on to do other things. Their Film Group experience will, in some way, form part of who they are and what they do. Maybe they'll become newspaper journalists that know how to edit their own videos for online distribution. I think that that's the real strength of the Film Group, and the thing that binds it together with all of its "graduates," if you will. I'm not so sure that Winnipeg is an important contributor to the history of Canadian cinema, in terms of the canon—even though, when I was at the Film Group, I liked to think that it was, or was hoping that it was. I think that seems too calculated. I think that history doesn't necessarily work like that. Maybe the films of Guy Maddin will be remembered, but maybe not.

KN: Anything else about the Film Group?

WF: I am just getting into the thick of talking about it! The Cinematheque is really the public face of the Film Group. It's the penultimate act of the cinema-making process—to show your movie on the big screen, to share with audiences—and, as such, Dave is really the guy at the finish line with the Gatorade cup, for every filmmaker there. He is an amazing person.

I think another thing about the Film Group that's really interesting is the perspective that you get, in terms of who was "good" or what work was "good." When you're at the Film Group, you are a bit blinded by certain things—context, friendships, hubris, whatever—but I think that some of the best work that was coming out of the Film Group, and some of the most exciting makers that I know, are people that, when I was at the Film Group, I didn't think were the most exciting makers. I'm very excited by people like Leslie Supnet or like Clint Enns. I don't even think Clint Enns is a good filmmaker; I think Clint Enns is an amazing photographer, and those weren't things that I necessarily thought when I was at the Film Group. That's interesting to observe, stepping away from the Film Group.

KN: You stepped away, but it comes back to you.

Party invitation from l'Atelier national du Manitoba. Courtesy of Walter Forsberg.

WF: I helped some people at the Film Group and I really pissed off some people at the Film Group, and it was all great. I just think that it's a special experience for young people to learn about political processes—things like hierarchies and seniorities in organizations, or even just the nuts-and-bolts of building a community. There's a lot of human knowledge that you gain from being a card-carrying member of the Winnipeg Film Group. I learned a lot about that. I feel great about not being at the Film Group. I love the Film Group and I appreciate the Film Group for what it gave to me, but it's great to not think about it too much anymore.

DISCOUNT

MATTHEW RANKIN

Matthew Rankin was born and raised in Winnipeg and first took workshops at the Winnipeg Film Group at the age of thirteen. He moved to Quebec to study history, obtaining an undergraduate degree from McGill University and a master's degree from l'Université Laval. He returned to Winnipeg and lived there from 2005 to 2008, during which time he collaborated with Walter Forsberg and Mike Maryniuk as l'Atelier national du Manitoba, culminating in the found-footage feature Death by Popcorn *(2006). During these years, Matthew frequented the Winnipeg Film Group and worked part-time at the Cinematheque. He lives in Montreal, making movies.*

20 JULY 2016, LONDON, ENGLAND

KN: Where did you get your start?

MR: I got started in film through animation. My parents learned quickly that if they just left me alone with a pen and stack of paper, I'd keep myself occupied for days on end. I just drew, literally all the time, and eventually this transformed into making little animated films with my friend's video camera. Then, when I was about thirteen, I took the Basic Filmmaking Workshop at the Winnipeg Film Group. That was my point of entry.

Matthew Rankin. Photo by Mike Aporius, 2006. *Winnipeg Free Press.*

KN: Talk about your experience when you walked in the door of the Winnipeg Film Group.

MR: George Godwin was the first person I spoke to and, somewhat begrudgingly, he allowed me to take the Basic Filmmaking Workshop. At that time, in the mid-nineties, there was no "Teen Workshop," so I was thrown right into a cohort of lost adults, most of whom were maladjusted thirtysomething bachelors. I was, of course, a naive kid and I remember Dennis Valdron and Dean Naday, then Film Group stalwarts, lecturing me at punitive length about how hopelessly unrealistic all my ideas were. But other people were very nurturing. Patrick Lowe and Winston Moxam were really encouraging and supportive and helpful, a real positive force in my young life. I was real naive and that's a vulnerable state.

KN: I think that's necessary—to have a measure of innocence and naivety as an artist—because if you really knew what you were to face, you'd never do it.

MR: That might be true. Later, I would teach that very same Basic Filmmaking Workshop and it always draws in same sort of novice filmmakers. I think it's really important to encourage people in their creative enthusiasm, make the Film Group a safe zone for that. We're all learning, all the time. There is a new workshop, specifically for teens, which would have been so great in my day.

KN: Let's work out your chronology. You were hanging around the Winnipeg Film Group and then you went away to Montreal?

MR: I didn't go to film school. I got a scholarship and went away to McGill, where I studied history and I ended up doing graduate studies in Quebec City, at l'Université Laval. And I also went on a number of extended trips in the Middle East. While I was gone, I found myself thinking about Winnipeg a lot and found I had a lot of feelings about it I wanted to express. I also figured out that I didn't want to be an

---

Matthew Rankin with Bolex, 1995. Courtesy of Matthew Rankin.

academic; I wanted to just do art all the time. I made the decision to go back to Winnipeg and do art.

KN: When you were away, did you have specific ideas about Winnipeg? When we're away, we become more objective about a place. I'm curious about your thoughts about the place.

A Winnipeg Aesthetic

MR: Yeah, it was lots of things. I got really excited about what I thought of as the "Winnipeg School" of filmmaking—the pattern of obsessions and pathologies, both visual and thematic, that seemed to create a singular film culture. I do think that you can speak about Winnipeg cinema the way you can speak of Quebec cinema, French cinema, Iranian cinema, and other coherent national cinemas. To me, the only thing that connects all filmmakers in Canada, into something that might be termed "Canadian cinema," is citizenship. There is no artistic dialectic happening on the Canadian level, to my eyes. But in Winnipeg, there definitely is!

So, that inspired me. I think the first time I ever watched a movie and understood it as something more than entertainment, it would have been Richard Condie's *The Big Snit* [1985]. In that movie, I recognized something about the city I belonged to, the culture I was part of. It was transcendental. Guy Maddin's *Careful* [1992] was also like that for me. And this just continued on. Patrick Lowe had given me a full doctoral seminar on the films of John Paizs and those films became so deeply meaningful to me. In these images, I could see my city in all of its ironies and unfulfilled longings, and I recognized them as my own.

KN: How would you paint a quick picture of Winnipeg?

MR: Well, the easy answer is that Winnipeg is remote and isolated from the rest of the world. It's a thing people always say and, while it might be true, I think it's an artistic cliché. What I find more interesting about Winnipeg is not so much its geographic isolation, but its exclusion from mainstream "Anglo-America."

My own reading of Winnipeg history is that there has been, throughout time, a constant tension between two systems of identification. On the one hand, you have what you might call the New Nation. For me, this is the Winnipeg that emerged out of Louis Riel's Provisional Government, during the Red River tensions of 1869–70. To me, Riel was totally punk-rock, and built up this brave, anti-establishment coalition, which would resist the brazen entitlements of mainstream Anglo-America and insist upon a new idea of nation. To me, that spirit is still shining bright, particularly in Winnipeg artists, and forms one major ventricle in Winnipeg's beating heart. The other ventricle—the right ventricle, let's say—falls under the metaphor that I will call the Orange Lodge. For me, the Orange Lodge is a Winnipeg that rejects the originality of the New Nation and seeks to crush it. This is the Winnipeg of John Christian Schultz, the Citizens' Committee of One Thousand, of Portage Place and CentreVenture—it's a pro-establishment, pro-development Winnipeg.[68] A Winnipeg that seeks to conform to mainstream Anglo-America and revel in its ill-begotten economic spoils. As you might guess, I'm not a big fan of the Orange Lodge. But the point is, these two contradictory elements are what make Winnipeg whole. There is a constant tension between them, throughout our history, and it continues on to this day.

For me, as somebody who works in art, I find this tension to be deeply creative and inspiring. It's hard to have a coherent relationship with Winnipeg. It's why Winnipeggers always see the fallacy in the unrelenting boosterism of the Winnipeg Chamber of Commerce and other Orangemen. Anything that we can affirm about Winnipeg can be swiftly and easily contradicted by its absolute antithesis. There's an irony we just can't escape—and I love that.

KN: Let's talk more about the Winnipeg film aesthetic. The Winnipeg School?

MR: I think of the Winnipeg School in film as a brazenly anti-establishment spirit, almost an outsider art. It can be loosely defined by three main tenets which, of course, are constantly shapeshifting through the prism of individual artists. First, there is an obsession with the materiality

Poster for *Garbage Hill: A Retrospective of Discarded Winnipeg Film and TV*, film screening event poster, 2005. Courtesy of l'Atelier national du Manitoba.

of film emulsion and/or video static. Second, there is a pathology for reprocessing of outmoded film language. Third, there is a very keen sense of weird humour and the absurd. These three aesthetic tenets generally unite a very large cross-section of Winnipeg media artists, from Erica Eyres to Shawna Dempsey and Lorri Millan, to Solomon Nagler, and Rhayne Vermette. Added to this, there is a reigning irony. Winnipeggers are not a very earnest bunch, for the most part. I also observe a consistent preoccupation with the apocalypse, from Richard Condie to Noam Gonick. And of course, I think it can be said that *all* media artists in Winnipeg, regardless of their aesthetic affiliations, eventually begin to obsess over the meanings of Winnipeg itself. The Québécois filmmaker Denis Côté once complained to me that all Winnipeg filmmakers ever do is make films about Winnipeg. And he's right! But of course, try taking the Quebec out of Quebec cinema. The joy of watching a movie is in the discovery of a new world, precisely defined; and there are feelings about

where we are from that just urgently compel expression.

L'Atelier national du Manitoba

KN: At what point did you consciously start to express those feelings?

MR: I came back to Winnipeg in 2005, with a lot of stuff I wanted to say. I met Sol Nagler and Mike Maryniuk and Deco Dawson, and I was so excited about what they were working on, so inspired by what they had achieved. My friend Walter Forsberg and I started working on lots of different Winnipeg-focused projects. I wanted to do a whole archival retrospective of locally produced Winnipeg TV commercials, from the analog glory days in the 1980s. Walter and I started digging through every VHS tape we could find, fast-forwarding through CKND broadcasts of *Jaws* and *T.J. Hooker* and plundering the commercial breaks. Simultaneously, the performance artist Daniel Barrow happened to be working on a

---

Walter Forsberg and Matthew Rankin. Courtesy of Walter Forsberg.

Filmmakers Mike Maryniuk, Matthew Rankin and actor Andrew Cecon, 2007. Courtesy of Walter Forsberg.

similar project about VPW, Winnipeg's public-access broadcaster, which would go on to become his celebrated curation-performance *Winnipeg Babysitter* [2005–08]. So, we joined forces and created this far-reaching survey of lost Winnipeg television, which we named *Garbage Hill* [2005]. This was the pre-YouTube era and the project amassed real cultural energy. Winnipeg screen culture was in the zeitgeist and there was a real appetite for it.

Doing that project, you realize how truly amazing Nick Hill was. Nick Hill was, of course, Winnipeg's most iconic furniture salesman but I also think of him as a great video artist. His boisterous TV commercials for Kern-Hill Furniture Co-op are, to my way of seeing, great works of art. Nick might have never consciously thought about his TV spots as anything more than promotion but, to me, they are visionary. A sophisticated set of aesthetic decisions is at work. In each spot, Nick appears wearing a ten-gallon hat inside a levitating, ectoplasmic bubble. For thirty seconds, he screams at you about discount dinette sets or wholesale microwaves, while urgent optical titles flash across utilitarian images of furniture. Again, a new world is discovered, precisely defined. Nick Hill is also a supreme example of simultaneity within screen nationalism. We all recognize Nick Hill as an image of ourselves and, in a strange but real way, he unites all Winnipeggers in a common cinematic experience. I've never bought a dinette set. But I suspect that more Winnipeggers have encountered a Kern-Hill Furniture spot than have seen *Stand!* [2019], the musical film about the 1919 General Strike, for example.

Anyway, the world of Winnipeg screen culture became fascinating to me, while I was abroad. Maybe I was homesick? But I think we do art to find out where we are from, and Nick Hill seemed to offer some clues.

Around this same time, Walter Forsberg and I got a call from the video archivist down at the now-defunct CKY television studio. At that time, CKY, a local CTV affiliate, was being shut down and consolidated into the Toronto head office and decades of video were being thrown in the trash.

The soon-to-be-retired archivist called us and said: "You should come down and take all these tapes. Otherwise, they're just going to the dump."

We ended up taking two carloads of old cassettes—some two thousand tapes in all imaginable video formats. Going through it, what we found was overwhelmingly old Winnipeg Jets footage, including a lot of historic material about the total collapse of the franchise in the mid-1990s. The real clincher was this one incredible tape of Burton Cummings suiting up as honorary Jets captain, circa 1990. Walter and I were completely obsessed with Burton Cummings and listened to his 1980 record *Woman Love* almost daily, in our apartment. So, this felt totally cosmic and we knew we had to do something about it. Mike Maryniuk knew much more about Jets history than Walter and I, and he had made some extremely accomplished collage films, which Walter and I really loved. So, all three of us started digging through this mass of tape, with the idea of building a collage film out of it.

We also felt like we were on a sacred mission. The fact that all of this material was just being tossed in a dumpster felt like a massive crime against Winnipeg history. When we were working on *Garbage Hill*, we had seen firsthand the terrifying fragility of Winnipeg's audiovisual heritage. At one time, VPW had a complete archive of Winnipeg public-access television, but, when it was taken over by Shaw Cable, the new management just carted it all off to a landfill as if it was worthless junk. You can't just go to the Manitoba Archives and consult the Nick Hill fonds. There is no Nick Hill fonds! It was as if nobody realized the value of this stuff, didn't care about it. TV ephemera is fragile material and seems to have escaped the kind of preservationist concern that protects "heritage buildings" from demolition, for example. So, when this CKY video archivist called us, we felt like this horrifying cycle was about to repeat yet again. We felt like we were duty-bound to save the Jets—at least in video form.

Matthew Rankin on the Winnipeg Cinematheque's concession stand in the Artspace Lobby. Courtesy of Walter Forsberg.

MEDIUM COMBO
$4
COMBO
$8
MONSTER POPCORN
$5
En français
avec plaisir!
in English
FRESH

Death by Popcorn

KN: What happened next?

MR: So, Mike and Walter and I started jamming out these little mashups, more or less independently from each other, and then stringing them together into an epic, sixty-one-minute omnibus film. We named it *Death by Popcorn: The Tragedy of the Winnipeg Jets* [2006], in honour of the box of popcorn that was mysteriously scattered upon the home ice during the 1990 playoffs, which, according to NHL historians, ruined Winnipeg's only real shot at the Stanley Cup.

The film is mainly comprised of snarky, remixed video fragments, but it nonetheless builds an argument and draws together a synthesis. We were inspired by *Tribulation 99* [1992], the mammoth experimental feature by Craig Baldwin, whom Walter and I idolized. I like it when experimental films transcend pure formalism and integrate narrative elements, and that's what we tried to do. *Death by Popcorn* is very surreal and abstract, crude and cunning; but, in a weird way, it's actually an articulate testimony to the existential crisis and civic self-loathing provoked by the collapse of Winnipeg's NHL Franchise. It's a city symphony about a very real, foundational trauma for "the saddest city in the world."

It was released in 2005 and, of course, at that time, there was still not even one hope that the NHL would ever return. The film became something of a Class F blockbuster and was widely reported upon, both in Winnipeg and across the country. Every screening was sold out. Again, there was a hunger for this material in the zeitgeist. Mike is always a very level-headed person, but Walter and I just went completely wild with hubris in TV interviews, brazenly gloating about how we had rescued precious Winnipeg artifacts from a corporate colossus who sought their destruction. I remember I actually said on camera, to one CTV journalist, that the scrapping of this sacred video archive was tantamount and equal to the burning of the library at Alexandria. It was really out of control.

Anyway, maybe a month after the release, we received a frightening letter from CTV. They instructed us to go down to the station and sign a paper confessing that we had stolen the tapes out of the dumpster. They accused us of violating copyright law by remixing their discarded footage; they ordered us to destroy every single copy of the film and return all the videotapes, so they could be definitively carted off to a landfill. Legal action was darkly threatened. It was scary.

Somehow Val Ross, a journalist at the *Globe and Mail*, caught wind of this sad story and wrote a long piece about it. This was a real blessing down from heaven, because she really took our side in the matter and made a strong case for reasonable artistic exceptions to copyright law in Canada. Her article resulted in a lot of bad press for CTV and, a few weeks later, the president of CTV's Winnipeg studio sent us a friendly email and said: "Let's go out for lunch and resolve this. My treat. Choose any place you like." So, we chose the Wagon Wheel Restaurant and the president *loved* his clubhouse and McCain Superfries. He told us he thought we were trying to make money with *Death by Popcorn*. He said he didn't understand how or why anybody would make a film just for the fun of it—just for art—without any moneymaking scheme. But he said that as long as we didn't try to sell it for TV broadcast, we'd have no more problem from him. It was a strange case of the Orange Lodge and the New Nation making a deal and shaking hands.

Winnipeg Film Group

KN: How is this flurry of activity happening in relation to the Winnipeg Film Group?

MR: The key was Dave Barber. Nothing would have happened without Dave. *Death by Popcorn* was made swiftly and it had to be presented somewhere. Same with *Garbage Hill*. Same with everything that followed. Dave follows the work of local creatives very closely and is a huge ally. He was generous, encouraging, and made space for us, found a way to present our work. The Film Group, writ large, was also full of great energy at that time. Walter and I took Solomon Nagler's hand-processing workshop and I remember what a massive inspiration that was to us. We got to know Victoria Prince and Heidi Phillips, and learned so much from them. Darryl Nepinak was just emerging, at that time. There was a real critical mass of singular talents and we were all helping each other and collaborating on each other's stuff. It was wonderful. It's what artist-run centres are supposed to be like.

KN: Is there a reason why the Film Group isn't always that way?

MR: I don't know. Winnipeg definitely has a mean streak, don't you think? Embittered artists are everywhere, but some Winnipeg filmmakers have really declared war upon civilization itself. I think it goes in cycles. You found that meanness in the films being produced in the mid-1990s, too. I remember, at one point, the Film Group put out a DVD called *The Sensationalists* [2004], which curated a number of significant short films produced in the 1990s. Nearly every one of them was overwhelmingly nasty, with the exception of Barry Gibson's *A Question of Reality* [1997], which really is his masterpiece. And Noam's film *1919* [1997] is one of my favourites. But the rest of the curation is almost gleefully callous. The shorts by Jeff Erbach, Gord Wilding, and Paul Suderman—all of which were prominent titles in their day—were driven by a real sadistic affectation. The spirit of the work is much like a rat revelling in human squalor. It's how I remember the reigning vibe at the Film Group in the nineties.

Don't get me wrong, though: Jeff Erbach was a major talent. An acid wit and a born leader, Jeff was surrounded by an adoring cohort of acolytes, who were absolutely devoted to his misanthropic vision. He was a true subversive and all of his films systematically undermined the old W.O. Mitchell cliché of nostalgic prairie wheatfields. The Orange Lodge has provided us with no shortage of overly empowered institutional voices telling us how perfect everything is in Winnipeg. Jeff's voice emerged in the cultural ecosystem to apply some severe, anti-establishment counterweights. This was all to the good. But the misanthropy reached its apotheosis and then mysteriously wafted away.

KN: What do you hear from other people? Do you say you are from Winnipeg?

MR: Oh, I always do.

KN: What do they say? What is their impression of Winnipeg?

MR: It is, by and large, a meaningless place out in the world. Most Québécois I meet think Winnipeg is in Alberta. It's kind of a non-entity. In Toronto and Vancouver, I have sometimes found Winnipeg to be an object of condescension. Though my favourite thing people say, when you tell them you're from Winnipeg, is: "Winnipeg, hey? Heard they got a good ballet."

KN: Are you permanently an expat Winnipegger?

MR: I don't know. I don't know where any of us are from, really. But certainly, I am tethered to Winnipeg for life. I've long cherished the notion that I could one day become a cosmopolitan, internationalist being, but the fact is I am deeply parochial.

Still photo from Matthew Rankin's short film *Negativipeg*, 2010. Courtesy of the Winnipeg Film Group

MIKE MARYNIUK

Mike Maryniuk was born in Winnipeg but raised in the rural backcountry of Manitoba. A completely self-taught film virtuoso, his style is an inventive hybrid of Jim Henson, Norman McLaren, and Les Blank. He was the production coordinator at the Winnipeg Film Group from 2004 through 2011.

13 MARCH 2016, WINNIPEG

Dave Barber: How did you find your way into film?

Mike Maryniuk: It probably wasn't until I was in my early twenties. I was working a construction job. Some friends and I had just made a short film for the NSI [National Screen Institute] amateur film contest, called *Tony Baloney*. It was really bad, but I thought it was really good and really funny. Right around that time, on this construction job I had, we were tearing down this building called Oretzky's Shoes, and it was right beside the Palace Theatre. They'd insulated between the roof and the ceiling with these movie posters from the 1920s. I climbed up on this half-collapsed roof, after seeing this image fall to my feet of a very 1920s-looking woman's face. I thought it was maybe an advertisement. Sure enough, it was full of posters and there were probably 350—there

---

Mike Maryniuk on set shooting Walter Forsberg's short film *Fahrenheit 7-11*, 2010. Photo by Jennifer Stillwell. Courtesy of Walter Forsberg.

was about a quarter of the building left, at that point. There was a two-storey drop, with tangled broken beams, two-by-fours, and parts of pipe. I'm trying to lift these laths off of this half-collapsed roof, hoping that the whole thing doesn't tumble into this mess. I was able to save thirty of those posters.

Kevin Nikkel: It strikes me that at some point, that image has to make it into a film you'll make. It's a great origin story.

MM: Yes, right.

DB: So, seeing those posters inspired your films?

MM: What ended up happening was: I had all these posters, so I just started researching the titles. I thought, that's Stan Laurel's face—I'm sure of it. I spent every weekend after that at the downtown library, going through microfiche and through the old archives from 1926, to see what was playing at the Palace Theatre. I rented a lot of them from the library. So, I got the strange education that no one would get, strictly based around 1926.

I was starting to get into independent cinema, and I went and saw *Tales from the Gimli Hospital* [1988] because I heard it pissed off a lot of Icelanders, of which I am one. I'm an Icelander soiled by Ukrainian blood (so that kind of cancels my Icelandic-dom). I had seen that with a few friends that went with me, and they said: "That movie was really bad. I think you could do better." I was like: "No way, that movie was perfect." It was just a perspective thing because I was seeing the same stories that I had heard growing up—about John Ramsay, about all these Icelandic folktales—being brought in and torn apart or reimagined, told in a way that was more exciting than the way I'd previously heard them told. And it was self-deprecating.

The image of him squeezing the fish, and the goop going onto his hair and then styling it up, I thought was hilarious. It had those elements of silent cinema. It was the missing link between that era that I had immersed myself in, and traditional cinema now, which is boring dramatic stuff.

Joining the Film Group

DB: Can you recall the first time you walked into the Winnipeg Film Group?

MM: Yes. I think, for most people, the first time they walked into the Film Group is probably with an enormous amount of fear. I guess I knew about it from seeing those early Guy Maddin films. I walked up to the front door—it was closed. There seemed to be something going on there that was more important than me walking in, and I don't think I walked in. I think I looked at the board outside. I wrote something down and then left. That was something that—later, when I started working there—I thought long and hard about: how difficult it is to actually step foot into the Winnipeg Film Group. You want to be taken seriously and most people who are walking in for the first time don't have the same degree of cinema knowledge, or know anything about cameras. What is 16-mm film? What is the difference between 4K and 3.8K? I imagined that there was some sort of really intelligent conversation going on behind the doors, that I wouldn't be able to be a part of. It turns out that wasn't the case.

DB: Do you remember who you talked to first?

MM: Sure. I came back, probably a few months later, and I would've talked to Brendon Sawatzky and Jeff Erbach, and I signed up for the Basic Filmmaking Workshop. The Basic Filmmaking Workshop was great, and it was lots of fun. There were people in that class that I still work with. That was the most important part: going through that process and being in a peer group that are all entering into it, and getting advice from someone like Shereen Jerrett and Paul Suderman. John Kapitany did one of the camera classes.

Probably the biggest takeaway from those first sessions at the Winnipeg Film Group—someone asked a question to Shereen: what would you change if you had an opportunity to change anything? She just stopped. Her dogs were in the class with us, running around her feet. She looked at the dogs, walked over to the window, and stared for thirty seconds. Then half-looked back at the class, and she said: "I would've moved to

Toronto." She just kept looking out the window. Then she said: "Okay, class dismissed." Everyone got up and, awkwardly, left.

DB: Did you take Sol Nagler's workshop?

MM: There was this opportunity to do this hand-processing class. I had a pretty good idea of what that would've looked like, shooting on 16-mm black-and-white. It had this old-timey look. I was going back to my accidental film education through those movie posters that I discovered from 1926, at that construction site. It just made a lot of sense to me to take the class, and so I signed up. It was huge. I made *Chicken Scratch* [2003] in that class and learned how to hand-manipulate film. Just the concept of that über-DIY concept of filmmaking was really interesting to me.

DB: Then you hung around the Film Group and, eventually, you started to work there as the production coordinator.

MM: I started working there one day a week—in the back, just cleaning at first. I'd used the Bolex once or twice, and I think the game plan, at that point, was to go to the U of W film school. I was in the process of applying, and I had got a call from the University of Winnipeg and it was someone from the film department. They asked if I wanted to be the lab technician for Film One.[69] I thought it was a total joke—because here I was going to *pay* to take these classes and they were asking me to *teach* them. I didn't really know what I was doing, but I knew how to use a Bolex. So, then I started teaching the lab stuff at the University of Winnipeg.

Two years later, after I started working one day a week, David Zellis broke his arm. He felt it was time for him to quit the Film Group. So, there I was: I guess I'll work at the Winnipeg Film Group. I was working already, as a camera assistant, and I was just getting somewhere with that. I always told people that it was a reconnaissance mission and I really

---

Still photo from Mike Maryniuk's short film *Carrot Teen*, 2005. Courtesy of Mike Maryniuk.

didn't want to do it for the rest of my life because camera assistants were notorious for being jerks.

I made a deal with Jaimz Asmundson: we would split the job. And so, that's what we did. We both decided it was a good idea to watch the Winnipeg Film Group's history. If we are to be working there, we should know how it started. What were all these relics of the past, that were sitting in the archive and had been long forgotten about? I think that came from coming across those posters and digging into an era of long-forgotten cinema. For Jaimz, it came from his father being in the community for a long time, and seeing all these people that he grew up with. Jaimz essentially grew up in Video Pool. So, we started watching all these old films and it really brought us up to speed pretty quick, as to what the organization was, or could be.

DB: What did you learn, watching all those films?

MM: I learned that documentary existed in Winnipeg—because it didn't during that era. One of the first things that I grabbed was *Havakeen Lunch* [1979]. I just thought it was a weird title—I didn't know what it was. Noam Gonick came in to rent some gear. He hadn't been there in a while. The VHS of *Havakeen Lunch* was on my desk, and he said: "Well, this is a good sign. Any new person that would have *Havakeen Lunch* on their desk is alright with me."

It just was weird to me that no one really wanted to watch these old films. It was fascinating to me to have someone walk in the Film Group, and usually to talk to the people at the Cinematheque. I'd see this filmmaker walk in for this or that. Then they'd walk out. I'd ask, who was that? That was Robert Lower and Elise Swerhone. There were always people coming and going, and so I got to meet a lot of people.

After my first interaction with the Winnipeg Film Group—when I walked up to the front door and couldn't walk in, because I thought they'd think I was not qualified—now, I had some knowledge about what the Winnipeg Film Group was and what some of the old films were. I could be a part of the conversation or I could reference something. I was absolutely interested in it—and I think that put me in a different class than the typical type of filmmaker, who was really just there as a stepping stone on their way to Hollywood, or Toronto, or to River Heights.

L'Atelier national du Manitoba

DB: Do you recall when you first met Matthew Rankin and Walter Forsberg?

MM: Walter was in town, doing this optical printing workshop, and he stayed for longer than he thought. Matt moved back from Montreal. And they were interested in Winnipeg for different reasons. We would talk about all these different things and they thought it was funny that I played hockey.

Walter and Matthew were investigating finding some old Winnipeg commercials and trying to find some old VPW stuff. I guess they made a contact at CTV Winnipeg and someone let them know that they were throwing out some of their archives. They got a phone call from the archivist, who said: "They're just throwing it all out. We did the first dump in the BFI today. We'll be doing dumps every day, at two o'clock. You guys gotta do something with the stuff. The city's audiovisual memory is being eradicated."

It's no surprise that Walter Forsberg is now a really big person in the archival community in North America, specifically in the United States. In Winnipeg, they were just making space, just downsizing. They're just moving to a new location—there's nothing to those memories.

So, it was almost more about making this political point, from Walter's perspective, about archiving. Then, from Matthew's perspective, it was about Winnipeg's self-hate. Then, for me, it was about my experience with the Winnipeg Jets leaving. So, you take those three things, put them in a bottle, and shake it up. Walter's rationale for making the film infected my thought process, and that's what working collaboratively can be.

Walter had gotten two tapes digitized, and came over to hang out and showed me one of them. It was one of the tapes of Burton Cummings putting on his hockey equipment. It was really interesting because, on one tape, you would have the Burton Cummings thing, and then you

Winnipeg Cinematheque guide promoting l'Atelier national du Manitoba's *Death by Popcorn*, 2005. Courtesy of Winnipeg Film Group.

would have player bios of the Winnipeg Jets. I loved seeing that stuff. I was a huge hockey fan up until I was twenty-two, and then, for about four or five years, I just stopped watching hockey. Now I am obsessed with it. It was great to get back into that childhood hockey card trading mentality where suddenly you got all this extra information. Did you know that Randy Carlyle was a great fisherman? It was just crazy, to go through all those tapes. One of my biggest jobs was to actually digitize all those tapes and do notes. We were all doing it. It was such a huge task. Then the film just came into being.

DB: The film caught fire. CTV wasn't too happy that it was out there.

MM: Yes, the film caught fire. The funny thing is that we never really said, at any point, let's make a film—let's make a documentary about the Winnipeg Jets. It just started happening. We had this one tape we made—a little two-minute thing—about Burton Cummings. We made a little thing about Paul MacLean. Then we just kept going. More and more stuff came in and more and more stuff came in, and then, soon, we started talking about the larger narrative.

We decided that Wayne Gretzky should be in the film because he was the evil presence. There were lots of conversations about how I was a huge Wayne Gretzky fan, as a kid. I went to this game—Jets versus Oilers. All these guys are screaming: "Gretzky sucks! Gretzky, you MF'er!" I was there with my dad. He had to fend off rows and rows of people swearing about Gretzky because I was there to see Gretzky. That's a hard task—even for a burly cop.

We just made the film and it was great to see it come together. It was great to see it in the theatre. It was great to see that the press covered it like crazy. There were two articles in the *Free Press* competing against each other, and it just was a pretty good exercise in getting to know how an audience reacts to things and what is too far, what's not far enough, how you build up characters.

We ended up getting in some trouble with CTV Canada. The president of CTV Canada came to Winnipeg to meet with us and so we went to Wagon Wheel Lunch. All five of us—Rob Hardy was also there, representing Manitoba Moments. The president of CTV Canada wanted to potentially acquire the film, he said. But he'd written a cease-and-desist letter, right before that, so we knew that that wasn't the case. He was really trying to get a sense of who we were and why we were doing this—and why we thought that we could make a film with copyrighted material and get away with it.

But the truth was that we were never even trying to make a film for public consumption. We were just making a film because we thought it was funny. Matt had driven up on this really ratty bike and Walter's car was falling apart. I took the bus there. This guy assessed our assets and realized that this was a lost cause, in many ways. He wanted all of the tapes back and wanted all the copies of the DVDs to be destroyed. There would be no lawsuit if we followed through on that. That was the end of it with CTV. We gave them most of their tapes back.

Motivation and Mistakes

DB: It just struck me that the way that you talk about working with Rankin and Forsberg in making the film—here are some independent filmmakers making films out of a sense of fun, with their friends. That's why they're doing it. I think Guy Maddin would say the same thing, in his early films.

MM: When I was working at the Winnipeg Film Group, I couldn't believe how many people were coming in and would begin a sentence with a panic attack. That's something that happens to all of us, but you really got a sense that there was this feeling, within every filmmaker, that there was only one chance at this. You can't screw up, or it's over. You will never make another film in your life.

Those people have the hardest time. Those are the people, when they start making a film, they walk into the Winnipeg Film Group and they would just quiver because this is their one shot. If they screw up, their Hollywood dream is over.

KN: Whereas, what is the alternative to the "one shot" mentality?

MM: The people that survive are the people that continue to make films. They are just doing it for themselves, or doing it to have fun, or doing it to be a part of the community. Or doing it to be a part of something. That fun translates in the film—you can see it on the screen—as opposed to the extreme-anxiety-ridden director.

People who approach filmmaking with a sense of fun, exploration, and that it's an extensive, collaborative journey, are successful. The people that are overcome with anxiety, of only having one shot to make a film and can't screw up, are the ones that generally fail. Generally. That fun translates onto the screen. You see it. It's those mistakes.

Still photo on set of Mike Maryniuk's short film *Give Beef a Chance*, 2007. Courtesy of Walter Forsberg.

Still photo from Mike Maryniuk's feature film *The Goose*, 2018. Courtesy of Mike Maryniuk.

MEAT
PEACE
MEAT
no name

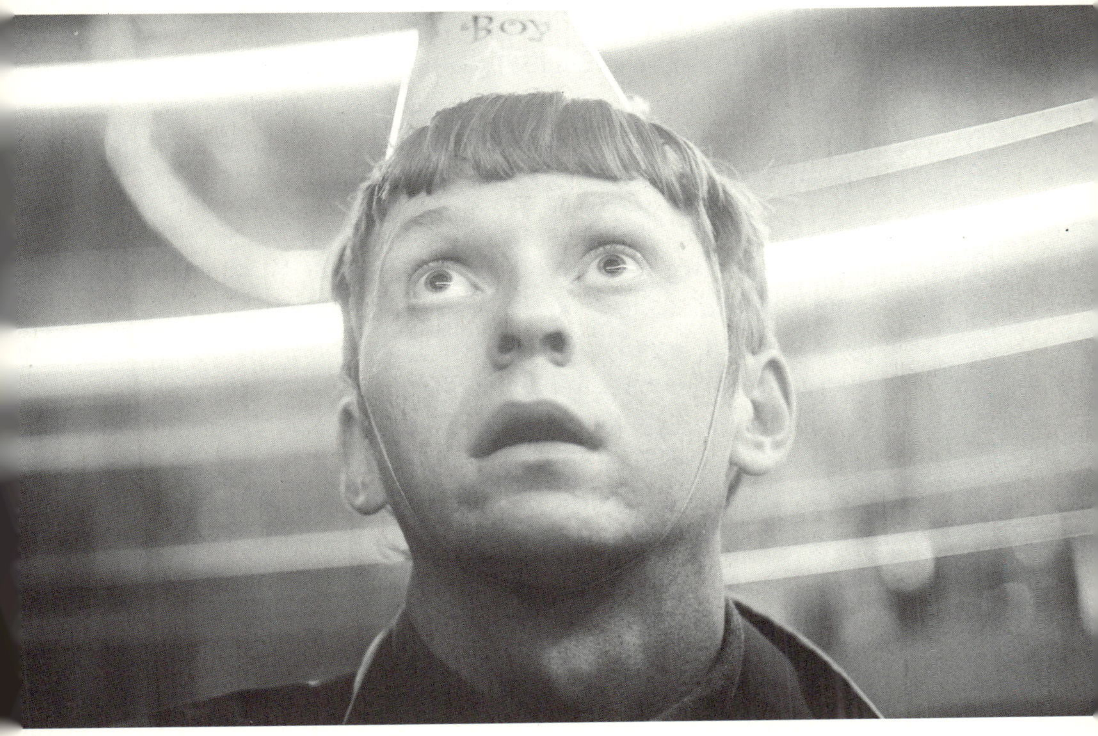
Boy

Some of those Film Group elders were coming in, when I started working there, and I'd say, how did you do this? They would say: "It was a mistake. We screwed up. We kept it in the film, though." Most of the really interesting things that were captured on film, in the Winnipeg Film Group archives, were actually mistakes. You can learn to embrace the mistakes, and let mistakes happen. You hear that so many times, working at the Winnipeg Film Group, that it becomes your reality. I don't care! I'll make a film without a crew. I'll make a film without an actor.

DB: That suggests the importance of being in a place where you can experiment and fail.

MM: John Kozak said: "The Film Group should always be a place where you can make a crappy film." That's the most important thing about the Winnipeg Film Group: it should absolutely be a place where you can fail because that's how you learn. That's how most people learn, is by failing.

DB: Any opinions on how the Film Group has changed over the years?

MM: Obviously. There are these cycles of bureaucracy and artistry, and they just flip. The bureaucracy fails and the artists take over. The bureaucracy builds up and the staff levels are through the roof, and then something fails or the Canada Council intervenes and there's less staff. And then the artists make films—the cycle happens over and over and over again. We're just in a cycle of bureaucracy right now.

I watch very smart and talented filmmakers descend to a place of profound frustration, trying to figure out what to do with the Winnipeg Film Group, or how those changes will take place. I think back to one day at the Winnipeg Film Group: there was a knock on the window. There was a guy at the door. He had a plastic bag with him and there were a bunch of film cans in it. I said, "Come in, the door is open." I walked over. He said, "Can we go in the back door?" We went to the back, to the equipment room, and I let them in through there. He said: "Thanks. I made a promise to myself that I would never step foot in this place again." I think it was Dean Naday. He said: "I met this Walter Forsberg. I promised him I would bring him a 16-mm film, but I can't go into the office. I made a promise to myself, many years ago, that I would never do this." That's not the only story like that.

Winnipeg Film Group History

KN: Other characteristics of the current era, or the changes?

MM: There is ebb and flow—different generations. I think I was a part of three eras. I transitioned out of the sensationalist *Erbachian era*—that's in reference to Jeff Erbach—of pseudo-horror, campy films that were being made at that time. A very kind of male sensibility within it—even filmmakers like Cindy Murdoch, who were making films as part of that sensibility.

Then next is the hand-processing era, with filmmakers like Jenny Bisch, Allison Bile, Cecilia Araneda, Danishka Esterhazy, Rob Haacke, Robert Pasternak, and myself. Deco Dawson was in the class. There were all kinds of films that were made. Sol Nagler was the instructor of the workshop and he encouraged this kind of poetic approach to filmmaking, which was very different from the films that were being made at the time. But it was in keeping with the Canadian tradition of experimental film. This was a workshop that he adapted from Phil Hoffman, who was doing the Film Farm. He asked me to help out, the second year, and do some scratch-animation classes with it. Then, the third year, Sol left and I took over. I started teaching classes for three or four years, with John Kapitany.

For me, Sol was one of the most important characters in my development because, even though my films were very different from his, he saw something and encouraged me to continue. I think what it was—I had a pretty strong work ethic at that time, where I was totally manipulating my films. I would try as many things as I could with them. I was staying in the studio for long periods of time and helping other people with their stuff. I was an assistant by default, just by being there the most. I knew why a certain chemical wasn't working—because someone had accidentally poured two quarts of beet juice into it—and it didn't have the right qualities.

Then the third era was this post-hand-processing world, where documentaries all of a sudden re-emerged. Those people, who were hand-processors and weren't content with just hand-processing films, they wanted to take it to a whole different level. So, you see filmmakers like Scott Fitzpatrick, Aaron Zeghers, and Rhayne Vermette doing really experimental stuff and winning awards all over the world. Heidi Phillips was already working throughout all that era, as well.

There were important things that happened at the Winnipeg Film Group—like the Mosaic Women's Film Project saw a few great films that were made: Caroline Monnet, Hagere Selam Zegeye-Gebrehiwot, Miriam Sainnawap, and the list goes on and on. And now the Winnipeg Indigenous Filmmakers Collective is an important thing happening, that will really start to emerge in a couple years.

What I see, the new members are seventeen years old, they're sixteen years old. They're high school students. This is the new lifeblood of the Winnipeg Film Group. There were only a couple of young filmmakers, that I can remember, able to infiltrate the Winnipeg Film Group culture back in the day. Matthew Rankin was one of them; he was making films when he was fourteen.

DB: That is a good synthesis of the history.

KN: Things have gotten more formal at the Film Group in recent years, wouldn't you say?

MM: When the Film Group excels, the sense of humanity is through the roof. It's: don't worry, we like your film. There are some problems, but I had the same problems. It's that mentorship. It's all of those human qualities that make the world a special place to live in. That needs to happen from filmmaker to filmmaker—that sense of community support. It's all of the good things in life. That's when a community thrives, or an arts organization thrives. But when you take that away and you're no longer members, but you're called *stakeholders*? That corporate mentality has no place in an arts organization. The bylaw changes take out any emotional attachment to the place. So, a twenty-two-year-old member thinks, I'm not a stakeholder

Self portrait of Mike Maryniuk, 2008. Courtesy of Mike Maryniuk.

of anything—I don't even know what an RRSP means. I don't understand the term *stakeholder*, but I understand what it means to be a member.

KN: Can you think of ways the Winnipeg Film Group does things right?

MM: I had a phone call, one day, from a guy who had an animation stand and he was trying to sell it to the Winnipeg Film Group for $20,000. And I wasn't going to buy it. But I got a phone call one day. He said, you got twenty-four hours. You come pick up this piece of crap, but you gotta take every single bit of it. I rented a U-Haul and I just did it. I called in Aaron Zeghers, who was assisting at the Winnipeg Film Group at the time. Jonah Nepon walked in and I asked him what he was doing that day. He said he could help volunteer, as long as there's no heavy lifting involved. There was a lot of heavy lifting involved.

We loaded that animation stand into the U-Haul and brought it into the Winnipeg Film Group. That was very much a spur-of-the-moment decision. We just went for it. It's done. Now it's built, and it's the envy of North American animation societies. Sometimes you just gotta make those decisions on the fly and be confident in your decision making, and know that it's going to be something special.

LESLIE SUPNET

Leslie Supnet describes herself as "experimental filmmaker from the Filipino diaspora who creates media works that explore themes of loss, change, and the passage of time." She got her start taking workshops at Video Pool and the Winnipeg Film Group. She completed an MFA *in film at York University.*

12 DECEMBER 2015, WINNIPEG

Kevin Nikkel: How did you end up in the artistic life?

Leslie Supnet: I got into animation. I actually took a workshop at Video Pool, which is right next door to the Film Group, right across the hall. I took a circuit-bending workshop. We were playing with the circuits of these small sound toys. I heard about Video Pool and the Winnipeg Film Group through the Winnipeg Cinematheque. I started frequenting both Video Pool and Winnipeg Film Group through workshops. But it was through watching films at Cinematheque, being at Artspace, and getting to know people—seeing the same people over and over, and at workshops. It just kind of happened that way.

KN: What had you heard about the Film Group?

LS: The only thing I'd heard about the Film Group that was very foregrounded was Guy Maddin. It was basically Guy Maddin *everything*.

Leslie Supnet. Courtesy of Leslie Supnet.

That is about it for my knowledge of the Film Group, before getting too heavily involved. But then I found out there is way more going on in the background. It was mostly through the artist-run workshops that I was able to find out where I fit in within the Winnipeg Film Group. I was introduced to a lot of different kinds of filmmakers.

KN: Where did you fit?

LS: I knew I fit into the experimental film world, more so than the animation, NFB world. More than the narrative filmmaking world. It was the experimental film scene, the people who were doing weird experiments—like, in the bathtub or in a dark room—directly onto the film. That's where I felt like I could really channel my material interests with cinema.

I think I was signing up for the 16-mm Bolex Experiment, with Mike Maryniuk and John Kapitany. I walked into the production office—that was the first time I met Mike Maryniuk, too. I didn't know what to expect. Video Pool was kind of weird and awkward, too; but there was this film stuff all over the place and there were movie posters everywhere. That was my first encounter at the Winnipeg Film Group. Do you want to hear about my first Cinematheque encounter?

KN: Yes.

LS: So, the first time I went to the Winnipeg Cinematheque, I actually went by myself. This is before I knew anybody. I used to draw a lot. That was my entry point into the visual arts world, but I didn't publicly show yet. I just wanted to see an art-house movie. I can't remember what it was, but I remember walking in. It was wintertime. I went up to the counter and it was Matthew Rankin. I didn't know him at the time; he was the ticket-and-popcorn guy. "I'll have one for *Seven Samurai*"—I can't remember. He said: "Are you a member of the Winnipeg Cinematheque?" I'm like, "No, I'm not. I don't know if I should become a member." He was very animated and he sold me on the whole thing. I got really excited. I'm part of something great! I filled out an application, I gave my money, I got my popcorn. I thought: this is great! But then my membership card never arrived. I told him about this and he said: "I don't remember this at all."

KN: Then you took a workshop.

LS: Yes, Mike Maryniuk and John Kapitany—the 16-mm Bolex Experiment. That was the first project workshop I took, and that ran for four to six weeks. It was really great.

KN: Where did you think that could take you?

LS: I was still very new to the world of cinema and to the world of animation. I had no idea how to make a film at all. I'd never shot on celluloid at all. It was really intimidating. I remember before the workshop even started, I got really nervous. There's all these technical details. I looked up the Bolex. I understand it now, but it took so long. It took so long to understand how to read a light meter. What is ISO?

After the first class, after being in what's now called the Black Lodge Studio—the Winnipeg Film Group studio—it totally changed everything. It was so casual. Mike taught me everything I know about animation and experimenting, and just goofing around. John was so technical, but so helpful and so lively. He was like, "Make sure you don't drink this bleach. Don't get it in your eyes." He was very conscientious—maybe a little paranoid, actually. It was really fun.

After the 16-mm Film Experiment, it continued to be a place for learning, getting more comfortable with the film medium, and meeting other filmmakers who were trying to do what we love to do. It ended up becoming a real passion for me—especially the material aspect of it. I was still back and forth between Video Pool and Film Group—working with video, animating with a scanner and drives, and After Effects, and whatnot. I'd still come to the Film Group to sign up for the One Take Super 8 or for other contests. There was lots of contest-driven filmmaking happening during my prolific time at the Film Group, using the space. It really gave me a sense of community, which I was really looking for because I wasn't a graduate of the [University of Manitoba] School of Art. That's its own community and its own world, that you cannot break into if you are not a graduate of the school. It's not going to happen. Having the Film Group was this kind of informal art school for me, one that was completely affordable. I quickly learned that filmmakers have their own unique anxieties and dreams and whatnot, that are every specific to them.

Women in Film

KN: There is a lot of criticism that the Film Group is a boys' club. Do you want to talk a bit about that?

LS: Yeah, there was definitely a gender disparity there, in terms of who was working there, the workshop participants, and just the filmmaking community that was around. I didn't personally feel ostracized. It could have easily happened, if I let technical issues come into play. When I was there, during the Mike Maryniuk era, when Darcy [Fehr] was around and Arlea [Ashcroft] was around, I didn't feel any negativity about that, or ostracized; but for some reason, there wasn't many women around, except for Heidi [Phillips]. And, later, Rhayne [Vermette] came.

When I talk to older artists about their experiences with the Film Group, it was very different than mine. Even after a ten-year gap, the experiences they had were way different. But also, they were still able to overcome whatever issues they were having with the place—the boys' club of the time. I definitely reaped the benefits of people like Shawna Dempsey, Lorri Millan, and Hope Peterson—the struggles of previous women filmmakers and what they've achieved before my time there. But I feel like it can always get better. Even now, there needs to be more of a shift, more of an outreach. I know there are specific programs, but there needs to be a way to retain women filmmakers. I don't know what the answer is. For me, it is to keep making work—which I feel is a main struggle for all filmmakers, too.

I think, in general, there is a lack of focus on women directors. I feel like it's not just a Winnipeg Film Group problem; I feel like it's just a worldwide problem. Even just recently, there was an article written in the *Globe and Mail* about analog filmmaking in Winnipeg. The article

Still from the Leslie Supnet's short film *gains + losses*, 2011. Courtesy of Leslie Supnet.

did not mention one woman filmmaker, at all. At all. It was completely insane. No contemporary people working in analog or, historically, women filmmakers who have been working in film—like Norma Bailey, for instance, who is famous in her own right. But the focus is very disproportionate. It's a constant struggle. I feel like all my women filmmaking friends are constantly challenging each other and making sure that we are now focusing on different demographics of voices, so that we're not just repeating history constantly.

Leaving Winnipeg

KN: You left for Toronto?[70]

LS: I left because I was getting back together with my boyfriend at the time, Clint [Enns, also a Film Group member]. And also, I was set up to go to graduate school at York University, the film and video production program. I left Winnipeg, very eager to be in the big city, and the Film Group, in many ways, really helped me in terms of knowing how to ask for certain things, in terms of artist-run centres and knowing the politics and the community.

Because Toronto is so huge, there are so many different scenes out there. There are so many different artist-run cooperatives there. It's like, what the heck, where do I go? LIFT [Liaison of Independent Filmmakers of Toronto] is very specific to analog films—that was easy. But with animation, there's so much going on over there. For me in Toronto, looking back at Winnipeg, I was always very nostalgic for the small community that I was a part of. That really kind of shaped who I am. Even now, even today, I think back to those times, during the contest era, or when things are still new and exciting, and all the friendships I made that have lasted through all of the drama. It just keeps getting stronger.

KN: When you were still in Winnipeg, what was your thought about Toronto?

LS: I knew Toronto was a film hub, in terms of everything: for documentaries, TIFF, HotDocs, the experimental film scene out there,

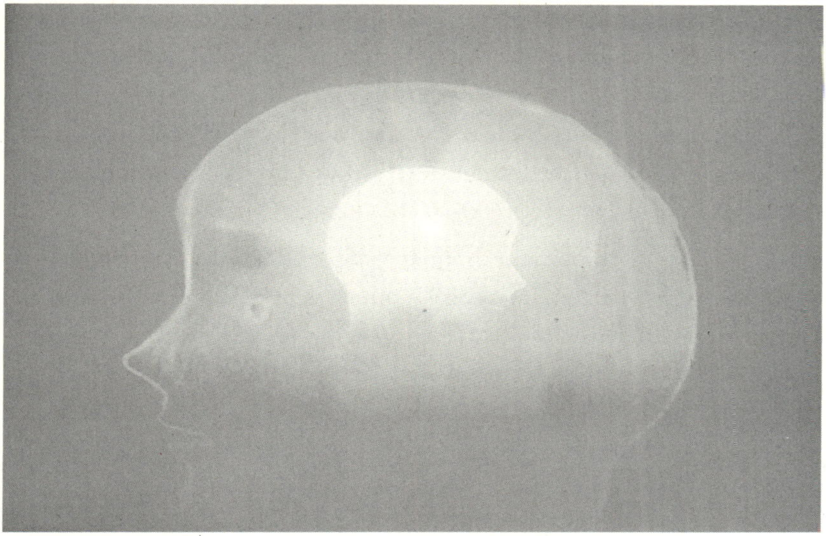

Still from the Leslie Supnet's short film *The Peak Experience*, 2018. Courtesy of Leslie Supnet.

too—more so in terms of being able to see work. I found, in Winnipeg, I was more productive in terms of making work. Being in Toronto, you're just working to make money all the time, whereas here the rent is not so high. You have the leisure time because you don't have to work as much to continue making work: funding your own projects, having a community of people to help you out during a shoot. My perception was, it's a big city. Big-city filmmaking. It's really the hub for being able to see whatever you want.

Winnipeg Aesthetic

KN: The folks in Toronto—when they heard you were from Winnipeg Film Group, what was the reaction?

LS: Programmers and people in the know—I'll bring up Guy Maddin again—who know the works that come from Winnipeg, and the art scene in general: their impression of Winnipeg, and Winnipeg artists, is we're just really strange. There is this edge that the work that comes out of Winnipeg has—surreal, strange. An awkward kind of edge, that a lot of Toronto expects to see. It is true.

Regionalism is a complicated thing, but there is something different about the work that comes out of Winnipeg that work from Toronto just doesn't quite have. It's not as polished, but it's also just way riskier. Winnipeggers take these weird risks and are not afraid of coming across being too strange. I think there is someone—who was it? John Kneller—who described Mike Maryniuk's work as *fun formalism*, and I think that can be said for a lot of the work that comes out of here. There is a good mix of very formal structure, but also there's a fun aspect to it.

KN: So, regionalism is a strength.

LS: Lots of people have this idea of it being this cold, depressing, isolated, sparse hellhole. Which could be true. It might be true for some people. I feel Winnipeggers exploit that, in a lot of ways. We have this self-hatred but also crazy pride. There's this constant conflict. We're so contradictory all the time. I feel I'm contradictory all the time. That's why I'm always so back-and-forth.

DB: Do you think your work was influenced by being in Winnipeg versus the work you were making in Toronto? Was it different?

LS: Oh yeah. Place is a big influence on the kind of work I make. When I was here, I was making a lot of paper cut-out, under-the-camera animations—all character-based and all very sad. The stories were tragicomedy. There're funny and sad, about an isolated character trying to overcome certain demons. I stopped making that work when I went to Toronto. I stopped drawing, too. I don't know—it is because of the place. In Toronto, I was very much looking for quiet and looking for just a way to deal with constantly being around people all the time. I wasn't dealing with loneliness anymore. I was dealing with a different problem, of just needing space. I don't know if the work actually reflected that? The work became more abstract. It became more about colour and form, whereas the work in Winnipeg I was making was dealing with loneliness, dealing with isolation, and dealing with depression. I just was not facing that problem anymore, in Toronto.

In Winnipeg, you walk down the street and you're completely by yourself. The wind is howling and it's seven o'clock, but there's no one to talk to. In Toronto, you're on the streetcar at seven o'clock and there are people breathing on you. You're just sardines and you just try to get away from it. So, place did affect my work. The work I did in Winnipeg is very distinct. I've had studio visits before where a curator or a programmer would ask me, "What happened to that weird, funny work, with those weird characters?" I'd say: "Oh, yeah, I don't make that anymore." It's interesting. It might be because I'm getting older, too.

Resilient Filmmaking

KN: Do you think, if there is a next-generation Leslie Supnet, would it be easier for a person who is similar to you—of your personality and sensibility—to emerge and join the Film Group, or would it be harder?

LS: With artist-run centres, there's always going to be problems. There is the idea of the arts utopia—that is just a lie. I think any new artists coming in will just realize it. You just keep going and keep working. You have to keep making work.

KN: What will the future hold?

LS: Well, the future is generally kind of bleak. Ha ha! Filmmaking is really life-affirming for me. It gives me a reason to want to be around. The best times I have are when I'm either watching stuff on screen for the first time and being able to discuss the work afterward, and helping people make work. And discovering new work—because the world is so big. The future is so big. It's why I continue to make things. It is a real helpful antidote to the depression about the coming apocalypse.

SCOTT FITZPATRICK

Scott Fitzpatrick is a visual artist from Winnipeg whose film and video work has screened at underground festivals and alternative venues worldwide. He obtained a bachelor's degree in film studies from the University of Manitoba, and began conducting lo-fi moving-image experiments in 2010. In addition to producing his own work, Scott also presents works by other filmmakers, currently as program director of the WNDX Festival of Moving Image and formerly as co-founder of the Winnipeg Underground Film Festival and Open City Cinema.

14 JANUARY 2017, WINNIPEG

Kevin Nikkel: Was there any sign, in your earlier days, you'd become the artist that you became?

Scott Fitzpatrick: I guess I was always a creative kid. Those were the projects I excelled at in school. Any opportunity to do a video assignment as an alternative to something else, I would do that. So, I always had an interest. Once I finished high school, I went straight to the University of Manitoba. I didn't really know what else to take, so I started doing English, film, and theatre, and I went from there. But I didn't start making my own stuff, actively, until engaging some of the local filmmakers in the city, which wasn't until later.

Photo of Second Star at *Film in the Present Tense*, 2017. Courtesy of Scott Fitzpatrick.

Guy Maddin

KN: As you're finishing your degree, you're starting to notice the local scene?

SF: Yeah, I got lucky because Guy Maddin was teaching some classes at the University of Manitoba at that time, and I was in those, which I really liked. I didn't really have a relationship with him at all, but a friend of mine did. My good friend I went to all my classes with, she was this really wild-looking blonde girl. He had asked her to be in a couple of shorts and she used that to weasel her way behind the scenes in his world, and I just tagged along. I was like, I'm coming along now. He didn't even really know who I was. He knew I was a student—but I wasn't invited. I started going to his shoots and stuff. On one of his bigger ones was where I met Mike [Maryniuk], Heidi [Phillips], Aaron [Zeghers], and Clint [Enns].

Dave Barber: Which one was it?

SF: *Keyhole* [2011]. The first ones I worked on were *Night Mayor* [2009] and *Glorious* [2008], the two shorts. But *Keyhole* was the big feature, with the *Séances* [2016] project on the side, that I was part of. It was really fun. That was like, a big breakthrough for me.

KN: What were you doing on that?

SF: He was doing the *Séances* project—a project where he reshot 100 or 200 lost films, and they get garbled up in this online generating website. Originally, he thought it wasn't feasible to shoot them all himself, so he got a whole bunch of deputy directors together, set up a studio system, and we would all be making the shorts under his producer's vision. I somehow got on, doing that. I got to direct two of these little short films under him, along with a bunch of other kids that he'd flown in. It was really amazing to meet all these people, who I otherwise wouldn't have been exposed to. Just a lot of art direction and stuff, making mini-Guy Maddin movies on a big Guy Maddin movie.

KN: Is Guy Maddin an influence on you in any way?

SF: I think he was, for sure. I can't say he's not an influence because that project, in particular, and the people he exposed me to, were really informative for the first few films that I made. You definitely feel him on them, which I think is the case with a lot of emerging Winnipeg filmmakers, especially in their earlier works—the melodrama and silent-film signifiers, intertitles, and Vaseline on the lens. But I think I've shed most of that in my stuff, now. Now I'm working in more structural modes and it doesn't resemble his stuff in the same way. I'm just getting further away. I think a lot of filmmakers in the city have had a similar arc.

Early Work

KN: Talk about your first couple of films.

SF: The first two that I made were both [done through] incubators for the Film Group. One was the One Take Super 8 [contest], which Mike Maryniuk encouraged me to do. *Keyhole* wrapped in September, so it was perfect timing. You have to shoot it in one take. Then, at the same time, they were doing the 90 Second Quickie [Filmmaking Challenge], where you made a film ninety seconds or less [in length]. Those were presented on that LED screen, at the corner of Portage and Fort. I wanted to play on that screen downtown! I made films for those events and they were both really well received. The first Super 8 was called *Down* [2011]. It's black-and-white. I put a static camera in the freight elevator at one of the buildings on Ross, where Frame Arts Warehouse used to be. I set up miniature narratives on each set, using all of the sets that we had offloaded from Guy's movie. You could recognize all the furniture, in my movie, from *Keyhole*, which is fun.

Artistic Practice

KN: Let's talk about the craft. How would you describe the stuff you're doing now?

SF: The stuff I'm doing right now is very engaged in handwork and craft: using different technical, overlapping processes; or misusing technologies, running film through this printer, for example. Or just finding different backdoor ways to come up with my own way of making a 16-mm film. I started doing laser printing on film, in a workshop at the Film Group that Mike Maryniuk was doing called "I Shot it on 16." I shot this 16-mm footage and it looked terrible. I tried to do these multiple exposures, but I'm really not a great cinematographer. I can shoot stills really nicely, but I'm really bad at shooting on 16-mm. I've never shot anything that's looked decent at all. I had this really awful footage and was frantically trying to figure what to do with it. I just cut it up and started printing onto it. From that point, I have just been seeing how much space I can excavate inside this really small gesture: the singular technique. So, that is what I'm doing now.

KN: What is the actual process to get an image onto the surface?

SF: I'll start on my computer. The first films I did in this mode, I was using Microsoft Paint. Excel. Word. Those were more primitive ones. Now, I use InDesign or Photoshop. I'll have an 8½ x 11-inch document and I'll print that off, just on paper. Then you cut the film into manageable strips, tape that down overtop of the image that you're intending to print, then run it back through. You can do it as many different times as you want. But you're captive to that cut rate of working with these strips.

KN: So, you're actually taping pieces of clear leader.

SF: Yeah, onto images that are already printed on the paper. So, that's how you align it properly, through the printer. I use only the manual feeders, so it's the clearest, most direct path through. There really isn't much intrusion there. I print as if I'm set for transparency, so the drums are really hot. So, it's going to adhere to the leader. It's just a lot of trial and error.

KN: How many of those per page?

SF: I usually do eight because that's a nice measurement. You can fit twelve across, if you're really trying to cram them on. I've done it on 35-mm, too, which is more time-consuming and much harder to get the alignments proper, and much more trial and error. You have to put more on, too, because you can only put three seconds on a page. More tedious. But you can get maybe ten or twelve seconds on a page, running it through as 16-mm.

KN: How did you come up with this idea?

SF: I stole it from Mike Maryniuk. He has a film called *Tattoo Step* [2008], which is a direct animation where he took clear 35-mm leader and covered it with temporary tattoos. It's totally genius—an amazing Film Group masterpiece. At the end of it, his credits are just: "a Mike Maryniuk film." It's a picture of his high-school yearbook photo. He used an inkjet printer to print that on. So, I'm like: "What's that, at the end? Oh, you printed your credits! That's cool. I'll just do that." That's where I took the technique.

I understand that it's in the Helen Hill, *Recipes for Disaster* book, too. There is definitely a history of people using Xerox and printers and stuff, to put an image on film. It's not like I pulled it out of the air, or whatever. But I don't think many people lean into it, or have really done much to create a body of work with that technique. I see it a lot as a workshop technique; or, like in Mike's film, it's the credits on his movie.

KN: So, now you have your own industrial photocopier.

SF: I didn't always have a printer like this, on my own. I used to do it at my office, afterhours, or really covertly. They had a colour printer, away from everyone else, and I would covertly send things to it and sneak around. Misuse their printer. But those days are over.

KN: That's funny. I can just see something getting jammed, and then having to call the tech guy and explain why there's film strips in the machine. "What are you guys doing here?"

SF: Yeah, you can't. You have to figure it out yourself. After that, my office moved, circumstances changed; I couldn't use that printer anymore. I started working at Staples a lot, and Staples had none of it. I would use their self-serve machines, but they would come up to me and say, "You're really not supposed to be doing that." Then, the Canon people would start saying: "No, you can't do that. Get away!" I eventually got banned from the one on Pembina Highway, so I had to move again. I eventually just needed to get my own.

KN: That's a great story.

SF: It actually got really awful because it was really expensive—when you are trying to do trial-and-error stuff and you're off by, say, 0.5 millimetres. I'd have to adjust and, every time, it's $1.30. I was printing on ledger size, at the time, so it was getting really expensive, fast. It was really stressful and I couldn't keep it up. I was really glad to get kicked out of Staples, actually. Put me out of my misery.

KN: What is the difference between the machine you have here and a normal printer?

SF: I've had some people who insisted that I don't need a printer this large. I know a couple filmmakers who do printing on film, and they use just home use–size printers. I've had home office–grade printers. I find that the drums don't get as hot, and so they don't adhere the toner to the film as well. The prints don't hold up. So, after multiple projections, they scratch off more easily. Even just rubbing it, you can just rub the toner off. But using this machine, it is set for printing on transparencies and it's a commercial machine, so the drums are used to turning out a really high volume. The print quality is good enough that it can hold up after multiple projections. The colour holds up. When I used to use a home office–grade printer, I couldn't do colour. It would slough off immediately. So, I find an office-grade is the only way to get colour to adhere to the film properly, and look vibrant or rich at all.

KN: At what point did you lock in and say, "I'm onto something"?

SF: There is a film I made at the end of 2011 called *Wingdings Love Letter*, that's really tossed off. It was the first time I really clued in to the sound strip on 16-mm film, and how much opportunity there was, there. It was also the most abstract one I've made so far, in terms of colour and composition. With that film in particular, I really felt I opened up all these different possibilities and was really excited by all of them, and it screened really well.

I always tell people: I'm working up to making a feature like this. I want to make a feature, narrative film on laser print—the whole thing—and make it look like a Lichtenstein comic book–type thing. That would be horrible. I don't want to do it! But I kind of want to do it.

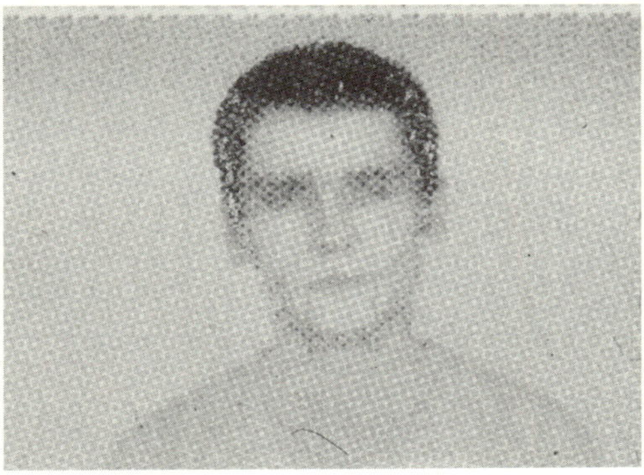

Still frame from Scott Fitzpatrick's short film *Second Star*, 2017. Courtesy of Scott Fitzpatrick.

Still frame from Scott Fitzpatrick's short film *Dingbat's Revenge*, 2015. Courtesy of Scott Fitzpatrick.

It's been at least the last five years that have been about, how much can I excavate in this small gesture? So, now, I do sound performances with this, where there is no image at all. It's just the sound generating. I do silent films that are all about the image or just the colour. I shot video of myself, too, and printed that video onto film, in *Screen Test 1 (Self-Portrait)* [2015].

KN: You're starting to print images onto the surface, as well.

SF: Yeah, there are basically two different ways you can look at this technique. You can really stay true to the frames that you're given by the film-strip standard—the 4 x 3 aspect ratio—and the way those frames are distributed on the strip. Or, you can deviate. The film strip is a rigid frieze pattern and you can try to match it with what you print, or you can make your own scale and pattern. So, things can get more abstract, scroll, come in and out of the bounds of the frame, like in *Wingdings Love Letter*. Or, you can stick to the standards, adhering to the box where the frames can be, and have a more or less static image, like in *Screen Test 1* or *Immortal Cats 1* [2015].

I do a lot with video. I break it down into still images and then put those in each frame. So, sometimes I'm working as if I'm painting across a strip. Sometimes I'm working within the frame and upholding that. That lends itself more to using video with moving images, which is really exciting but really tough.

KN: Where do you think it's going?

Expanded Cinema

SF: I'm not sure right now. I'm really excited by the performance stuff. Lately, the last couple years, my filmmaking practice has been mostly devoted to performance, which is really just a bridge. I've always wanted to be a musician, not a filmmaker. I'm like, wow, look at this backdoor way I found into doing a rock show—just with 16-mm projectors or something. That's what I'm most excited by, right now.

KN: What does that look like?

SF: I've done a lot, lately. *Expanded Cinema*, you could call it, a phrase loosely meaning any time you can deviate from the traditional theatre setup—projector at the back, projecting one image taking up a certain amount of real estate within a frame. Expanded Cinema can be anything from multiple projectors across—like a diptych, or a triptych—to overlaying projectors or refracting images with crystals or mirrors. The possibilities with it are limitless.

DB: Of the performances I've seen, you seem fearless when something goes wrong. You feel it is part of the performance?

SF: People love that, too. That's even another way that you can play with the dynamic of the theatre—if I had the projector at the back of the room but people are still aware of me, as a performer in the back of the room, because I'm tossing things around and manipulating the film. I did this one performance called *BCKGRNDS, PTTRNS, TXTRS + TNTS* [pronounced: backgrounds, patterns, textures, and tints; 2013] with these repeating patterns that I lifted out of design manuals, and I was overlapping them with multiple projectors, projecting with coloured gels and stuff. The second performance, I got really drunk and was unruly, and I kept loading them in wrong. I kept loading the loops with the perforations facing the wrong way. I would fire and it wouldn't move; so, instead of trying to fix it, I would just grab it and run it with my hands and just pull it through. That was great, and I learned through that. How I made those films was using Scotch Tape to lift images out of the books: I'm using clear leader plus Scotch Tape, and I realized that if you let it linger a bit, you can totally burn Scotch Tape, but the film is fine. So, you can burn the tape on the film. I got to do these really cool things. I'd let it melt. People loved it. So, now, when I do that performance, I always will purposely load them in wrong. Occasionally, I'll melt loops.

Analog and Bricolage

KN: How important would the Film Group be to your development, for supports, resources?

SF: I feel the more established I get, the less I depend on the Film Group. But they still have equipment that I need. I use their JK optical printer, which is rigged up to a digital camera. That's how I make digital versions of all of my films. Every direct animation I've done, I've run through their optical printer and I get really great copies. So, that's a resource that the Film Group has, that I need. That being said, that machine is in total disrepair. It gets moved from room to room; there's really very little respect for the machine because it's falling out of favour for what people are doing now. It's not digital—it's not the RED. It's not a really snazzy handle for your iPhone, to make it into a Steadicam. So, it just collects dust, mostly. I have conflicted feelings about that. Sometimes, I want to buy that machine. Would I have to go to the Film Group at all? But at the same time, it was those incubators and things that really got me actively practising and actively making movies.

KN: The analog field is overgrown from lack of use. Do you notice it's harder to get supplies to do the work, or to perform the work?

SF: It's very niche, almost even fetishy—so much so that I think, if you really want to get your movie playing around, finish it on 16-mm. If you have a 16-mm print or a 35-mm print (which, lately, if you're coming from digital videos, can be cheaper to make than a 16-mm print), that will play everywhere, just because there's a desire to show prints at so many festivals.

I think interest is probably increasing, actually. There's a reverence for analog stuff. It's not that hard to get your hands on film. Kodak just recently announced they're bringing back Ektachrome on Super 8. That's great, and I'm sure it will probably be available on 16-mm too, eventually. We'll see. Me, I just use clear leader. When I started, I would raid the Film Group stuff and I would bleach down the 35-mm trailers and literally recycle stuff. Now, I buy clear leader online—that's where I go. My practice has always been about bricolage and about working with trash, anyways.

Winnipeg Aesthetic/Fun Formalism

KN: Is the mentality that you're embodying—this "poor man's craft"—a Winnipeg thing?

SF: I think so. I think there is a rich history of bricolage in Winnipeg, particularly with Maddin—and, probably, Mike Maryniuk would be the other really important bricolage filmmaker. He'll use anything. He'll shoot on 16-mm. He's using found footage, different kinds of techniques on film: puppetry, stop motion, everything. He is just omnivorous and will do anything. That's the best way to develop an aesthetic, is to not always have what you want, the first thing that comes to your head. If I could make this perfectly, what would it be—if you don't have that, then what do you do? That's how you come up with an aesthetic. That's how you really find out what you look like, as opposed to what the ideal looks like—the consumer image. I think that all the best filmmakers in Winnipeg have that mentality. It's pretty prevalent, here. I don't know if it is everywhere else. I mean, I don't know. I don't think it is—especially now that I get to see a lot of artist-driven experimental work. Not a lot of glossy stuff comes out of Winnipeg. There is an attitude about stuff that seems to come out here, that it's faster and messier than a lot of other places.

KN: Why? What shapes that?

SF: I'm not sure. I think it's a transgressive thing. I think it comes from feeling left out, probably from being left out of the bigger picture of things. From being geographically isolated, culturally isolated. We're not Toronto. We don't get the big exhibits. We don't get as many films, so there's a reactionary feeling behind it. I think it's a little punk. That's probably where it comes from.

DB: How do people react when you travel places? How do people react to Winnipeg work?

SF: I like showing the Winnipeg regional programs because I think there is a very recognizable ethos, aesthetic, and attitude behind them. They almost never take themselves too seriously. I'm sure there are some very self-serious Winnipeg filmmakers, but I don't know them and I'm not programming them. Clint Enns talks about *fun formalism*—a term that was actually coined by John Kneller. He says that's the genre that guides the avant-garde in Winnipeg. We're a bunch of fun formalists. A lot of very serious, thoughtful work, with modes and media—but it's all fun. You're never going to alienate your audience. Sometimes, seeing regional programs from other cities, they don't have that concern as much.

I feel that Winnipeggers don't want to alienate their audience, ever. It's like you're always throwing a bone. When I look at the successes that I have had, to have my work play, my work has played all over the US but not much in Canada. I almost never play in Toronto. Toronto is too serious for my work. I have never played at Images or Wavelengths, or any of those festivals. But other cities don't have this problem, I don't know why. They're pretty buttoned up. Unless you're a name—then you can have fun.

DANISHKA ESTERHAZY

Danishka Esterhazy is a Winnipeg-born writer and director. She took the Winnipeg Film Group's Basic Workshop and found her way into filmmaking. Her first short was made through the Film Group's hand-processing workshop, and she has served on the organization's board. Danishka continued her training at the Canadian Film Centre and the National Screen Institute. She currently works in directing and splits her time between Toronto and California.

12 SEPTEMBER 2016, WINNIPEG

Dave Barber: How did you get into film?

Danishka Esterhazy: I don't think I naturally wanted to be a filmmaker from the beginning. I think my got my start as a storyteller. I've always been a writer, so, back in junior high, I had a writing group. This group of friends and I, we all created characters and we would write stories with each other's characters interacting, and that went multigenerational. We had that story-writing group for years after high school. So, I was always really driven to tell stories, but I didn't really know what medium I was going to use. I tried a few different mediums. I was a musician for many years and I wrote songs. Then, one day, I stumbled into filmmaking and then never looked back.

Danishka Esterhazy. Courtesy of Danishka Esterhazy.

Winnipeg Film Group

DB: When did you first hear about the Winnipeg Film Group?

DE: I first heard of the Winnipeg Film Group from an article in the *Winnipeg Free Press*. I didn't know any filmmakers. I didn't know anyone from the Film Group and really had no access to that world. I read some article showcasing the Manitoba film industry and I thought, Manitoba has a film industry? I had no idea. I was completely surprised and shocked because I thought to be a filmmaker, you had to be a millionaire from Hollywood. I just had no exposure to that world. I thought, wow, ordinary people like me can just go and make films! I'm going to try this. So, I went down to the Film Group.

DB: Do you remember who you met when you went down to the Film Group?

DE: I remember the first time I went to the Film Group. I walked in and everyone who worked there was a dude. They were all the quietest—if not surly—dudes I'd probably ever met. Ha ha! They turned out to be great, actually. Victor Enns was the executive director at the time. He was very welcoming and he really encouraged me, and so I stayed. I signed up for some classes and I met some people. But the face of the Film Group has really changed from the first time I walked in.

DB: One of your early films has hand-processing in it. Did you take the hand-processing workshop?

DE: I took Sol Nagler's processing workshop and I made my very first short film, called *Embowered* [2002]. It got picked up in a number of film festivals around the world, which I found deeply encouraging. I probably have to blame *Embowered* for being a filmmaker because, if that hadn't taken off, I probably wouldn't have continued. I found the processing class really inspiring because it allowed us to break the rules and the conventions of commercial filmmaking. It gave us permission to say, we're not trying to make a film that looks like something from Hollywood. We're going to make something that looks absolutely the opposite. That kind of tactile, hands-on processing in the darkroom with the chemicals, physically damaging the film—it gives you a certain kind of creative ownership that is very unique, and it's liberating in every way.

DB: Can you comment on any influences on your filmmaking?

DE: When you talk about the Film Group and who was an influence, everyone is going to start with Guy. How can you not be influenced by Guy Maddin? He's amazing. He's a force. But I think, for my personal interaction and in the mentoring that I received, I think my biggest influence was Sean Garrity. I took a number of classes with Sean. He's a very generous mentor, a great instructor. I've learned a lot about preparing for my future work through Sean. I hope that I've also been able to give back, at the Film Group. I hope I've been able to be a mentor and inspire filmmakers as well.

DB: You produced a short by Guy. Did you learn anything from that about how he works?

DE: I produced a short film by Guy Maddin called *Fancy, Fancy Being Rich* [2002], a BravoFACT project.[71] I certainly learned a lot, working with him closely on that project. I was very inspired by his work ethic. He works really hard. He treats his crew with such respect and that became a model for how to work on set. But also, his commitment to his vision: he demands his own creative freedom and then he sticks to it. How can you not be inspired?

Shorts versus Feature

DB: You made a number short films, and then a feature. What led you to that?

DE: I made a number of short films. I also wanted to make longer-format films. That had become my dream. I took every class I could possibly take at the Film Group, with every instructor, trying to get ready for that. Then, after the Film Group training, I went to the Canadian Film Centre, where my instructors were John Paizs and Greg Klymkiw—so you really can't escape Winnipeg. Then I came back to Winnipeg and

did more training with the National Screen Institute. Then, I guess I was ready. I got my first feature in Manitoba and that was *Black Field* [2009].

DB: Did you learn anything through making that feature, compared to making shorts?

DE: It's hard to describe making your first feature. I think I felt prepared because I had made a lot of shorts and I loved making shorts. They had some great success; so you think, okay, it's a lot like making a short, but it's just longer. But it's not simple math. It's not just ten times more work than a short. The depth of skill and storytelling you have to bring to make a long-format film is very challenging. But it's also the best feeling on earth. *Black Field* was really hard for me to make. I almost died of hypothermia. We were out in a field in spring, and it was wet and the temperatures would go down, and we'd get stuck in the mud, and there was ice everywhere. We couldn't get the trucks out of the mud. One of my actresses was almost killed by a horse. These are the things that happen in filmmaking. It makes you such a stronger storyteller. It's quite addictive. I've only made two features now, but I'm working really hard to make my third.

Women in Film

DB: There's been a lot of talk about lack of opportunity for women and the Film Group has been perceived as a boys' club. Do you think that has changed now?

DE: The film industry is unwelcoming to women—it's just a fact. If you look at the stats for Telefilm, our major Canadian funding body, in 2015, the women directors that were funded in the micro-budget were

---

Rebecca Gibson, Ashley Hirt, and Danishka Esterhazy, members of the Red Czarina collective. Courtesy of Danishka Esterhazy.

Danishka Esterhazy on set filming *Level 16*, 2018. Courtesy of Danishka Esterhazy.

21 percent; and the women filmmakers funded in the main budget area were 4 percent, which is insane.

DB: Why do you think that is?

DE: Tradition. Sexism. The industry has been very exclusive for a long time. It didn't start that way: if you look at the history of silent film, there were a lot of really great women filmmakers involved in the beginning. But once it becomes about money—and it takes a lot of money to make a film: there's a lot of gear and you have to pay a lot of people—people traditionally don't want to give money to women. They're not willing to put their faith in our ability to lead a set and to be the creative force behind a film—which is just crazy. Hopefully it is changing. Everyone's talking about it now, which is really great. People are pointing out just how unequal it is, but that doesn't mean it changes and it's easy to get.

DB: Let's talk about how the Film Group has changed.

DE: When I first went to the Film Group, there were no women working there and very few women in the classes. It was still a welcoming environment, but it certainly lived up to its name, of the boys' club. I do think that's changed. I think Cecilia [Araneda] has put so much work into making the Film Group more diverse and to engage different communities. I know there's so many wonderful filmmakers coming to the Film Group now, who are women. I feel that the Film Group has really transformed and I'm really happy to see it.

Danishka Esterhazy on location. Courtesy of Danishka Esterhazy.

DB: Do you think the inequality is the same in the independent sector, as well as the more commercial?

DE: The film industry has a lot of obstacles and barriers for women. It's hard for us to get funding. It's hard for us to get jobs. That's just a fact. Is it better in the indie world than the commercial world? That's a really tough question. I wouldn't say it's *much* better. I think maybe it's changing in the independent world faster than it's changing in the higher-budget world. I think women filmmakers are making their own opportunities—but there have to be commitments. The NFB is committed to funding 50 percent women in all its funding. I think that's wonderful. I applaud that. The Swedish Film Institute has done that. Institutions all over the world are committing to gender parity in their funding. I don't know how anyone can argue against that. It would be great to see all the film funders of the independent, commercial level commit to gender parity.

Winnipeg Identity

DB: You're now in the US. Have you noticed any difference in the independent film world there, compared to Canada?

DE: Now that I'm spending half my time in California, I certainly appreciate the Film Group even more. I see how hard the arts organizations struggle there, to support the filmmakers. They don't have the same level of funding. Certainly not the same level of government funding. So, they just can't provide as much to emerging filmmakers. When I went to the Film Group, I could get training and distribution, and incredible, hands-on experiences. Amazing access to equipment. It was all very affordable. I wouldn't have been able to become a filmmaker if access to training and equipment hadn't been so affordable at the Film Group. I know that's not the case everywhere, in Canada or in the States. I think people in Manitoba need to know how lucky they are.

DANIELLE STURK

Danielle Sturk is an award winning Franco-Manitoban filmmaker. Beginning her career in dance, she was attracted to film while studying in the film program at the University of Winnipeg. After she graduated, she became a member of the Winnipeg Film Group and later served on its board. Danielle works in both English and French, often in documentary but with live event production as well.

25 SEPTEMBER 2016, WINNIPEG

Kevin Nikkel: How did you get into film?

Danielle Sturk: After my dance career, I had my first two children. I was wanting to go back to school, to keep my brain working, and I realized I had only five courses left for a filmmaking degree. Filmmaking is a visual form, not unlike dance, where I was a choreographer. You have a frame: in the case of dance, it's a stage; and film, it's the same thing. You know what's in the frame, what is not in the frame, and where we are drawing the eye. It seemed like that was a nice fit for me artistically. In modern dance, I felt like a lot of the choreography was extremely abstract and sometimes people understood, sometime people didn't understand it. In filmmaking, with narrative form, at any rate, people could understand

---

Danielle Sturk, 2020. Courtesy of Danielle Sturk.

a lot more. People can understand what story you're telling. That appealed to me.

KN: Have you always been based here in Winnipeg?

DS: When I was eighteen, I had a dance job for a dance company in Vancouver, so I moved out to BC. Then back to Winnipeg. Then to Montreal, for all of my twenties.

KN: You got to see the artistic climate in BC and in Montreal, but you decided to come back to Winnipeg? Was that a difficult decision?

DS: It was a personal choice. It was a family choice as opposed to a professional choice. So, for myself, here I'd be back home, which was great. I had not lived here as an adult. I had my first daughter, Elena, in 1994 in Montreal, so returning to Winnipeg was a choice: for me, for her, for family reasons.

The dance environment had really changed. When I started out, I had full-year contracts, with dental plans. By 1996, when I returned to Winnipeg with Elena, contracts were three weeks here, six weeks there. Really hard, with childcare, for me to make that work. I did that for a year, danced with Winnipeg's Contemporary Dancers. But I was thirty and a single mom, and I can't live off of $3,000 to $4,000 a year, and find daycare, and in French. It was very difficult, so I needed full-time work to have that happen.

KN: Tell me about your film training at University of Winnipeg.

DS: When I went through filmmaking school, I was in my thirties and a mom. And I was pregnant with my third one. I arrived to class with a bunch of eighteen-year-old guys, basically. I think there was a couple of other women. It was strange to be with young men. I think their parents still cleaned their socks, made them dinners. It was a weird kind of mix—especially when you're writing stories that were very different. I mean, the mass amount of the class was concerned with zombie movies and picking the cutest girl in class to film, and I was writing stories about old people falling in love—like, *really* old people—and ice fishing. It was a little different context.

But technically, I think the experience is really good at University of Winnipeg. I really liked the tactile-ness of working with film itself, and the Steenbeck. I really liked doing that work and I think it is really a good base. Even though my interest was more documentary and experimental forms, the training around story making and storytelling through just basic shots was a really useful background for me.

Winnipeg Film Group

KN: What was it like when you walked in the door of the Winnipeg Film Group?

DS: I'm trying to remember, now. I'm going to back up a little bit. One of our courses at University of Winnipeg, in the film and theatre program, was to do a short film on Bolex. Mike Maryniuk was our mentor, for that particular film. Then we followed up with another one on 16-mm, and he also mentored us. That was our connection to the Winnipeg Film Group. So, there is a beginning there, where I believe we went and picked up some equipment to support our student projects.

KN: Was the climate at university, with the students, comparable to the Film Group?

DS: Walking into the Film Group, the feelings I've always had coming into that space was very relaxed, very welcoming. I can imagine walking into another type of film production centre and feeling intimidated or, especially as a student, feeling like it's beyond your scope. But there's none of that feeling at the Film Group. I felt welcome. I felt at ease and at home, and felt like this was a place where I belonged. I don't know how that energy was created—probably just the fact that there was a lot of buzzing-around of people that were more experienced, but also people that were less experienced, that were using the space.

Early Work

KN: You graduated from the University of Winnipeg and began making films. What films came after that?

DS: I worked a lot in the francophone community and also worked a little bit as a radio producer with Radio-Canada, through my time studying and raising children. Somebody who worked there was running the Festival des Vidéastes du Manitoba, which is a festival for young teens to create their own films, *en français*. It's through school divisions that encourage this, and they have a screening gala with prizes, etc. The man that ran that, Jean-Marc Ousset, a colleague at the time at Radio-Canada, was working with Pluri-elles, a francophone powerhouse women's organization, who had funds to make a doc on literacy with francophones in Manitoba. He basically said: "Do you want to make a half-hour film on literacy?"

I remember driving out to St. Pierre, Manitoba. I had just graduated from the U of W film department. This was the new career, after dance. It just felt like such a page turning. An actual vocation again. I met this woman and pre-interviewed her, and was completely unaware of the personal information she was going to load onto me. I wasn't prepared for that at all. I drove back and I was like, wow—how lucky to be able to have access to people's lives. And to be able to be gifted with this crazy environment, in this bubble, where people trust you with very intimate things. I think the sense of responsibility around that was very huge: having to care for that personal information that they willingly gave you and consider the context in which each individual does that, was really strong. But also, the sense of freedom that I had—I get to tell stories the way I want to do it. This is a work that hardly feels like work! It just felt like a freedom to express myself. What a gift to get to know people. If you're lucky, you get paid for that too, which I do.

Still photo from Danielle Sturk's short film *ciel(s)*, 2010. Courtesy of Danielle Sturk.

KN: Absolutely. The opportunity to have permission to ask questions and be curious, and people being generous enough to answer you.

DS: One thing that was missing in a three- or four-year university program was the documentary end of things. I feel very strongly about the ethics around documentary filmmaking, and one of the ways that I develop my own sense of ethics around documentary filmmaking was doing it. There were many opportunities through the Winnipeg Film Group, WNDX, and the Gimme Some Truth Festival, that brought in amazing filmmakers and offered master classes with amazing speakers. Through the exposure to those things, that really helped develop my sense of ethics. I think I have a strong ethical sense to start with. That very first film, with this woman in St. Pierre—I asked her if it's okay if I film our first interaction. I just put a little video camera on the counter, as I met her. I said: "I just want to record sound, so that I can remember when I come back, what types of things I'd like to discuss with you." I didn't know she was someone who had been highly abused, and then she shared highly traumatic events with me. I asked the simplest question—like, how many family members do you have—and then, it just turned into a very intense exposure of her life and the abuse that she had survived. I left shocked and thinking: what do I do with that material? I never looked at that footage, ever, and destroyed it because I just thought, that's not what the film was about. It was just not a place for it, in that film. But the shock of hearing that information—I was just completely unprepared.

Filmmaking Community

KN: You eventually began to associate more with the Film Group. How did that happen?

DS: I became a member of the Winnipeg Film Group right away. I think I was involved in the first Super 8 One Take Event, and that [resulting] short film, *reeds/quenouilles* [2008], travelled to a lot of film festivals. So, that was a really encouraging thing. There were ways to create films in small bites, at the Film Group. I didn't need to apply for a huge grant or get a producer to do this first film. It felt like, here's $30. You can make your first film and you get $30 back after screening it. Then the film travels and you get screening fees. It is an awesome program, the One Take Super 8 event.

With distribution, at the Film Group, there's an engagement around artists being paid for their work. If you look at opera singers and symphony players, and then you start moving down the track to dancers, the conditions are very poor. In dance at the time I was a dancer, there were very few rights and people were asked to work for free all the time, and they did. So, that's always bothered me. I think that being an artist is a very important role in society and I really think that all artists should be paid for their work. Yes, of course, we do stuff for free—but once you've trained and once you gained some experience, I think it's extremely important to be paid for your work. So, that really aligned itself well with Winnipeg Film Group's distribution model, where they would distribute films to festivals that paid screening fees. That already made a lot of sense to me.

Women in Film

KN: What were some of your experiences through the Film Group?

DS: I just felt really welcome. When I walked in there for equipment, chatting with people, the environment of casualness—which some might seem to think that is not professional—I think is totally the gem of the place. You are able to stop and talk and listen and exchange ideas. I don't know how many times I've been in there and one of the production guys says: "Hey, Danielle, have you ever met so-and-so? She's a new filmmaker." Connecting the dots, affecting people—we're a community. Let's talk about our work, let's exchange ideas. I see that in the Film Group's women's film network, as well. I don't go to all the meetings, but I do follow them on the website.

I got a production grant from the Film Group; I'm forgetting for which one. I've served on juries, as well. I had the opportunity to be a mentor for the Mosaic Women's Film Project. That was a really fantastic experience, with Kristin Snowbird. At the end, with the release of the film, I really saw her vision from the start. I think she is a very strong filmmaker—nice to have that new voice in there. Mentorship is a huge thing. I think it's really important for filmmaking, whether it's casual mentorship, going for lunch, talking about our work to each other; or more formal, in the way of the Mosaic project or even the First Film Fund.

KN: Were there mentors for you at the Film Group?

DS: Shelagh Carter was a filmmaker who came to me and asked me to be director of photography for the first 3D dance film made in Winnipeg. It was a great fit for me, but I refused, saying that I am not a camera operator—even though I have shot some of my own work. She wouldn't have it. She insisted and I accepted, with a mentor to support me—so, Brian Rougeau, a very talented director of photography and a gentle, generous artist, accepted, and I shot Shelagh's short dance film. I never really thanked her enough. It was a small film, but a great learning moment for me—and I have passed that on to others. Just do it. Yes, you can do it. Step into the arena. Traditionally, our society has trained women to ask permission before doing something. Time to drop all that bullshit. Try and fail gloriously, but try.

I think everybody needs mentorship. There is a whole lineage where you pass on knowledge. You can go on the net and get information, but it's also the human connector, of the actual action of passing on knowledge to somebody else. I think that human piece of it is super-important. I cannot, off the top of my head, remember a mentor. I'm trying to think of women because that would've affected me quite a lot. I felt quite

On location during the shooting of Danielle Sturk's short film *ciel(s)*, 2010. Courtesy of Danielle Sturk.

Model by Peter C. Graham, from Danielle Sturk's short film *El Toro*, 2018. Photo by Gabriel Levesque. Courtesy of Danielle Sturk.

SANDWICHES
HOMEMADE PIES

Danielle Sturk with Super 8 camera, 2019. Courtesy of Danielle Sturk.

isolated, actually, leaving the U of W at the age I was, in my mid-thirties—starting a second career, being a parent.

There weren't a lot of parents, when I was in the Film Group. There weren't a lot of women and, if there were women—in the dance world, as well—if they worked, they weren't parents. That's changed a lot since fifteen to twenty years ago, but there weren't a lot of people that I could relate to. Or the idea of starving artist versus artist married, or in a relationship where there are two incomes. There was a certain difference there, and I felt very isolated that way. When I made the Governor General's Award video with Reva Stone, who is in her seventies, she mentioned that same thing: she mentioned being a mom and a married person, and that she also felt isolated in the visual arts world. You have to be a certain type, or you're regarded as some kind of housewife or some kind of supported dependent, that's able to do art as a hobby. It's a sexist perception. I've never heard many people relate that kind of descriptor to men that are in relationships and are parents. That double standard has always been a pain in the arse.

KN: Things have changed—especially at the Film Group. What has been the motivation for the changes that allowed the evolution to happen? What has been the tipping point?

DS: I think, socially, things have changed a lot. I think being part of the board of directors, I had a sense where the Canada Council required certain things. It's great that we're giving you this national money, but the people there are all white, or people are all this age group, or people are of this gender. We need to see more of a mix of people from society, there. I think that's probably pretty normal—for any group of the age the Film Group was. It's natural that it would keep evolving. Well, actually not natural, because there is and has been much resistance to change, to inclusivity, to giving space to others that are not in the male, white club. It would be nice to think this would be a natural evolution but, in fact, history has shown that things change only when people really push for it or are forced to make a change. Change makes people uncomfortable. Too bad. Being excluded for centuries is pretty uncomfortable, too.

Working in Winnipeg

KN: Do you think there are enough opportunities in Winnipeg or would you have better chances emerging elsewhere?

DS: I certainly wouldn't have settled elsewhere for filmmaking.

Dave Barber: Because?

DS: I think, first of all, I am actually overly busy in film, which is a weird thing to say. I've been very lucky. I think that being able to do the live experience and television work balances out my own personal filmmaking—*film d'auteur*. Then there's some television production lately that's happening that I've been able to direct for, which has been a total pleasure because I don't have to produce it. I don't have to finance and have to worry about hiring everybody. I get to hone my skills as a director, so that's been really amazing. I don't think I'd get more work somewhere else right now, actually. I think a lot of that is, I love Winnipeg. I grew up in Winnipeg. I really love it. I love the place. I feel very supported here, both at the funding agency level and even colleague-wise. If I felt really lonely or isolated, I could call you up and say, let's go for lunch and tell me what you're doing. I've done that with people—because it can be an isolating experience.

That's the world I want to live in. I think that world is here. I think that generous-spirited filmmaking world is here in Winnipeg. I may be wrong, but I certainly wouldn't want to do film in Vancouver or Montreal right now. The sense I have is that the industries are big, really big. I've never had an interest in working in big-production narrative film. I'd rather make a short, small Super 8 film myself than pull cord for somebody on the set, doing traffic controlling for films that I really don't care about. Not interested! Life is too short. I'm not a star-attracted type of person, so it's really about the work, and saying what you want to say. I think, here, there's not a lot of hindrances. I also feel that as a population, in general, we're way less sexy than Montreal, Toronto, and Vancouver. We just are. We don't dress as nice. We don't have as nice stuff. We couldn't care. It's fricking cold out!

So, I think all that big-city kind of business is not present here and I thank God for it because we get to cut right to the heart of it. You know, for even Buffalo Gals [Buffalo Gal Pictures], I've done mostly work in French; and for them to give me a shout to propose a pitch for a project, for this nun documentary [*Soul Sisters*, 2016], that's great news. Or Eagle Vision, years ago. I did artistic direction for stage stuff, for Festival [du Voyageur], so there's been opportunities there with Rivard [Productions Rivard, a French-language TV and film production company], for their live-music shows for TV. I never would have had those opportunities elsewhere, I don't think. And to raise four daughters and do the work here.

Franco-Manitoban Filmmaking

KN: What is the place of Franco-Manitoban filmmakers?

DS: I've actually felt very welcome as a francophone at the Film Group, or never felt it's been an issue at all. I've never felt any discomfort. There never has been any kind of "Check that at the door. Act a little more like this to fit in." As a Franco-Manitoban filmmaker, I've never felt that I couldn't make a film in French.

I felt, with my francophone films, that the French community is behind me a zillion percent. People really like your stuff. So, I felt welcomed. And I think Dave's been very open and inviting, and has reached out to the French community with the program of Québécois films in French and local films from the French community.

KN: Anything else you want to say about the Film Group?

DS: Did I mention Dave Barber enough? Other than to encourage people to be part of it? That I hope it stays around? If I imagine Winnipeg without the Film Group, that would be a huge loss. There'd be a huge hole there. Something else would emerge for sure, but I really think it brings a lot of the different pieces together and holds it together. So, maybe the Film Group is the pot and the members are the spaghetti? Maybe. I think the Film Group does really contain all that craziness, that bubbles up occasionally over the sides.

CAROLINE MONNET

Caroline Monnet is an Indigenous filmmaker from Quebec who spent five years in Winnipeg. She completed a degree at the University of Winnipeg. During that time, she discovered the Winnipeg Film Group through the organization's Mosaic project, for which she made Ikwé *(2009). While in Winnipeg, she founded the* ITWÉ *collective with Kevin Lee Burton and Sébastien Aubin. She made several celebrated, experimental shorts and documentary films in Winnipeg before moving back to Quebec. Her visual arts practice has expanded to include installations in galleries around the world.*

11 JUNE 2017, ATLANTIC FILM FESTIVAL, HALIFAX

Solomon Nagler: Talk about your journey to Winnipeg. How did you end up there?

Caroline Monnet: I ended up in Winnipeg unexpectedly. I was doing a project in South America and then, when I came back, had to be in Calgary for a few days. I had never been outside of Quebec or visited the rest of Canada, so I decided to take the bus from Calgary back to Ottawa. I was joined by my partner and we stopped in Winnipeg to visit his family. The plan was to stay one week. Within a week, our lives changed. We met some Indigenous artists through Urban Shaman, we

---

Caroline Monnet. Courtesy of Caroline Monnet.

found an apartment, and had job offers.[72] I didn't really speak English at the time, so I decided this would be the perfect opportunity to become fully bilingual. I registered at the University of Winnipeg.

The first thing that really struck me, when I got to Winnipeg, was the vibrant Indigenous presence. I went into a supermarket and three-quarters of the people were Native. That's not something I was used to, growing up in Gatineau. Besides my own family and visits to my mom's community, I didn't really have many First Nations models in my surroundings. I thought Winnipeg was vibrant and exciting. There was room for growth and possibilities. I felt at home. As I started dwelling in the urban nation community, I met numerous architects, lawyers, arts administrators, and other intellectuals. It was an exciting and inspiring time. Winnipeg felt like a place I was looking for, for a little while. The plan was to stay six months and we ended up staying five years.

SN: How is it that you ended up discovering your filmic voice while spending those five years in Winnipeg?

CM: I was quite young when I moved to Winnipeg. I was only 21. It was in 2007 and I was studying sociology and communications at the time, and registered at the University of Winnipeg to finish my degree. I was working at the French CBC, as a part-time job. My intentions were to be a journalist, as a way to be useful to the world and have the opportunity to travel. But I quickly realized that working in the newsroom was not a format suitable for me. I wanted to go deeper into the subject matter and this is how I got interested in the documentary form. I worked for Productions Rivard, in St. Boniface, for a little while. They were great people and I learned much about the Franco-Manitoban community. But once again, the TV format wasn't exactly what I was looking for and it didn't really work for me. I learned quite a bit of how to be in the field and how to do interviews, and working with a camera person. I got introduced to camera equipment and people working in the industry. I value the learning I did, while working there. But for me, it all really started when the Winnipeg Film Group started the Mosaic Women's Film Project, and I made my first video, *Ikwé*, in 2009. I discovered experimental films, and I was hooked.

Winnipeg Film Group and the Mosaic Project

SN: How was your experience at the Film Group a different experience?

CM: The Winnipeg Film Group was a much smaller thing. They trusted me. They didn't pressure me. They nurtured the creative process and understood that sometimes it takes time to find the story and make the film. I had a one-on-one meeting with Monica [Lowe] and Mike Maryniuk. It was more like, "Okay, let's sit down and see what you want to do." Cecilia [Araneda] was also very supportive. I felt they were excited to see what I would create. I had five months to make a film, in total creative freedom. Because it's an artist-run centre, because the resources are there, you feel in a safe space to focus on the work rather than the expectations. Also, just to be able to go to the Film Group and rent camera and sound equipment as you wish. I discovered the Nagra sound recorder and it's one of the most beautiful sound-recording devices that I was fortunate to work with. I made the entire film in my living room.

SN: Can you talk about the Mosaic Project?

CM: The Mosaic Project is targeted to women of minority. The mandate of the program gave me the tools to start: to look at women and what it can represent from an Indigenous perspective. I did some research and talked with some Elders. Their stories often referenced the Moon as our oldest grandmother. I started writing a contemporary tale, where I would converse with the oldest grandmother in my lineage of grandmothers: the Moon. *Ikwé* is about teachings passed down across generations. But it also speaks about how I was removed from my culture, using the metaphor of buzzing lights: human activity making the Moon's teachings harder to reach me. I was working around those concepts.

SN: The Winnipeg Film Group was a place where you essentially started making films?

CM: I remember one time, when we had the screening of the Mosaic Project, and Monica, the distributor, came up to me and said, "I would like to distribute *Ikwé*." I didn't even know what a distributor was!

I learned everything from the Winnipeg Film Group. She's like, "We're going to want to submit to TIFF." I didn't even know what TIFF was. One day, she called me to say we got into the festival. She was super-excited. And I said, "Cool, I am excited, too!" It was only after, seeing people's reaction, that I fully realized what it meant. TIFF is a big deal, I guess.

SN: Did you go to the festival?

CM: I did. I loved it.

SN: Did the Film Group influence you in any way, making work together as a group?

CM: The Winnipeg Film Group gave me the opportunity I needed to make my first film, and that film gave me the opportunity to keep making films. Because *Ikwé* travelled to festivals, I gained the credibility to apply for Canada Council funding and make the next one. I started surrounding myself with filmmakers and was more interested with the community of filmmakers. Kevin Lee Burton became a very solid collaborator, at that time, because he had been working on editing *Ikwé* and we just wanted to keep working together. We both wanted to work with youth, to use filmmaking as a way to bring back self-confidence.

I felt like it worked for me. Film, as an art form, brought me a level of self-confidence that I didn't have before. I wanted to share that with youth from northern First Nation communities, arriving in Winnipeg for the first time. We made three films with three youths. They are all distributed by the Winnipeg Film Group.

SN: Can you talk about those projects—the three portraits: *Tashina*, *Warchild*, and *Kwoni* [all 2010]?

CM: It's a trilogy. It's three documentaries on three youth that have to leave their northern community to access education in the city. It's to celebrate their resilience and to talk about their experience. The culture shock, when you arrive from a small community in northern Manitoba to the city, can be daunting. Imagine if you never took the bus before, never had to deal with groceries because there's only one store in your

Still photo from Caroline Monnet's short film *Ikwé*, 2009. Courtesy of Caroline Monnet.

community. All these things that we take for granted can be intimidating for some youth. I wanted to celebrate them and also talk about the future. We always go to our Elders to talk about the future and get advice, and I felt like, with the youth, what was important right now is to really reflect on: what is the future is going to be? They are the ones we need to listen to.

So, that trilogy was about that. The beautiful part is that it gave them a level of self-confidence, a sense of belonging and pride. One of them applied to theatre school at the University of Winnipeg, after playing in one of the films. The other one was pursuing studies in law. Every time she felt a bit down, she would rewatch the movie to remind her that she can do it. Filmmaking is an important tool for empowerment, I think.

SN: Can you pinpoint a certain style or influence from your time learning at the Winnipeg Film Group and making work there?

CM: I guess when I was living in Winnipeg, I used to go a lot to the Cinematheque and be surrounded by the community of filmmakers.

That community had an influence on my work. I always felt Winnipeg had some kind of a gritty underground scene that really spoke to me and I felt connected to. Especially working with 16-mm, working in film, black-and-white—that's all influences that I'm convinced are coming from Winnipeg.

I guess because my first film was made through the Winnipeg Film Group, I naturally just stayed there. I could have worked more as a video artist, with Video Pool. I don't know, but those two are kind of the same community, in a way. But for sure, it influences the work that I have been doing and maybe also in terms of Indigenous cinema—the kind of experimental essays that are connected to personal stories. My sound is often not synced with the image, something I was doing a lot at the beginning. It's only with *Roberta* [2014] that I started doing things with synced sound, and it marks my move to Montreal.

A Winnipeg Aesthetic

SN: You were saying that this work, produced in Winnipeg, has a certain heaviness to it. I wonder if you can speak to that? What is that Winnipeg aesthetic, in your mind?

CM: I think we're sponges, in many ways. I think we, as artists, we're always observers of what we are surrounded with. We talk about the things in our everyday lives. The work is quite instinctive also, so, if you're in a certain space and place, then it's going to be reflective on the work that you do. And Winnipeg is full of contradictions. It can be pretty rough. It can be pretty dark. It's very cold. But at the same time, there's a certain warmth to it also, in terms of community and in support.

Still photo from Caroline Monnet's short film *Tashina*, 2010. Courtesy of Caroline Monnet.

Still photo from Caroline Monnet's short film *Warchild*, 2010. Courtesy of Caroline Monnet.

I think that the earlier work has grit and talks about the things that are important to talk about; but also, I think, in terms of my trajectory, moving to Winnipeg was also kind of reconnecting with my Anishinaabe culture, something that I didn't really have in Gatineau, growing up. It was not as celebrated, growing up. As a teenager, I was the only Native in the school I went to. Going to Winnipeg, I really wanted to grasp onto it, express it, and celebrate it.

When I moved out of Winnipeg, I didn't want to be labelled as just the Indigenous filmmaker. I started exploring other things, like industrialization—maybe because I was starting to live in a bigger city. Themes of migration, loss, tension, architecture—exploring different themes. Winnipeg, in terms of the landscape—it's flat land, everything is slower. Aesthetically, it's just different.

SN: What is there, in terms of arts groups, that allowed you to find a connection within Winnipeg? Who are some of the colleagues you found?

CM: In Winnipeg, there is room to be different. In Winnipeg, there's room to grow. I wouldn't be where I am now, if I hadn't moved to Winnipeg. I'm convinced of that. There was a lot of room and thirst for different types of voices. There's a freedom to experiment—like Guy Maddin's films, that are not conventional. They're beautifully crafted. Matthew Rankin and Mike Maryniuk are also people exploring forms and style, and being true to their creative process. The Surrealist era is one of my favourites of all the art movements; I felt Winnipeg could embody a little bit of that—with its humour, that I didn't quite understand at first, but knew I liked it. It was a kind of dark humour, almost used for horror films. This grittiness was exactly where I was at in my life, at that particular time. So yeah, just to have room to experiment. I think I was making work really fast because I had this urge to express myself, to be productive, and to learn more about myself.

SN: You were really prolific. How many films did you make while you were in Winnipeg?

CM: I spent five years in Winnipeg. I made four films in Winnipeg.

SN: What about your visual arts practice? Let's talk about your sculptural works.

CM: I started doing video installations in Winnipeg. My first one was at Urban Shaman gallery, where I started using projections on sculptural elements.

SN: Which one was that?

CM: It was with *RESERVE(d)*, an exhibition [2010] in collaboration with Kevin Lee Burton. We had video projection in the gallery and I was projecting photography on Plexiglas. It was my first venture into exploring projections in a non-traditional format. I love the cinema experience, but I felt that my work could also get rid of those walls. I've always tried to make film as a physical experience. I was looking to have people move around the art, interact with the projections. I got interested in exploring more visual arts in my work and went on a residency at OBORO, in Montreal, while I was still living in Winnipeg. I started developing more sculptural work, using video projections to complement the concept. Montreal was an exciting place to discover, at the time, and I was exposed to a lot of great artists working in video installations.

There was one thing that was important for me, when I left Winnipeg in 2011—that I would keep a connection there. I would come back, maybe twice or four times a year, working on different projects. I haven't been back as often as I wanted to in the last years, but it is still a place that I want to go back to.

Leaving Winnipeg

SN: So, why did you leave Winnipeg?

CM: Winnipeg is a place that if you're from there, you've got that real connection with Manitoba. My family, and territory, is all in Quebec. Parents are getting older. Childhood friends are having kids, and you want to see them grow. I was missing speaking and working in French. I wanted to be closer to my Anishinaabe culture and my mom's community of Kitigan Zibi. My work was starting to deal more with territory and land. It was hard to be away from my foundations. You reach a point where you know your work needs to evolve; I needed that change in order to grow.

SN: Do you think you see yourself evolving more into a Quebec filmmaker?

CM: Of course, my style is evolving, and that's just normal. If I would be in Berlin, maybe people would say my work looks like a Berlin filmmaker's. I think it is just, I'm exploring different avenues and I'm always experimenting with myself and my work, trying to grasp as much as I can. I'm also Anishinaabe and French—that must influence my aesthetics as well.

Since I moved to Montreal, I've started working in colour. I'm trying to bring more humour in the work, but the grit is still there. I can still notice the Winnipeg influence in works that I'm doing recently. Actually, my latest documentary looks like a Winnipeg film.

SN: Which one is that?

CM: The train documentary, titled *Tshiuetin* [2016]. It's shot on 16-mm, in the middle of a rough winter. I'd be happy if the Winnipeg aesthetic continues to show up in the work that I do. But it's not something that I do on purpose, or plan. It's all very instinctive.

SN: Did that inform your work in any way?

CM: Absolutely. I remember winters in Winnipeg. Every February, I'd get pretty low and tell myself: last winter, last winter. We're leaving. And then spring would come, and there would be such a burst of energy and freedom and creativity. It would be the most beautiful summers—such a bliss. Then you do another year. Then February would come again. I think the Winnipeg winters have a real influence on the work being made. It's nurturing for creativity: you enter a bubble. I think that's why so many good artists are coming out of Winnipeg. I remember long, cold nights, just talking and brainstorming, watching movies, listening to music, and simply creating for the joy of creating. I even started painting in Winnipeg, as a way to occupy my time.

SN: And also, the artist-run centres are in Winnipeg. Do you want to talk briefly about the artist-run centres that you worked with, that helped you and influenced you?

CM: One thing that I missed, when I moved to Montreal, is how the artistic community in Winnipeg is mixed. Dancers, architects, musicians, visual artists, and filmmakers—all together. The artist-run centres have a connection, they support each other. In Montreal, it is much more specific to your discipline, to your niche. The visual arts in Montreal don't necessarily mix with the filmmaking industry, and there's no real bridge; whereas in Winnipeg, you can sense that support. I worked a lot with Martha Street Studio, Urban Shaman, RAW Gallery of Architecture and Design, Video Pool, and Winnipeg Film Group. I sat, briefly, on the board of directors of Urban Shaman.

SN: There is a different level of intimacy where, in Winnipeg, people look out for each other—but the level of quality they expect from their peers is very high in Winnipeg. They really expect you to work your butt off, to make work that is of international calibre. And that is something remarkable.

CM: There's also a high level of collaboration between different artists. It's not as competitive, I think. There's a lot of support from the community in Winnipeg. It feels that if someone from Winnipeg makes it big, there will be support for that person. It's beneficial for the entire Winnipeg community.

SN: Do you have any concluding remarks that you'd like to make?

CM: I wish all the best to the Winnipeg Film Group. I'm excited to see where it goes next and hope it can continue to nurture new artists, as it did for me years ago.

ACKNOWLEDGEMENTS

Establishing Shots grew out of my passion for history, film culture, and the local community of Winnipeg. My work is sustained through the support on the home front by my wife and adult children, my enthusiastic extended family, and my dear friends. Of the friends that made this work possible, I have to begin with my collaborator, Dave Barber. I, and so many filmmakers across the country, and Winnipeg in particular, owe so much to the life's work of this man—he helped launch and sustain so many film careers. Dave's passing in 2021 left a void that we now have to fill, as he contributed so much to our community. Our documentary *Tales from the Winnipeg Film Group* was not possible without his extensive knowledge of local film and his insider's understanding of the history of the Winnipeg Film Group since he joined the staff in 1982. *Establishing Shots* is an extension of the work we did together on that film, and Dave's voice and presence exists throughout this volume. Thanks, Dave.

More thanks are due to the support that we received in the making of the documentary, particularly the funds available at the time from MTS TV Stories from Home and their team, Cam Bennett and Kim Bell. The production demanded that we track down filmmakers in Manitoba, Saskatchewan, Ontario, Nova Scotia, Los Angeles, Washington, and London, England. There was extensive behind-the-scenes production help by a dedicated and creative crew of camera operators that also lent their opinions and comments about the topic of Manitoba filmmaking before, during, and after our interviews. Thanks goes out to Ryan Herdman, Tyler Funk, Mike Maryniuk, Sean Parenteau, Andrew Luczenczyn, Charles Lavack, Lauren Dial, Ryan McKenna, and Derek Eidse. Additional thanks for help from filmmaker and NSCAD University instructor Solomon Nagler, who conducted the interview with Caroline Monnet while attending the Atlantic International Film Festival in Halifax. I also am grateful to my collaborators at Catacomb Microcinema: Bevan Klassen, Blair Dagdick, Frank Zappia, and Matthew Etches. We didn't realize at the time that our recording of the Q & A with Winston Washington Moxam following the screening of his film *Barbara James* would be such an important addition to this volume years after his death.

The staff at the Winnipeg Film Group deserve a big thank you as well. Over many years now they have offered friendship and collaborative support for the making and distribution of my films. They were essential with their advice, photos, and research help on this book. Thanks to past and present staff including but not limited to: Monica Lowe, Dylan Baillie, Ben Williams, Greg Klymkiw, David Knipe, Jaimz Asmundson, Cecilia Araneda, Karen Remoto, and Jillian Groening. I cannot help but mention Dave Barber again here as well.

I am lucky to have the University of Winnipeg Oral History Centre in my home town and the support of past director Alexander Freund, who offered suggestions in the early phases of this oral history project. I also benefited from the support of Parks Canada and the Manitoba Arts Council's Deep Bay Artistic Residency at Riding Mountain National Park. My time spent at the Deep Bay Cabin was essential for getting an early draft of the manuscript completed.

One of the best parts of this project was the opportunity to collaborate with a host of filmmakers, many in Winnipeg, but others further afield. The list of people Dave and I interviewed for our documentary *Tales from the Winnipeg Film Group* is long and unfortunately many great interviews didn't make it into this volume. I hope to include discussions with many of these filmmakers, and others, in subsequent interview collections as opportunity permits.

The book would certainly not have the life it has without the generosity of filmmakers and local photographers donating their photos for use in this volume. The illustration of the early years of the Winnipeg Film Group are a credit to the foresight of Brad Caslor to bring his camera along to member meetings and events in the mid 1970s. Thanks also to the support of the

Winnipeg Film Group staff for allowing me access to the organization's archives—and Dave Barber again needs mention here, as his collection of prints was so important to bring these interviews to life with photos. The archives of the *Winnipeg Free Press* were also a valuable source to fill in missing photos.

When it comes to the manuscript of *Establishing Shots*, I have to thank Dave Barber for reviewing the early drafts before he passed away. Patrick Lowe was a helpful proofreader of the Introduction to get the Winnipeg Film Group history right. I also valued discussions with the late Howard Curle, Gene Walz, and Andrew Burke on aspects of our local film culture and history. I am grateful to Walter Forsberg, who gave encouragement and first looks at the manuscript and inspired me with his own publication on his years in Winnipeg (see note 24 in this volume). Thanks also to Kelly Milne and Caden Nikkel for helping with transcripts along the way.

Finally, I have to thank the staff at University of Manitoba Press for their support: past director David Carr, Glenn Bergen, Jill McConkey, and editor Edwin Janzen for their careful attention that was essential to get this book finished.

NOTES

1 Dave Barber, "Tales from the Winnipeg Film Group," program guide (Winnipeg: Matchbox Cineclub, 2020), 3.

2 Andrew Burke, *Hinterland Remixed: Media, Memory, and the Canadian 1970s* (Montreal: McGill-Queen's University Press, 2019), 11.

3 Agi Ibranji-Kiss, "Winnipeg Symposium: The Turning Point," *Cinema Canada* 13 (April–May 1974): 14.

4 Katie Fitzrandolph, "Gloomy Mood Prevails at Film Symposium," *Winnipeg Free Press*, 9 February 1974, 23.

5 Ibranji-Kiss, "Winnipeg Symposium," 14.

6 Ibid.

7 Winnipeg Film Group, "Statement of Principles, Objectives and Structure" (Winnipeg: Winnipeg Film Group, 1974).

8 Penny McCann, "Forty Years @ 24 Frames Per Second: Film Cooperatives in Canada," curatorial essay in *Reflecting Light: 40 Years of Canadian Cinema*, Winnipeg, 6–9 May 2015, 14–16.

9 AA Bronson, "The Humiliation of the Bureaucrat: Artist-run Spaces as Museums by Artists," in *Museums by Artists*, ed. Peggy Gale and AA Bronson (Toronto: Art Metropole, 1983), 30.

10 Ryan Takatsu, "Video Pool Media Arts Centre – Origins," Video Pool, accessed 3 April 2021, https://videopool.org/vp-orgins/. Established in 1972, Plug In began as a not-for-profit artist-run centre but, in the late 1990s, adopted a broader vision and changed its name to Plug In Institute for Contemporary Art, or Plug In ICA.

11 Space prevents an extensive listing of the range of films produced by Winnipeg Film Group members over the decades. The Film Group's distribution department maintains an excellent online database, with many of the films available on DVD and via streaming through VUCAVU. See: http://www.winnipegfilmgroup.com and http://vucavu.com.

12 David Demchuk, "A Confected Reality, A Reality of My Own: An Interview with Filmmaker John Paizs," *Prairie Fire* 5, no. 4 (1984): 48.

13 Geoff Pevere, "Prairie Postmodern: An Introduction to the Mind and Films of John Paizs," *Cinema Canada* (April 1985): 12.

14 John Kozak, "Isolation in the 1980s," curatorial essay, DVD insert, *Isolation in the 1980s* (Winnipeg: Winnipeg Film Group, 2005).

15 Gene Walz, "Review of *Dislocations*," *Canadian Journal of Film Studies* 5, no. 2 (Fall 1996): 140.

16 Geoff Pevere, "Greenland Revisited," in *Dislocations* (Winnipeg Film Group exhibition catalogue), ed. Gilles Hébert (Winnipeg: City Press, 1995), 41.

17 Brenda Austin-Smith, "Strange Frontiers: Twenty Years of Manitoba Feature Film," in *Self Portraits*, ed. André Loiselle and Tom McSorley (Ottawa: Canadian Film Institute, 2006), 248.

18 Paul McGrath, dir., *Why Make Movies in Winnipeg?*, news documentary, *The Journal* (Toronto: CBC, 1991), https://www.cbc.ca/player/play/1747745622.

19 Pevere, "Greenland Revisited," 50.

20 Walz, "Review of *Dislocations*," 143.

21 Northrop Frye, *The Bush Garden: Essays on the Canadian Imagination* (Toronto: House of Anansi, 1971), 222.

22 Deco Dawson, interview by Kevin Nikkel and Dave Barber, Winnipeg, August 9, 2017. We interviewed Dawson for our documentary film *Tales from the Winnipeg Film Group* (Winnipeg: Five Door Films, 2017).

23 Quoted in Walter Forsberg, "Plain-speaking on the 'Peg," *Uptown* (Winnipeg magazine), 11 October 2007.

24 Walter Forsberg, *Starvation Years: Album de l'Atelier national du Manitoba 2005–2008* (Winnipeg: L'Atelier national du Manitoba, 2014), 15. *Nips* refers to a much beloved hamburger offered by Salisbury House, or Sals, an iconic local fast-food chain.

25 Burke, *Hinterland Remixed*, 115; Forsberg, *Starvation Years*.

26 Carole O'Brien, "Ladies First: Ladies' Firsts," curatorial Essay, DVD insert, *Ladies First: Ladies' Firsts* (Winnipeg: Winnipeg Film Group, 2005).

27 Randall King, "Winnipeg Film Group Announces Departure of Executive Director," *Winnipeg Free Press*, 19 March 2021, https://www.winnipegfreepress.com/arts-and-life/entertainment/arts/winnipeg-film-group-announces-departure-of-executive-director-574025222.html.

28 Lorri Millan and Shawna Dempsey, "28.1," in *decentre: Concerning Artist-Run Culture*, ed. Elaine Chang, Andrea Lalonde, Chris Lloyd, Steve Loft, Jonathan Middleton, Daniel Roy, and Haema Sivanesan (Toronto: YYZBOOKS, 2008), 82.

29 Austin-Smith, "Strange Frontiers," 239.

30 Gilles Hébert, "Dislocations," in Hébert, *Dislocations*, 10.

31 Lucy R. Lippard, *The Lure of the Local: Sense of Place in a Multicentered Society* (New York: New Press, 1997), 36–37.

32 Shawna Dempsey and Lorri Millan, "The Winnipeg Effect: Should I Stay or Should I Go?" (keynote presentation, Centre for Contemporary Canadian Art 20th Anniversary Symposium, Winnipeg Art Gallery, 3–5 November 2016), http://ccca.concordia.ca/winnipegeffect/symposium/keynote.html.

33 Rhayne Vermette, interview by Kevin Nikkel, Winnipeg, 25 January 2017. I interviewed Vermette for the documentary film *Tales from the Winnipeg Film Group*, directed by myself and Dave Barber (Winnipeg: Five Door Films, 2017).

34 Kenneth Frampton, "Toward a Critical Regionalism: Six Points for an Architecture of Resistance," in *The Anti-Aesthetic: Essays on Postmodern Culture*, ed. Hal Foster (Port Townsend, WA: Bay Press, 1983), 29.

35 Cited in Pierre Théberge, *Greg Curnoe: Retrospective* (Ottawa: National Gallery of Canada, 1982), 12–13.

36 Joel Faflak and Sky Glabush, *(Re)imagining Regionalism* (London, ON: McIntosh Gallery Curatorial Study Centre, 2013).

37 James Reaney, "Editorial," *Alphabet 4*, June 1962, 3.

38 Dave Barber, email to the author, 19 April 2021.

39 K. George Godwin, "Far from the Maddin Crowd: Thirty Years of Winnipeg Film Group," *Cinema Scope* 20 (Fall 2004): 17.

40 Stephen Broomer, "The Unfamiliar Messenger: Clint Enns Interview," *The Seventh Art*, 10 October 2014, http://theseventhart.org/clint-enns-interview.

41 Clint Enns, interview by Kevin Nikkel and Dave Barber, Winnipeg, October 1, 2016. We interviewed Enns for the production of our documentary film *Tales from the Winnipeg Film Group* (Winnipeg: Five Door Films, 2017).

42 AA Bronson, "9.1," in Chang et al., *decentre*, 36.

43 Howard Curle, "Introduction: Remembering and Projecting," *Prairie Fire* 20, no. 4 (Winter 2000): 5.

44 Gene Walz, "Manitoba Film-making: On the Brink," *Arts Manitoba*, January 1983, 9.

45 Leon Johnson's *Yardmen* (shot in 1977) had its premiere at the Winnipeg Cinematheque in December 2022 as part of a program of films I curated titled *Not Forgotten Docs: Winnipeg Documentaries from the 1970s*, which included *Main Street Soldier* (1972) by Leonard Yakir, *Havakeen Lunch* (1979) by Elise Swerhone, *The West Quarter* (1974) by Joanne Jackson Johnson, and footage from two other unfinished Winnipeg Film Group projects: *Scenes from the Winnipeg Children's House*, (1975)—from an unfinished collaborative film about an inner-city Winnipeg daycare centre by Nancy Edell, Joanne Jackson Johnson, and Val Klassen; and *Scenes from the Winnipeg Folk Festival* (1975)—from the unfinished documentary portrait of the second-annual Winnipeg Folk Festival at Bird's Hill Park, a collaboration by Winnipeg Film Group members.

46 The Interlake is a southern region of Manitoba located between Lake Winnipeg and Lake Manitoba which includes the town of Gimli, popularized in the films of Guy Maddin.

47 Valgardson was an Icelandic-Canadian author noted for his poetry and fiction.

48 The Third Story was a children's television show produced by Square One Media and Mennonite Brethren Communications that ran from 1977 to 1990: https://www.squareoneworldmedia.com/our-history.

49 Vladimír Valenta was a leading Czechosolvakian film and TV actor that fled to Canada during the Soviet era. He worked with the National Film Board for many years. He visited the Winnipeg Film Group to teach a drama class for members in the 1970s.

50 Kroeker's dramatic films for CKND included: *The Catch* (1982), *The Prodigal* (1983), *Hunting Season* (1984), *Tramp at the Door* (1985), and *In the Fall* (1985).

51 Women in View is a national not-for-profit organization dedicated to strengthening gender representation and diversity in Canadian media both on screen and behind the scenes. https://womeninview.ca/.

52 The Core Area Initiative was a tri-level governmental initiative launched in 1981 with $196 million in funding to address issues of decline and urban decay in Winnipeg's inner city. The revitalization program's overall results were mixed, but the Winnipeg art scene was a clear beneficiary.

53 With the federal election of 1980, Lloyd Axworthy became the Liberal Party's sole elected MP in western Canada, giving him a position of prominence in Pierre Trudeau's government, including two cabinet postings. He used these positions to direct much federal funding and resources back home to Manitoba during his time in office.

54 Lockport is a small town located on the Red River about thirty minutes north of Winnipeg on the way to Gimli.

55 Garbage Hill is the popular name of Westview Park, a rehabilitated landfill at the edge of Winnipeg's West End, which has become a local landmark. The park has another connection to cinema: in 2018, somebody erected an improvised GARBAGE HILL sign, in large, blocky letters in the style of the famous Hollywood sign. Civic authorities removed the sign but, in response to public outcry, later replaced it with a professionally made sign. The park was also the location for Noam Gonick's first feature, *Hey, Happy!*, discussed in his interview below.

56 McGrath, dir., *Why Make Movies in Winnipeg?*

57 A popular large-sized fountain drink served at 7-11 convenience stores throughout Winnipeg.

58 Jay Scott, "Half-Cooked *Crime Wave*: Winnipeg Director Can't Quite End It All," *Globe and Mail*, 14 September 1985.

59 Manitoba Film and Music was originally created in 1987 as a joint initiative between Manitoba and the Government of Canada, and was known as the Cultural Industries Development Office (CIDO).

60 McNally Robinson, founded in 1981, is an independently owned Canadian bookseller chain that pushed a large-store approach and was thus able to compete against the influx of big corporate competitors such as Chapters and Indigo.

61 Emanuel Jaques was a Canadian youth sexually assaulted and murdered in Toronto in 1977. The incident sparked outrage in the city that was credited to the regeneration of Toronto's Yonge Street downtown area.

62 See note 54 on Garbage Hill above.

63 Shoal Lake straddles the Manitoba-Ontario border and has been the source of Winnipeg's potable water since an aqueduct was constructed, in 1919. It is home to two First Nation bands, Shoal Lake 39 and Shoal Lake 40. In 2019 a road was finally constructed to Shoal Lake 40, which had been cut off from road access for a century after Winnipeg's aqueduct turned the community into a man-made island. Only in 2021 was a new water treatment plant installed to provide clean drinking water for Shoal Lake 40.

64 Member of the Legislative Assembly (MLA) of Manitoba.

65 The collective l'Atelier national du Manitoba, comprised of Film Group members Walter Forsberg, Matthew Rankin, and Mike Maryniuk. See the interviews with Forsberg, Rankin, and Maryniuk in this volume.

66 VPW, operated by the company Videon Cablesystems, was a public-access TV channel in Winnipeg that featured some very diverse, very unorthodox programming, all locally and independently produced.

67 Forsberg, *Starvation Years*; see also, Burke, *Hinterland Remixed.*

68 Sir John Christian Schultz was a prominent Winnipeg businessman and politician as well as Manitoba's fifth lieutenant governor, from 1888 to 1895. He was one of Louis Riel's key opponents and was, in fact, an Orangeman.

The Citizens' Committee of One Thousand was a secret cabal of local businessmen and professionals organized to oppose the Winnipeg General Strike, of 1919. Even today, aside from a handful of individuals from its executive, the committee's full membership remains unknown.

Portage Place is a shopping centre in downtown Winnipeg. Opened in 1987, it was hoped that Portage Place would help revitalize the inner city by providing a countervailing force against the city's various suburban shopping centres, and bring customers back to the downtown. Critics maintain that it has had the opposite effect and that its construction actually displaced several blocks of an existing and quite vibrant commercial area.

CentreVenture is an arms-length agency of the City of Winnipeg, established in 1999, aimed at expediting development in the city's downtown core. Its approach has been criticized as not doing enough for the inner city's poor and primarily Indigenous residents, if not seeking to displace them altogether.

69 Film One is the first-year program of film studies at the University of Winnipeg.

70 Leslie has since moved back to Winnipeg to continue her artistic practice. In 2022 she became the executive director of the Winnipeg Film Group.

71 Established by the television channel Bravo as a fund to support the creation of short films and videos, BravoFACT was in operation from 1995 to 2017.

72 Urban Shaman Contemporary Aboriginal Art, established in 1996, is an Indigenous artist-run centre in downtown Winnipeg.

BIBLIOGRAPHY

Austin-Smith, Brenda. "Strange Frontiers: Twenty Years of Manitoba Feature Film." In *Self Portraits: The Cinemas of Canada since Telefilm*, edited by André Loiselle and Tom McSorley, 237–70. Ottawa: Canadian Film Institute, 2006.

Barber, Dave. "Tales from the Winnipeg Film Group." Program guide. Winnipeg: Matchbox Cineclub, 2020.

Bronson, AA. "9.1." In Chang et al., *decentre*, 35–36.

———. "The Humiliation of the Bureaucrat: Artist-run Spaces as Museums by Artists." In *Museums by Artists*, ed. Peggy Gale and A.A. Bronson, 29–37. Toronto: Art Metropole, 1983.

Broomer, Stephen. "The Unfamiliar Messenger: Clint Enns Interview." *The Seventh Art*, 10 October 2014. http://theseventhart.org/clint-enns-interview.

Burke, Andrew. *Hinterland Remixed: Media, Memory, and the Canadian 1970s*. Montreal: McGill-Queen's University Press, 2019.

Chang, Elaine, Andrea Lalonde, Chris Lloyd, Steve Loft, Jonathan Middleton, Daniel Roy, and Haema Sivanesan, eds. *decentre: Concerning Artist-Run Culture*. Toronto YYZBOOKS, 2008.

Curle, Howard. "Introduction: Remembering and Projecting." *Prairie Fire* 20, no. 4 (Winter 2000): 4–6.

Demchuk, David. "A Confected Reality, A Reality of My Own: An Interview with Filmmaker John Paizs." *Prairie Fire* 5, no. 4 (1984): 46–54.

Dempsey, Shawna, and Lorri Millan. "The Winnipeg Effect: Should I Stay or Should I Go?" Keynote presentation, Centre for Contemporary Canadian Art 20th Anniversary Symposium, Winnipeg Art Gallery, 3–5 November 2016. http://ccca.concordia.ca/winnipegeffect/symposium/keynote.html.

Faflak, Joel, and Sky Glabush, eds. *(Re)imagining Regionalism*. London, ON: McIntosh Gallery Curatorial Study Centre, 2013.

Fitzrandolph, Katie. "Gloomy Mood Prevails at Film Symposium." *Winnipeg Free Press*, 9 February 1974.

Forsberg, Walter. "Plain-speaking on the 'Peg." *Uptown* (Winnipeg magazine), 11 October 2007.

———. *Starvation Years: Album de l'Atelier national du Manitoba 2005–2008*. Winnipeg: L'Atelier national du Manitoba, 2014.

Frampton, Kenneth. "Toward a Critical Regionalism: Six Points for an Architecture of Resistance." In *The Anti-Aesthetic: Essays on Postmodern Culture*, edited by Hal Foster, 16–30. Port Townsend, WA: Bay Press, 1983.

Frye, Northrop. *The Bush Garden: Essays on the Canadian Imagination*. Toronto: House of Anansi, 1971.

Godwin, K. George. "Far from the Maddin Crowd: Thirty Years of Winnipeg Film Group." *Cinema Scope* 20 (Fall 2004): 14–18.

Hébert, Gilles. "Dislocations." In Hébert, *Dislocations*, 7–13.

Hébert, Gilles, ed. *Dislocations* (Winnipeg Film Group exhibition catalogue). Winnipeg: City Press, 1995.

Ibranji-Kiss, Agi. "Winnipeg Symposium: The Turning Point." *Cinema Canada* 13 (April–May 1974): 14.

King, Randall. "Winnipeg Film Group Announces Departure of Executive Director." *Winnipeg Free Press*, 19 March 2021. https://www.winnipegfreepress.com/arts-and-life/entertainment/arts/winnipeg-film-group-announces-departure-of-executive-director-574025222.html.

Kozak, John. "Isolation in the 1980s." Curatorial essay, DVD insert. Winnipeg: Winnipeg Film Group, 2005.

Lippard, Lucy R. *The Lure of the Local: Sense of Place in a Multicentered Society*. New York: New Press, 1997.

McCann, Penny. "Forty Years @24 Frames Per Second: Film Cooperatives in Canada." Presentation, Reflecting Light: 40 Years of Canadian Cinema national forum, Winnipeg, 6–9 May 2015.

McGrath, Paul. *Why Make Movies in Winnipeg?*, News documentary, *The Journal*. Toronto: CBC, 1991. https://www.cbc.ca/player/play/1747745622.

Millan, Lorri, and Shawna Dempsey. "28.1." In Chang et al., *decentre*, 82–83.

O'Brien, Carole. "Ladies First: Ladies' Firsts." Curatorial essay, DVD insert. Winnipeg: Winnipeg Film Group, 2005.

Pevere, Geoff. "Greenland Revisited." In Hébert, *Dislocations*, 37–51.

———. "Prairie Postmodern: An Introduction to the Mind and Films of John Paizs." *Cinema Canada* (April 1985): 11–13.

Reaney, James. "Editorial." *Alphabet* 4, June 1962, 3.

Scott, Jay. "Half-Cooked *Crime Wave*: Winnipeg Director Can't Quite End It All." *Globe and Mail*, 14 September 1985.

Takatsu, Ryan. "Video Pool Media Arts Centre – Origins." Video Pool. Accessed 3 April 2021. https://videopool.org/vp-orgins/.

Théberge, Pierre. *Greg Curnoe: Retrospective*. Ottawa: National Gallery of Canada, 1982.

Winnipeg Film Group. "Statement of Principles, Objectives and Structure." Winnipeg: Winnipeg Film Group, 1974.

Walz, Gene. "Manitoba Film-making: On the Brink." *Arts Manitoba*, January 1983, 9.

———. "Review of *Dislocations*." *Canadian Journal of Film Studies* 5, no. 2 (Fall 1996): 140.

INDEX